Picture Postcards of the Golden Age

Tonie and Valmai Holt

—

# Picture Postcards
# of the
# Golden Age

A COLLECTOR'S GUIDE

MacGibbon & Kee   London

Granada Publishing Limited
First published in Great Britain 1971 by MacGibbon & Kee Ltd
3 Upper James Street London WIR 4BP

Copyright © 1971 by Tonie and Valmai Holt

ISBN 0 261 63245 0
Printed in Great Britain by Western Printing Services Ltd
Bristol

To two pairs of parents, Sian and Gareth

# Contents

List of Plates                                                    *Page* 9

Preface                                                                 15

1  The Early History of the Picture Postcard                            23

2  The Mechanics of Collecting                                          43

3  Topographical Cards                                                  50

4  Topical and Commemorative Cards                                      65

5  Pictures from the War                                                79

6  Humour and Politic                                                   91

7  Portraits                                                           101

8  Advertisements                                                      117

9  Curious                                                             129

10  Miscellany                                                         149

### APPENDICES

1  British Official Postcard Issues, 1870–1899                         165

2  Chronological List of Postcard and Related Events                   170

3  Publishers of Picture Postcards with some Information on            173
   Trademarks and Series

4  Printing Processes                                                  187

5  How to Date Postcards                                               191

6  How to Value Postcards                                              195

7  British Exhibitions and Other Events Commemorated by
   Picture Postcards                                                   198

8  Some Postcard Dealers and Postal Magazines                         199

Bibliography                                                          201

Index                                                                203

# Plates

*Between page 64 and 65*

1 The World's first postcard
  Britain's first postcard
  Britain's first foreign postcard

2 British 'Officials', 1878–99

3 Foreign and Empire 'Officials', 1871–97

4 Victoria State: 'Beer & Baccy', 1895
  Red-Brown aerial postcard, 1911

5 Tuck: Heraldic card, c. 1901
  'Ja-Ja' Heraldic Series, c. 1905

6 Valentine's: Dartmoor, c. 1903
  D.F. & Co.: moonlight view, c. 1904

7 Card posted from the Rigi, Switzerland, c. 1904
  LL: Broadstairs, c. 1909

8 Valentine's: 'Russian outrage on Hull fishing fleet', 1904
  Anon: 'Illustrated Daily Post-card', 1905

*Between pages 96 and 97*

9 Tuck: 'Kings and Queens of England' Series—Edward VII
  Broom: 'Visit of the King and Queen of Portugal to Windsor Castle',
  1904

10 Typical 'Gruss Aus . . .' card, c. 1890
   Card posted from Vesuvius, 1904

11 Tuck: 'Oilette', c. 1905
   Valentine's: Newport, c. 1910

12 C. W. Faulkner: Bovril card, 1914
   Lord Kitchener and 'If', c. 1916

13 *Daily Mail*: 'Official War Photograph', 6 September 1916
   *Bystander*: 'Fragments from France', c. 1916

14 Tuck: 'British Army' Series by Harry Payne, c. 1900
   Tuck: 'Defenders of the Empire' by Harry Payne, c. 1914

15 C. W. Faulkner: 'Punting' by Louis Wain, c. 1903
   C. W. Faulkner, 'Dutch' card by Florence Hardy, c. 1913

16  Tuck: 'Phil May' Series, c. 1903
    Tuck: 'Write Away' Series by Lance Thackeray, c. 1903

*Between pages 128 and 129*

17  Japanese Official Postcard, 1904
    Jarrold's: 'The Great War' Series, 1914

18  Advertisement for Fry's Cocoa, c. 1904
    Advertisement for a musical comedy, c. 1904

19  'Popular Series': Christmas card, c. 1910
    Philco Series: 'Welcome Home My Boy', 1918

20  Davidson Bros: cartoon by A. Ludovici, c. 1903
    Tuck: Oilette—'The Zeppelin Raider', c. 1916

21  'Art and Humour': 'Leap Year' Series, 1916
    Millar & Lang: 'When Father Says "Turn" . . . ', c. 1903

22  Tuck: 'Modern Art' card, c. 1901
    Misch: 'World's Galleries' Series (Rubens), c. 1905

23  Tuck: 'Real Japanese' card, c. 1905
    WWI embroidered card, c. 1916

24  Klingenstein: Zeppelin I, c. 1909
    POW card issued at Alexandra Palace, 1915

*Between pages 160 and 161*

25  Cynicus: 'Our Local Express', c. 1906
    Card by Donald McGill, c. 1913

26  LE, Paris: 'L'Avarice' by Raphaël Kirchner
    James Henderson & Sons: Gibson Girl, c. 1906
    Rotary: Camille Clifford, c. 1906

27  Tuck: 'Gladys' by A. Asti, c. 1905
    G.B. & Co.: 'Hope' by Mailick, c. 1905

28  Crawford's War Map, 1904
    Shackleton's Oxo card, 1909

29  McCorquodale: advertisement for steamer line, 1902
    Embossed card with stamps of Mexico, c. 1904

30  *The Times:* 'Flying Scenes at Blackpool', 1909
    Alpha: fantasy composition, c. 1912

31  Card woven in silk by T. Stevens, 1905
    W. N. Sharpe: 'Fab' patchwork card, 1910

32   Ettlinger: midget card, 1904
      Rotary Book card: Edna May, c. 1902
      Rotary: Marie Studholme, c. 1905

# Authors' Acknowledgements

We would like to thank the following people for their generous help: Mr John Smith, Editor of the *International Postcard Market*, for much useful postcard material and information; Mr Peter Lawrence, Collector Extraordinary, for information, advice and the loan of cards; Mr R. J. Bradley, collector and expert on Raphaël Kirchner, for checking our passage on that artist; Mr Geoffrey A. Godden, author of *Stevengraphs and Other Victorian Silk Pictures*, for information on some of the postcard artists; the Rev. W. R. Saunders, for details of the Heligoland postcard; The Imperial War Museum, for permission to reproduce *Daily Mail* War Cards; Mr Henry Sandon, curator of the Dyson Perrins Museum at the Royal Worcester Porcelain Works, for information about Charles Baldwyn; Messrs Raphael Tuck & Sons, Bamforth's, Boots, Gale & Polden, Eyre & Spottiswoode and Jarrolds, for permission to reproduce postcards published by them; Messrs De la Rue and the Archivist of Reading University for information on that firm; the staff of the British Museum, the Victoria and Albert Museum, the National Postal Museum, Companies House, the Birmingham Public Library, the Liverpool Public Library and the Malvern Public Library for assistance in research; Associated Newspapers Ltd, for permission to reproduce articles published in the *Daily Mail*; the Post Office for permission to use material from their archives; Dr B. de Burca for information and encouragement; and many other knowledgeable and enthusiastic collectors who have provided us with much information and help in a variety of fields, and whom we regret not being able to name individually for lack of space.

Since this manuscript was submitted to the publishers Dr Alan Huggins has published his book *British Postal Stationery*. We deal with Official Postcards as the forerunners of Picture Postcards, and comment upon the lack of an authoritative reference work for the collector to use as a follow-up to the research we ourselves have done. Dr Huggins' book is an excellent summary of all currently available information on Official Postcards, and we wish that we had been able to refer to it.

# Preface

This book is designed to help the Picture Postcard collector at every level. It aims to give practical aid to the novice and to provide some new information for the more experienced collector. It also provides an attempt at a valuation of cards that are still readily available and others that are worth looking for; clear-to-follow appendices list the better-known publishers of cards, their trade-marks, processes and some of the sets they produced.

We also hope it will give the casual reader some sort of answer to the question we are always being asked: 'But *why* collect postcards?' The reasons for starting a collection are almost as varied as the types of card available. We started almost by accident. We had been experiencing a common human urge to collect something – but what? The outlay had to be small, that was almost the first consideration, and this meant it had to be something that not too many other people were showing an interest in. Nothing inflates the price of a simple article as quickly or as much as for it suddenly to become fashionable to collect. Fashions, especially in the fringe antique world, have a nasty habit of becoming unfashionable as with-it collectors move on to the latest fad. So it was no use jumping onto a band wagon that was already in motion. On the other hand it had to be something that other people might gradually start taking an interest in, or one's collection would not appreciate to keep pace with our ever-depreciating pound.

The solution came while poring through the long catalogue of a forthcoming local house sale. 'Six Picture Postcard Albums' – that was it! So off we went and bought the lot. Although we didn't realize it for some time, we had been extremely lucky. For these six albums had belonged to an avid Edwardian collector and contained everything from a silk to a metal card. We were there-fore made aware sooner than the average novice of the wealth of variety that lay in our chosen hobby. So that was how we became deltiologists.

Deltiology is only one of the terms coined at the height of the postcard collecting mania. We could equally have said 'cartophiliacs' or 'cartomaniacs' or 'cartologists'.

There are two interests which bring a large proportion of enthusiasts into the ranks of card collectors. One is an interest in one's locality. Many students of local history discover that a view card of their favourite town can give them a far fuller and more accurate picture of what life was like there sixty or seventy years ago, and what architectural changes have taken place, than any number of history books. Therefore you will find a collector who specializes in views of his own neighbourhood in almost every district of the country. Local museums too are now building up substantial picture postcard collections as an im-portant part of their local historical reference libraries.

15

The student of social history in its many forms is another common postcard enthusiast. Costume experts search for details of hats and bathing costumes and parasols; transport fans fall into subsidiary categories of tram enthusiasts, early motor car enthusiasts, those with nostalgia for horse-drawn buses or fire engines, and so on.

Military historians have a field day when they discover what a great source of knowledge the picture postcard can be. The Boer War, the Russo-Japanese War and of course the First World War are fully documented on the picture postcard.

Loyal subjects can follow every Royal event on commemorative postcards and stage-struck collectors can acquire second-hand memories of the productions and stars of a glamorous bygone age. The sportsman can collect portrait cards of his favourite local and national stars in such sports as cricket, football, golf, racing, motor racing and aviation.

Philatelists often start by looking through old picture postcards for stamped treasure on the back, only to become hooked on what is on the front too. The same applies to postmark collectors, who often graduate to card collecting. The philatelists often specialize when they turn to deltiology. Some will concentrate on postcards posted at sea, especially those bearing the sought-after 'Paquebot' cancellations, others on exhibition cards posted and franked at the exhibition itself. As you will learn later, these special postmarks can add greatly to the value of what is otherwise a comparatively worthless card.

Animal lovers find great scope in this hobby – from Louis Wain's delightful cat studies to the cuddly chicks that adorned Easter greetings cards during Victorian and Edwardian times. Animals were always a popular subject with the card producers.

The humorist is equally well catered for. Again there are many humorous fields to specialize in. Some will concentrate on cards drawn by a particular comic artist, such as Tom Browne or Donald McGill, others on the more genteel forerunners of the modern seaside belly-laugh raiser.

For the sheer aesthetic pleasure of collecting something beautiful, one would have to look far to beat old picture postcards for value for money. An outlay of a few pence in most cases will buy the most exquisite reproductions of classical paintings such as those produced by Misch & Co., glamorous girls in the style of Kirchner or Asti, artistic still lifes of fruit or flowers, to name but a few. The processes used were remarkably sophisticated in many cases and are seldom bettered today for true-to-life vibrant colours; and though such cards sold at about 1d each when they were first produced, today they would cost the manufacturer well over a shilling per card to make using these processes. Many of these 'artistic' cards still appear incredibly beautiful today. The purist may cry 'Sacrilege!', but, when framed, this type of card makes most attractive pictures for grouping in halls or landings or even down the stairs.

Today's commercial artist searching for new inspiration often turns to the

Edwardian picture postcard for source material, and comedian Ronnie Barker, an enthusiastic deltiologist, finds good material for his sketches in his large collection of comic cards.

The picture postcard, then, offers scope to specialists in many varying fields, and each of the categories mentioned so far will have its own chapter or part chapter later in this book. But what of the general buy-anything type of collector? What does he find so fascinating in what is so often someone else's damp and musty salvage? We think the answer must be in the fact that there is basically nothing more interesting to one human being than other human beings. The way our Victorian and Edwardian forebears lived, dressed and spent their leisure, whom they admired, where they spent their holidays, what they wrote from the trenches to wives and sweethearts, their politics, what made them laugh, their artistic values – all these facts can be gleaned from an average-sized collection of picture postcards. The quality and pace of life have altered so vastly over the years covered by our period that it is refreshing to be able to satisfy one's natural curiosity about fellow men from studying cases from an age made more attractive by its leisurely tempo and elegance. There are few hints to be found on the postcard of the hard conditions and poverty that the mass of people had to endure to make this elegance possible for the few. The seaside resorts are always peopled with fashion plates in their Sunday best – the scruffy urchins only crop up on the comic cards as appealing little ragamuffins, and the horrors of the First World War produced some of the most beautiful cards – the silk embroidereds sent by the thousand from France.

Moral qualities, too, were more noticeable in those days. Wars were a glorified excuse for the display of patriotism, a favourite theme for the picture postcard. And in war time and peace time cards that swelled the funds of any charity from the missions to the scheme to Send Bovril to Our Boys at the Front sold like hot cakes. Religious fervour was high, and favourite pin-ups were the local bishops or even vicars. Such horrors as 'Popery in the Birmingham Streets' were subjects for indignant picture postcards and Bamforth's produced many best-selling series of popular hymns such as 'Abide with Me'.

To the frankly nosy, the picture postcard is a boon. Buy a collection of them from a local house sale and you can get to know the family that occupied it far better in one evening's browsing than their neighbours managed to in years of peering through the net curtains. From the name of the admirer who sent a regular valentine to the exact itinerary of every family holiday – it's all there in the album. To the snooper, of course, the message side of the card is what matters. The whole story of family relationships and habits can be built up by this visual form of eavesdropping, and the private card made from a family photograph was a favourite inter-family missive. 'Just to remind you how Father looks. You may have forgotten,' writes sarcastic Mother to an obviously errant Emily in 1906 on the back of a card bearing a portrait of Father.

The collector in the family would make known to all the aunts and uncles, cousins, and in-laws that he had acquired an album. The result would be floods of cards, mostly bearing the words 'Have you got this one?', 'Another one for your collection', or 'Does this complete your set?' This would be followed, perhaps, by thanks for the pot of clotted cream or arrangements for an outing the next day. Yes, always the next day. What immediately strikes one is the utter (and to us extraordinary) reliability of the postal system and the complete confidence of the writer in his card reaching its destination within twenty-four hours. 'I shall be arriving tomorrow on the 2.15 train', is a frequent announcement. The efficient Post Office delivered up to six times a day and a card posted to any destination in the United Kingdom arrived within twenty-four hours. As a short form of communication the picture postcard supplanted the letter and was a satisfactory mass alternative to the telephone call, which was only just starting to have any popular function.

The picture postcard was a two-way status symbol. The album vied with the family photograph album for admiration and was always conspicuously placed in the drawing-room during calls. Cards from strange-sounding places with far-away names were always desirable inclusions. But it was equally one up to send a 'Wish you were here' card from the top of the Eiffel Tower or the Blue Grotto in Capri.

In its heyday the craze for collecting was frantic. Millions of cards were produced, bought and eagerly posted. It is a curious thought that these same cards are now being collected, with just as much enthusiasm, for the second time. At the turn of the century competitions and magazines for the collector were common and great rivalry was engendered between friends over acquiring the greatest number of cards. 'I have got 110 postcards', wrote a youthful beginner in 1903, 'send me a postcard there's a dear. From your loving cousin Mabel. P.S. Auntie Maud told me you were collecting.' The effect the postcard mania had on tourists was described by a visitor to the continent in a letter to the Editor of the *Picture Postcard Magazine* of August 1900 in the following words:

> The craze has a curious effect. The track of the tourist is lined with Postcard Pencillers. You enter a railway station and everybody on the platform has a pencil in one hand and a postcard in the other. In the train it is the same thing. Your fellow travellers never speak. They have little piles of picture postcards on the seat beside them and they write monotonously. Under the shady trees, by the shores of the lakes, in the public gardens and parks, every seat is occupied by a postcard writer. When a lady finishes her correspondence and rises, another lady with a stock of cards and a lead pencil instantly drops into the vacant place. Recently I went up the Rigi with a large party. Directly we arrived at the summit everybody made a rush for the hotel and fought for the picture postcards. Five minutes afterwards everybody was writing away for dear life. Nobody troubled about the glorious view. I believe that the entire party had come up, not for the sake of the experience or the scenery, but to write postcards and to post them on the summit.

The ascent, incidentally, had been made easier by the funicular railway which carried passengers to the top of the Rigi. It had been built on the rack and pinion principle by Riggenbach in 1872, two years after the first official post-card had been issued in Switzerland. (A card posted from the Rigi is seen in Plate 7.)

A great many of these 'Postcard Pencillers' were more than a little coy about the messages they scribbled. They went to great pains to ensure that the 'stupid' postman or the servants would not be able to read what they had written. The most common device for making their messages impossible for anyone other than the intended recipient to decipher was to write the message up-side down! Other frequent ruses were writing the message backwards – 'Ynam yppah snruter fo eht yad, Morf Htide,' – 1904; in shorthand, in Esper-anto, odd parts in code or French or Latin, or making oblique references that no-one else could possibly understand – 'I am still troubled with the . . . You know what I mean,' confided Lizzie to her girlfriend in 1904.

Not so discreet was the lover who wrote to his servant girl sweetheart in 1912, 'Darling my very own. Your time is drawing near now. I dare say your Mistress will be a bit nasty now on account of you leaving. But Dear take it all in good part.' Or the 'friend' who wrote to the Rev. N. S. Jenkins in 1904 for all the world to see, 'Now just you leave those girls alone or I tell your Ma.'

Not that one can take at face value all that one reads on a postcard. We got quite excited on finding a card that read 'Relief of Ladysmith just arrived.' What a truly historical card we had found! But on checking dates we noticed that the postcard had been posted on 14 August 1903 and Ladysmith was relieved in 1900. Perhaps the card just took a long time in reaching the Post Office!

A great deal of the appeal of collecting lies in the search: the compulsion that soon grips you so that you become physically incapable of passing a junk shop or missing a house sale. You can't complete a conversation with a senior citizen without asking him if by any chance he had an unwanted album of old picture postcards tucked away somewhere that he would like to dispose of – but more of the way to acquire cards in Chapter 2.

Collecting, however, is by no means an end – in fact it's merely the opening to the pleasure you can derive from your collection. We have seen how the specialist uses his cards almost like a set of encyclopaedias. The general col-lector can get just as much from his collection, even at the therapeutic level as a complete relaxation from the tensions of the rat race that is living today. The non-collector may call it escapism. Perhaps it is; but can it be so useless to be able to steep oneself in the atmosphere of another, much more gracious, era at the mere opening of an album?

Many involved theories have been propounded to explain why people get so fanatical about these small pieces of cardboard. The psychologists would main-tain that it gives one a sense of power to acquire, possess and handle small objects and that they could attempt a character assessment by studying the subjects that appeal to any one deltiologist. Peter Lawrence, a dedicated collector of our acquaintance who has built up a superb collection of over 40,000 cards over the years (from the purest of motives), describes his collection in these words: 'My cards are my time-machine, by means of which I can spend an evening with Edwardian actresses, climbing the Matterhorn, dancing the tarantella and flying by balloon to far away places to sing hymns – or simply hop on the Southend express for a day at the sea.'

A far-seeing lady by the name of Miss Margaret Mead exactly anticipated our present-day attitude to the late Victorian picture postcard. Writing in *Girls' Realm* in December 1900 she said:

> The Picture Postcard is a sign of the times. It belongs to a period peopled by a hurried generation which has not many minutes to spare for writing to friends. What with the express trains going at the rate of a mile a minute, with telegrams and telephones, the world has become a small place. We go all over it, we have acquaintances in all parts of it. When we rush from Rome to Paris, do the galleries of Italy in one week and those of Holland the next, fly [not literally of course at that time] off to the Holy Land, take Mount Olympus on our way, how can we pause to do more than send a signal of safe arrival and a sign of remembrance to our numberless acquaintances? The Picture Postcard is with us. It suits us. It meets our needs. It helps us to keep in touch with those we have left behind and gives them a glimpse of the places that for the time being form the background of our lives. I can imagine a future generation building up by their help all the life of today – our children, our pets, our adventurous youths, our famous old people, our wild and garden flowers, our outdoor delights, our life of sport, and our life of stress and strain, our National holidays, our Pageants, and traces of the drama of our political life, are all to be found thereon.

How modern she sounds, and how right she was.

1 Oxford Road,                                                                     T. and V.H.
Malvern, Worcestershire.

Picture Postcards of the Golden Age

# I

# The Early History of the Picture Postcard

The inventor of the Picture Postcard died in 1940 for the fifth time. When he first died in 1930 his name was Ludwig Zrenner, and he claimed that the cards that he had produced for the Nuremberg Exhibition in 1882 were the first picture postcards. The second time he died, in 1933, his name was Heinrich Lange, but when he died again in 1934 his name was Cesare Bertanza.

In March 1934, one month after Bertanza, he died again in the guise of a court photographer named Alfons Adolph, who claimed that the cards he had produced in 1879 in Vienna were the first picture postcards. In 1940 came the fifth death, this time of Pastor Ludolph Parisius, who believed that as a student in Göttingen in 1871 he had produced the first picture postcards. There will have been other deaths of the inventor that we have not noticed, but it must already be clear that it is almost an impossible task to say who he really was.

The men who most commonly share the credit for the introduction of the picture postcard are not mentioned above, and we shall deal with them later. But their claims cannot stand against the assertion made by a national newspaper in 1903 that the picture postcard existed in 1777, but that it was turned down because the open correspondence might 'stimulate the malignity of servants who could thus penetrate family secrets'. However, it is safe to assume that the object that we know as a picture postcard is a fairly recent invention, and we have no reason to depart from the view that the first cards were made towards the end of the nineteenth century. Although we are concerned here with picture postcards, their history cannot be examined without reference to the ordinary postcard. Indeed, for the first thirty years their development was closely allied, and in our early reading, aimed at finding out more about our own collection of cards, we became confused about this point. In the hope that others may avoid similar confusion, we consider the development of the Official Postcard in some detail, and in Appendix 1 list the earliest British versions.

There are three forms of British postcard in our period. There is the Official Postcard, complete with printed stamp, which appeared in 1870; there is the privately printed card, introduced in 1872, which had to be handed to the Inland Revenue to have a stamp printed on it; and there is the Private Postcard which could be used with an adhesive stamp, which was introduced in 1894.

This latter developed into the Picture Postcard, and we must look at the development of the other two cards before we can examine and understand its history.

There is, however, one more important point to make first. The words 'post card' have a technical significance in that they denote that piece of cardboard to be delivered by the Post Office at the Postcard Rate. This was normally half the Letter Rate, so firms and individuals were very conscious of the need to conform to the Post Office Regulations for Postcards in order to qualify for the lower postal charge. In our historical account when, for example, we say that 'the first cards bearing the halfpenny adhesive stamp were posted in 1894', we mean that the first cards bearing the halfpenny adhesive stamp which qualified for the Postcard Rate were posted in 1894. Pieces of paper, cardboard and even Correspondence Cards bearing small pictures, normally sent in envelopes as they are today, would have been sent through the post without a cover and bearing adhesive stamps before 1894. But they would not have qualified as postcards because no such category of postage rate existed. The stamps they carried should have been to the value required by the Letter Rate. Cards posted before 1894 with less than the Letter Rate should have been spotted by the Post Office sorters and surcharged or returned to the sender. However, since most of the sorting and processing was entirely manual, regulations were often confusing and the Post Office frequently overstretched by the volume of mail, many cards with adhesive stamps of less than Letter Rate value got through to their destinations. We own a vignetted, coloured view of Somerset House bearing an adhesive halfpenny stamp (Letter Rate was 1d) which got through in 1892, two years before Private Postcards were allowed.

## The Official Postcard and the Private Card Officially Stamped

In 1865 Heinrich von Stephan, later to be one of the instigators of an international postal agreement, suggested to the German postal authorities that they should introduce a postal card. In 1867 at a Postal Conference in Karlsruhe he repeated his suggestion, but on neither occasion did anything result.

On 26 January 1869, in an article in a Vienna newspaper, one Dr Emanuel Hermann, a professor at the Wiener Neustadt Military Academy, suggested that postal cards about the size of the envelopes then in use should be introduced. He advocated that a message of restricted length should be permitted and that the card should be allowed to pass at a reduced rate of postage. The Austrian postal authorities seized upon the idea, although they did not accept all Hermann's detailed suggestions, and the world's first postcard was issued by them a few months later on 1 October 1869. The card bore a printed two kreuzer 'Head of the Emperor' stamp on one side, and the other side was labelled as the space for the written communication (see Plate 1).

The first British postcards were issued exactly one year later by the General Post Office on 1 October 1870, having been printed by Messrs De la Rue under an exclusive contract, and were an immediate success. At some Post Offices the crowds were so large that police had to be called in to control them.

Half a million passed through St Martins Le Grand on the first day. The popularity of the cards soon attracted imitators, and many copies were clandestinely produced for advertisement purposes, a practice that increased to such proportions twenty-four years later that the Post Office had to issue a notice forbidding their production.

The first card issued (see Plate 1) was 122 mm. by 88 mm. and made of light buff cardboard much thinner than that used today, with violet printing and border. It was superseded for a practical reason about six weeks later by a similar card which measured 121 mm. by 74 mm. The notepaper used at the time, much of it illustrated, was generally about 114 mm. wide and in the region of 205 mm. long, and it was common practice to fold it into three before putting it into an envelope or sealing it. The second postcard was therefore designed to join the stacks of mail without sticking out and becoming damaged by the string used to tie up the bundles. However, the authorities wished to issue Britain's first cards on the anniversary of the world's first postcard, in the design of which letter size was not considered. Nevertheless they believed the postcard to be second class as far as postal treatment was concerned, for they warned '. . . When, owing to a great and unusual influx of letters, books etc., the transmission or delivery of the letters would be delayed if the whole mail were dealt with without distinction, Book Packets . . . and Postcards may be kept back until the next dispatch or delivery.'

The cards, which were solely for Inland use, could be bought only at Post Offices and sold for one halfpenny each, the face value of the stamp printed upon them. This brought complaints from the stationery trade. They pointed out that the public had to pay for the paper that they used for their letters and then buy the stamp. In their view the postcard, a Post Office monopoly, introduced unfair competition in that the cost of the card was included with the cost of the stamp.

The postal authorities acknowledged the soundness of this argument two years later, on 1 April 1872, when they introduced an extra charge of one halfpenny per dozen, the cards being available from that date onwards only in multiples of twelve at 6½d per dozen. During those two years, despite a Victorian feeling that the postcard was somehow vulgar, and comments in newspapers on 'the absurdity of writing private information on an open piece of cardboard, that might be read by half a dozen persons before it reached its destination', the card proved to be popular and about 150 million passed through the post. The general public and commerce found the new postcard of great value for such things as acknowledging the receipt of weightier communications, for confirming appointments, for sending out price lists or for circular communications to members of clubs or societies. From the first day the cards were used for advertising purposes by the addition to the blank side of small monochrome pictures of the wares for sale which surrounded the message space. This was an activity which extended quite naturally from the advertising circulars and envelopes that had been in existence for over thirty years. It is supposed that one of the first view cards produced in this country was made in March 1872, showing a sketch of St Paul's Cathedral, London Bridge with the Thames, the Tower and the Monument. It was published by Grant & Co. of Fleet Street, London and advertised an illustrated book on London by Gustave Doré, which was to be issued in twelve monthly parts at five shillings each.

This early acceptance of the postcard by the commercial world, and the greater freedom to produce private postcards on the Continent, led to agitation by business interests in particular for the breaking of the Post Office monopoly. The story of the years from the postcard's inception to the eventual official sanction of the picture postcard is one of conflicting interests between the Post Office, their printers De la Rue, commerce and the general public. At that time cards were printed for the Post Office by De la Rue and Co., who had the exclusive right to do so, and no other cards could be used. The pressure on the Post Office was sufficient to make it decide to relax its monopoly a little, but it was not able to change the situation without negotiating with De la Rue. The negotiations led to a new contract for the production of postal stationery by the company, in return for which they agreed to the loss of part of their monopoly of the printing of postcards. From 17 June 1872 anyone was allowed to print postcards (although these were not to be put on sale to the general public at Post Offices) provided that certain conditions 'acceptable to us', to quote Mr De la Rue, were observed. Among the more important of these conditions were the following:

The card had to look like the official card, but without the Royal Arms.
It was to be as nearly as possible the same size as the official card.
The cardboard used had to be whiter than the official buff board.
Anything could be written or printed on the back, but not on the address side.
After printing it was to be sent to the Inland Revenue Department to have the halfpenny stamp printed or impressed upon it, and once this had been done the card could not be altered.

Although the cards could not be used with adhesive stamps to pay the postage, they were welcomed by commerce as a step forward. It was cheaper to print the firm's acknowledgements, price list or advertisements on printer's board and then have the stamp embossed on the finished product than it was to supply the printer with official cards on which to print. Nevertheless, the Post Office charged the private printer heavily for embossing the oval stamp onto the cards, and agitation continued for further relaxation of the regulations.

The increase in mail during the previous decade contributed to by the introduction of postcards, led the Post Office to experiment with mechanical methods of cancelling stamps. At about the time of the introduction of the privately printed postcard, in 1872, machines that made holes or cuts as cancellations were tried out on postcards in five places. In Manchester the machines cut pieces out of the edge of the card in the shape of a pentagon, semicircle or vee. In Edinburgh and Birmingham the printed stamp was perforated with a single hole; in Liverpool the single hole perforation was used as well as an anchor shape; while in London the anchor as well as a series of holes in the shape of an inverted orb was tried. There was public dissatisfaction with such machines, however, because quite often part of the message on the postcard was destroyed, and they were discontinued after a year or so.

It is probable that the majority of postcard traffic at this time was commercial. Writing letters was a social grace that was an outward manifestation of the importance that society placed upon personal relationships. Thus the postcard was still vulgar, and had no room for the long flowing sentences that could go into letters. However, the card had obvious advantages for a generation to whom so much was happening, and provided the social barrier could be overcome almost everyone would find it acceptable. A lead in this direction was given by Mr Gladstone, who used a large number of postcards and was full of praise for them, except for their thinness. He suggested that the Post Office should have a thicker card, and they readily obliged him and issued what they called a 'stout', superior quality card. The new card was on sale from 1 February 1875 at 8d per dozen, and the original thin card, although it continued in production, went up to 7d per dozen. Neither variety could be sold in quantities of less than half a dozen.

In 1875, too, postcards were first allowed to be sent abroad. The year before, at the instigation of Heinrich von Stephan, a congress had been held in Berne to discuss the handling of mail between different countries. This congress, which was attended by twenty-two member countries, discussed the formation of a body to be known as the General Union of Posts, and agreed to the introduction of certain postal conventions between themselves. The Union Convention, as it is sometimes called, came into force on 1 July 1875, and one of its provisions was that postcards could be sent between member countries. Great Britain issued an official card, available from that date, which bore a $1\frac{1}{4}$d stamp and sold for that price. It was slightly larger than the official Inland card in order to allow for the longer addresses that would be used; an example is shown at Plate 1 and it is listed as Serial 6 in Appendix 1. In anticipation of the public rush to use the card, the Post Office made plans to engage extra staff – clerks at 10d per hour and messengers at $7\frac{1}{2}$d per hour.

The period of history with which we are concerned was one of great change. It is difficult today to appreciate the number and the importance of the changes and developments that were taking place, and it is impossible to get the flavour of those years by recounting dates alone without identifying them with particular events. We can make our point clearer perhaps by pointing out that between the introduction of the Foreign Postcard in 1875 and 1878, when the next postcard event of note occurred, General Custer made his last stand at the Battle of the Little Big Horn, Plimsoll's line was put into law, and the telephone and carpet sweeper were invented. The postcard, a brief and cheap carrier of messages, acknowledgements and advertisements, suited the era. It was advanced and, above all, it was modern. In the pressure of the inventions that were flowing from fertile minds and the struggles of governments to improve by war or commerce the stature of their countries, the need for communication was overwhelming. The telegraph had been invented in the 1830s and served as a communication link between countries and over great distances. The telephone had only just arrived and the wireless was still in the future. The postal service, then, formed the major link in the chain of communication and international efforts were devoted to making it as efficient as possible.

To this end discussions within the Universal Postal Union, as the Union had become known in 1878, led to the introduction of two new Foreign Postcards in Britain. One card, which cost a penny, was for use to those countries within the Union whose letter rate was $2\frac{1}{2}$d while the other, which cost $1\frac{1}{2}$d, was for those countries whose letter rate was 4d. Both cards were sold at their face value, were thicker than the Inland card but thinner than Mr Gladstone's stout card, and were available from 1 April 1879, the day on which the old $1\frac{1}{4}$d card became obsolete. One was to cause a storm of protest.

The 1d card (see Plate 2) was of light buff board and measured 88 mm. by 122 mm. The brown printed stamp denoting the postal charge was in the top right-hand corner, and a central heading in capitals said 'UNION POSTALE UNIVERSELLE'. Under that came 'Great Britain', then '(Grande Bretagne)', and below that 'Post Card'. Finally there was the instruction, 'The address only to be written on this side', and this was underlined. It was the words 'Great Britain' that caused the trouble.

Complaints from Ireland came thick and fast. One irate Irishman wrote to the Postmaster General, '. . . there is no such power in the world as "Great Britain"', and the press made a great play on the omission of 'and Ireland' from the heading of the postcards. Theories as to the reason for this ranged from 'official bungling' to a tongue-in-the-cheek opinion voiced by one newspaper that '. . . the Ministry, intending to let Ireland go at last, are gently preparing the public for separation by the initial step of ignoring Ireland on the face of their penny postcard'. The Post Office reacted very quickly to the criticism and a new penny card, headed 'Great Britain and Ireland', was printed and issued later in the year.

The $1\frac{1}{2}$d card also omitted to mention Ireland, but presumably because it was not used to Ireland did not cause such uproar. A replacement card with 'and Ireland' was not approved until three years later and not issued until a year after that.

The postcard was becoming more and more popular with each year that passed. By 1879 the annual total of cards dealt with by the Post Office was about 150 million, compared to the 70 million at the beginning of the decade. The privately printed card grew in popularity too, and the use of small illustrations around the edge increased, particularly amongst breweries and hotels. These cards were usually ordered by a customer from a printer, to the customer's design – allowing for the Post Office regulations. The printer arranged to have the cards embossed with the postage stamp by the Inland Revenue Department and delivered the cards in bulk to the customer. The charge made by the Post Office for embossing the stamp was considerable, and much persuasion was exerted, even through the House of Commons, to change the system. But the profits from the stamping of private cards were high and the Post Office held on to its monopoly. The newspaper *The Standard* was taken to task by the Postmaster General for incorrectly reporting one of his speeches in the House during a debate. The paper replied, '. . . the errors in the report are entirely due to the Postmaster General's inveterate habit of answering questions in so low a tone as to be quite inaudible in the gallery.' Although the Post Office was congratulated upon the issue of its first Reply Paid Cards in October 1882, it came in for more criticism in November 1884 when a complaint was received at Head Office about the cost of the official thin Inland card. The cards sold at 7d for twelve, unchanged for seven years, a price a little over the face value of ½d each in order to satisfy the stationers, as we have already explained. The writer of the complaining letter pointed out that the Foreign Postcard, made of better quality board, sold at twelve for a shilling with no charge for the board. 'Could someone explain this to me?' he asked. The Post Office found itself in the familiar position of being unable to please all the people all the time, and how they explained the position to the complainant we were unable to find out; however the matter was closed within the Post Office itself when one high official commented to another, in a memorandum justifying inactivity, '. . . no-one has ever complained before'. It was twenty-nine years before the charge for the board was removed.

Postcard development was faster on the Continent and by the end of the decade issues had been made to commemorate important exhibitions or events in several places, including Paris and Amsterdam. The first British Official Commemorative issue appeared in May 1890 to celebrate the Jubilee of Penny Postage. A Postal Exhibition was held at the Guildhall from 16 to 19 May, and a limited issue of 10,000 penny postcards was sold, the proceeds going to the Rowland Hill Benevolent Fund. The cards sold at 6d and had an enlarged drawing of the Arms of London as a central motif instead of the Royal Arms. They were printed in bright carmine on the largest sized card yet produced by the Post Office, and were so popular that by 5 July the newspaper *The Graphic* reported, 'These Guildhall postcards took the fancy of the public so much that they have since been sold for the high premium of a guinea.' How much they were a departure from the normal official card can be seen at Plate 2.

By the 1890s public and commercial clamour for a private postcard had forced the Post Office to consider how it best might relinquish its monopoly. As before when it changed its postcard policy, there were Messrs De la Rue to consider. They quite naturally were not keen to see their monopoly completely broken unless a new contract with the Post Office would compensate them in some way. Mr Adolph Tuck of Messrs Raphael Tuck & Sons made much of the need to allow free private printing of postcards, and together with Mr Henniker Heaton MP, a great postal reformer, was instrumental in forcing the issue to a successful conclusion. An internal Post Office memo of November 1893 speaks of the 'moral obligation to De la Rue of the Government' as being 'the difficulty' in the way of allowing the public to use adhesive stamps, i.e. allowing the use of postcards that were not printed by De la Rue or stamped by the Inland Revenue Department. Mr Henniker Heaton had his finger well on the pulse of public opinion and put down a question for the House of Commons for 15 February 1894. 'Why,' he asked, 'could not any card of the prescribed size bearing a halfpenny adhesive stamp be accepted as a postcard?' What was holding things up, he wanted to know, 'De la Rue?'

It is right to conclude that they were, but it was not a great delay from the time that the Post Office decided that it would have to give way to the pressure put on it. De la Rue acted as any reputable commercial enterprise would have done and negotiated the most advantageous terms they could get in return for an early termination of their still monopolistic contract. Eventually, on 1 September 1894, the production and use of private postcards was allowed, but even then there was public dissatisfaction. The Treasury Warrant of 24 August 1894 gives the details of the cards, among which were the following.

The maximum size to be as nearly as maybe . . . that of the Inland Official Postcard for the time being in use.

The minimum size to be 3¼ in. by 2¼ in. (82 mm. by 57 mm.).

Nothing shall be written, printed or otherwise impressed on the side of the postcard which bears the postage stamp, except

a. the address to which the card is to be delivered,

b. the name and address of the sender of the card,

c. any direction as to the mode in which the postcard is to be dealt with, such as Immediate, Local, Forward, OHMS.

Anything, including a letter, may be written, printed or otherwise impressed on the side of the postcard which does not bear the postage stamp . . . but nothing may be attached to it.

The Warrant goes on to say that infringement of the regulations will incur the Letter Rate charges.

It is apparent even from the extracts given above, which are neither continuous nor verbatim, that the regulations did not make the position of the private postcard very clear. The regulation concerning size, i.e. 'as nearly as maybe . . . that of the Inland Official Postcard for the time being in use', came in for particular criticism. The *Westminster Gazette* posted a selection of cards on 1 September 1894 from various places in London, so that they would have to be dealt with by different Postmasters. The cards were of assorted sizes, with and without attachments, and the official reactions to the same card ranged from Letter Rate surcharge through acceptance at the Postcard Rate to rejection and return to the sender. The *Gazette* came up with a best buy in Postmasters and lightheartedly recommended one part of London as the place to post the new cards with the best chance of getting them through. However, in its report on 3 September it concluded, '. . . the public wants to know what it may do, and may not do, with this new halfpenny post. This the public is hardly likely to find out so long as the Post Office doesn't know itself.'

Another major bone of contention was the 'correspondence' or 'court' card. This was a card often illustrated or decorated with a small picture, that was used as postal stationery. It was posted inside an envelope and most hotels and clubs kept them for the convenience of their guests. As the regulations stood, the court card could not be used as a postcard because its normal size, 115 mm. by 89 mm., could not be interpreted to be 'as nearly as maybe the size of the Official Inland Card' – 122 mm. by 75 mm. Manufacturers held large stocks of court cards and they enjoyed considerable popularity. Criticism of the new regulations which excluded the court card from the Postcard Rate filled the daily press, and the Post Office reacted very quickly to it. By September 14 the *Liverpool Echo* was able to tell its readers that it understood that court shaped cards would be accepted as postcards, because the Post Office had instructed Postmasters to let them pass. But there was still no official statement to the public. As before, Messrs De la Rue had to be consulted and they, in close consultation with the Postmaster General, produced a simple solution to the problem. Since the upper limit of size for the new private postcard was 'as nearly as maybe that of the official card for the time being in use,' all that they had to do was to issue a court size official card. De la Rue would have the extra business of producing the card to compensate them for the increase in the number of private cards that would be used, the public would be able to use the long-established court card as a postcard, and the regulations need not be changed. Five months later, on Monday 21 January 1895, the new court size official cards were put on sale. They were made of stout card, measured 115 mm. by 89 mm. (4½ in. by 3½ in.) and were issued in addition to the existing cards.

This was a considerable victory for the advocates of the private postcard, but the reformers were not yet satisfied. On the Continent restrictions on the production of postcards had long since been lifted, particularly in Germany, and many cards were posted to this country or sold in this country for posting back abroad. They were larger than the British size, being about 140 mm. by 89 mm. (5½ in. by 3½ in.), the maximum size allowed by the Universal Postal Union, and they were often pictorial cards. British manufacturers complained that their own cards were too small to take effective pictures and that they were not allowed to compete with the Continentals by producing larger cards. By 1898 a Post Office Postage Rates Committee was prompted to look into the matter and on 31 October they reported that

We have evidence of the extensive use of illustrated cards as postcards on the Continent, and most of them seem to be of the maximum size allowed by the Postal Union. . . . The Post Office could be accused of hampering trade because it doesn't allow manufacture of private cards larger than the official Inland size. The old argument that larger postcards would be damaged by the string used to tie up the bundles of envelopes is no longer valid now that most people have envelopes something over $3\frac{1}{2}$ in. wide, and court shape cards will just go into the same envelopes.

The committee went on to consider Government obligations to their contractors, De la Rue, and concluded that, in view of the contract with them and the framing of the regulations which governed the maximum size of the private postcard, 'it would only be fair to De la Rue . . . to arrange for the issue of a larger official card'. It was much the same solution that resolved the court size card problem. They recommended that two new cards of the larger size be issued, one for inland use and one for foreign use, and that, except for the court size Inland card 'which has a large sale', the existing issues be withdrawn. They also advised a change in the layout of the card which, four years later, was to account for a major step in the development of the picture postcard. The Inland card current in October 1898 had printed on the address side 'THE ADDRESS ONLY TO BE WRITTEN ON THIS SIDE', as in the top card shown in Plate 2. The committee suggested 'that this be changed to "THIS SIDE FOR THE ADDRESS", as the former does not correctly represent the present view of the Department'.

The 'present view' of the Department was that nothing could be written on the address side of the card that made it difficult to read the address, obscured the stamp or embarrassed the Postal Officials. The committee's recommendations were accepted, although the wording on the old card was 'THE ADDRESS TO BE WRITTEN ON THIS SIDE', and the new cards were on sale from 1 November 1899. A Foreign Postcard of this issue is shown in Plate 2. The issue date was anticipated by several private firms who had prepared their private postcards in advance. Among them was Raphael Tuck & Sons, the firm of Mr Adolph Tuck who had played such an important part in bringing about the new regulations. The British version of the Continental, or Postal Union, sized Private Picture Postcard thus became legal from that date, and from then began the development of the picture postcard as we know it today.

The story of the Official Cards does not stop here, but goes on throughout the whole of our period. Indeed, with the introduction of the new card size, the Post Office wished to stop imprinting the stamp onto privately produced cards of other than Continental or court sizes. This caused another confrontation with commercial interests, which had large stocks of the original smaller size, or oblong, cards. That struggle we will not go into here, as we have reached the beginning of the true picture postcard, but the official cards have, up to now, formed a neglected part of what is known as postal history. They have been lumped in with envelopes and covers in general. We hope we have made it clear that they are a vital part of postcard history, for without them there would have been no picture postcards.

Now that the postcard has passed its hundredth birthday, interest in all cards is rapidly growing and it is to be hoped that collectors will seek out the officials as well as the more readily obtainable picture cards. In America some official cards are changing hands at over £20 each, and prices are rising. In Britain they can generally be got for a few new pence, but the situation cannot last.

The official field presents an intriguing challenge to the collector, for it has been poorly cultivated until recently (see Alan Huggins in our Bibliography). There is opportunity for satisfying detective work and good financial investment. Catalogues of stationery published around 1900 by Stanley Gibbons, Campbell and Bright among others now sell for around £5 each and are worth hunting down – if only for the entertainment of working out which one had the correct information.

In case the reader may think that we have dwelt too long on these cards, and he still does not see them as the true forerunners of the picture postcard, we have assembled a few specimens of Foreign and Empire Officials in Plate 3.

Further, in order to show that Europe did not have a monopoly on postcards, an impression which is easily given, we have ventured further afield. As with stamps of that time, British official postcards were plain and uninspiring in appearance compared with foreign versions, and it was left to the picture postcard to brighten things up.

## The Picture Postcard

No date can be given for the first picture postcard as it was for the official card because, unlike the latter, it was not introduced formally but just evolved. That pictures found their way onto postcards is not surprising, for pictorial stationery was in common use in the 1840s, including the Mulready pictorial envelopes which attracted public scorn and satirical imitations. Christmas cards were in use in the 1850s as well as with pictorial envelopes advocating many things from Free Trade to the Abolition of Slavery. Elihu Burrit used the pictorial envelope to further the cause of a cheap Ocean Postage, and birthday and Easter cards were known in the 1880s. None of these qualify as picture postcards, however, although their development foreshadowed the way in which the picture cards were to evolve.

As we have seen earlier, the postcard progressed more quickly on the Continent than it did in Britain, and it is in France that the earliest recorded joining together of postcard and picture is to be found. During the Franco-Prussian War about 40,000 French troops were stationed at Conlie in La-Sarthe, France in 1870. They were mostly country men with little formal education who found letter writing difficult and tiring. A local stationer in the village of Lille-le-Guillaume, named Besnardeau, realized this and began to sell the men cards on which to write instead of the normal paper and envelopes. The cards were decorated with drawings of stacked arms, cannon, shells and various patriotic designs. At the top was printed '*Guerre de 1870*' and then '*Camp de Conlie*'. Underneath a scroll proclaimed '*Souvenir de la Défence Nationale*', and below that, '*Armée de Bretagne*'.

  In Britain small advertisements of the variety already described and in one colour only were printed on the official cards from 1870. They were not views, and it is likely that the term 'picture postcard' was not created until the view card was established. However, British cards posted on 1 October 1870 carrying pictorial advertisement designs are real treasures to own, and in retrospect would today be known as picture postcards. Isolated instances of cards having engraved views have been reported on the Continent for the period up to 1882, but it was not until that year that the next significant event occurred. The lithographer Zrenner produced a commemorative card for the Nuremberg Exhibition on 1 May and later claimed it to be the first picture postcard. It was probably the first commemorative card. It showed a sketch of the entrance to the Exhibition, but more as a design than a straightforward view. There will be discussions forever about the first picture postcard – or until one is found firmly dated the 1 October 1869. The Belgian card shown in Plate 3, which was first issued in 1871, could be argued to be a picture card. However, the first type of true picture card was a view card, and the earliest that we have seen, apart from the monochrome 1882 Nuremberg card, is one posted from Heligoland to Hamburg on 5 August 1889 which belongs to the Reverend W. R. Saunders of Kenchester. It is a large card, 140 mm. by 89 mm., of a size not permitted in Britain until 11 years later, and shows coloured figures of a fisherman and fisherwoman standing either side of a coloured view of the island, under which is a small space for the message. The card appears to be an official issue, judging from its address side appearance, and is headed 'Union Postale Universelle', 'Heligolande Post Karte'. It bears the Queen's head (Victoria) three halfpenny cum ten pfennig adhesive stamp. If it is an official card the picture may have been printed privately after issue. The stamp too is a puzzle, for Britain did not accept adhesive stamps on postcards until 1894, yet in 1889 the island was a British possession. It was ceded to Germany a year later and became part of Prussia in 1892, so there is little hope of tracing the card's ancestry there.

  Most authorities consider that the first picture postcards recognizable as such were those that were posted from the top of the Eiffel Tower at the Paris Exhibition in 1889. The tower had been built especially for the Exhibition and was by far the tallest building in the world at the time. It was pictured on the left-hand third of the message side of the card. The cards could be stamped and posted at the top of the tower, and usually 'X marked the spot' where this was done. This facility for the traveller to pinpoint for those at home, or for his own recollection at leisure, the exact extent of his travels caught the public's imagination. Holidays away from home were now becoming popular and possible for increasingly large numbers of people, and at the start of the last decade of the century view cards of hotels, mountains or holiday resorts were circulating widely, most of them bearing crosses. The Rigi mountain in Switzerland, mentioned in the Preface, and an advertisement card for Cook's tours available at the top of Vesuvius are shown at Plates 7 and 10.

In Germany in particular the development of new printing techniques enabled the printers to produce in quantity cards bearing small views. These grew rapidly in popularity and soon almost every town and village in Germany had its own card bearing two or three small unbordered (vignetted) views of the locality, and inscribed 'Gruss Aus' or 'Gruss Von' (greetings from). A typical card of this sort is shown at Plate 10, and it is worth comparing this private picture postcard design with that of the official card issued for the Budapest Millennium Exhibition shown in Plate 3, to see how much these early cards influenced design for the whole of the decade. The development of the phototype process in Germany around 1892 enabled the printers to produce more faithful pictures, and to do it more quickly. Cards were exported by the million to countries all over the world, including Britain, and colours began to replace the earlier black and white and monochrome views. In Germany itself the habit of collecting cards caught on and spread so rapidly that it became known as 'the plague of Germany'.

At home, however, the Post Office monopoly prevented the development of private cards and British manufacturers of postal stationery became more and more agitated at the flood of Continental cards which reached the country. They argued that, since the Post Office delivered these cards to addresses in Britain, surely British-made cards of similar size and design could be allowed. The Post Office did not agree. International postal agreements were one thing, and internal postage another.

The brightest and largest card printed and issued in Britain up to 1890 was the vermilion Official Postal Jubilee Card issued in May of that year. The heading of the card is shown in Plate 2. Its postal rate was presumably 1d, because it contravened the regulations on size. In June 1891 another interesting British issue was made at the Royal Naval Exhibition held at Earls Court. With the sanction of the Postmaster General, an official stout white card had printed upon its reverse a blue sketch of the Eddystone lighthouse. A model of the lighthouse was built in the Exhibition grounds and by posting the cards at the top of the model they could be cancelled with the special Exhibition stamp. Today these cards are fetching over £5 each. Two years later the lighthouse was used again with a special card at the Gardening and Forestry Exhibition.

At last, on 1 September 1894, the British Post Office allowed private postcards to be printed and used with the halfpenny adhesive stamp. They were for Inland use only and were restricted in maximum size to the same dimensions as the official card then in use (122 mm. by 75 mm.). There do not seem to be any such private cards in existence today – if they ever existed. The first picture cards produced appear to have been of the court size (115 mm. by

89 mm.), and had they been posted and properly treated by the Postmaster concerned, they would have been charged at the Letter Rate because they were too deep and would not have been within the regulations.

However, court cards bearing small pictures in colour had been used in envelopes for some years, and those manufacturers who took advantage of the opportunity to produce their own postcards almost certainly took some of their existing stocks of court size Correspondence Cards and printed 'Post Card' on the back of them. The first British-made view cards were probably the court size cards issued by Messrs George Stewart of Edinburgh, in 1894, showing small views of that city in the top left-hand corners. The Post Office soon accepted that court size private postcards were a fait accompli, and within a month had instructed Postmasters not to charge the Letter Rate for them. Four months later the official court size card was issued, and the private court size card then automatically conformed with the regulation that it be no larger than the official Inland card then in use, and became legal. Just to show that it does not pay to be too dogmatic about which were the earliest view cards sold in this country to use the adhesive stamp, we shall mention that in our collection we have a court size card that bears a coloured view of the Embankment, complete with carriages and horses, that is dated 25 December 1892. On the address side it is titled 'POST CARD'. Nevertheless, by our own earlier definition, it was not within the regulations at the time that it was posted and cannot be considered a true postcard.

It is surprising, in view of the clamour that they made for the end of the Post Office monopoly, that more British firms did not produce Picture Postcards from the first day that they were allowed to do so. Mr Adolph Tuck of Messrs Tuck & Sons explained this in an interview in 1900 by pointing out that even from 1895, when court size cards were permissible, the larger Continental cards, generally of full Postal Union size (140 mm. by 89 mm.), were much more suitable for printing pictures on. He led a campaign for the British manufacturers to have the same freedom as the Continentals, and finally on 1 November 1899 British-made cards of the Postal Union size were allowed to be made and used. Mr Tuck had been told of the impending change in the regulations about six months ahead, and so his firm were able to issue their first cards that day.

Very few of the major publishers of cards have any records of their products at the turn of the century. A decline in the postcard trade in the 1920s, two World Wars, fires caused by bombing and the cost of allocating floor space to the storage of papers have all contributed to the destruction or disposal of records. Messrs Tuck are no exception. However it is possible to single out what may well have been their first cards, or were at least among the very earliest, and details of these are given in Appendix 3 along with those of some of the more important cards of the other major manufacturers.

The collector, of course, can see here the start of a fascinating trail leading hopefully to the earliest extant copy of a Tuck's picture postcard. A card stamped 1 November 1899 would be a treasure and cannot help but appreciate as revived interest grows. But Tuck's are by no means the only manufacturers whose earliest card has yet to be found, and as we proceed through this and later chapters intriguing avenues of research are opened, all offering the thrill of the chase and the possibility of financial reward.

Before the turn of the century several well-known firms were producing picture postcards in Britain, including Valentine's of Dundee, who had been using the collotype process since 1895, the Pictorial Stationery Co., Blum & Degen, and Corketts of Leicester, who laid claim with George Stewart as the first British manufacturers of picture postcards.

Around 1897 the first artistic designs, as distinct from views, began to appear on postcards. Artists who had brought the design of theatrical and advertising posters to a high creative standard turned their attention to the postcard, among them Mucha, Cassiers and Kirchner, later to find fame with his pin-ups.

The final push that brought the postcard into everyone's home, and sent the annual consumption over the 500 million mark, was provided by the Boer War. Patriotism was a popular sentiment then, and the picture postcard of the new large size allowed from 1899 was the right medium to express it. The khaki uniformed soldiers, adopting the colour of the Indian battlefields and the name of field dust in place of the traditional red coats, figured prominently with proudly flying Union Jacks, and excellent cards were drawn by Harry Payne and Richard Caton Woodville.

Coloured cards became popular in Britain around 1900, and the collecting craze had developed to such an extent that in July of that year the *Picture Postcard Magazine* was published; 'the first magazine to combine travel, philately and art through a natural connecting medium, the Picture Postcard', to quote the Editor, E. W. Richardson. In the magazine, Tuck's announced a £1,000 prize competition for the largest collection of their cards that had passed through the post, and this accelerated the spread of the collecting habit. Automatic vending machines were installed at major railway stations, special pens were put on sale for the writers of postcards, portable and permanent cabinets were available to keep cards in, postal clubs were formed with branches all over the world, and many cards that filled the postman's bag were there not to carry a message, but to fill a hole in someone's collection. The Golden Age of the Postcard had arrived.

The following chapters tell the story of this age, of the use of photography, mechanical cards, the trouble that the Post Office had with glitter cards and metal cards, and many other facets of those exciting years. In almost every picture postcard venture the accent was on quality, and because so many cards were produced the latest and most refined methods of printing could be afforded. A contemporary writer commented that the picture postcard portrait was 'every bit as good as the shilling cabinet photograph', and the Editor of the *Picture Postcard Magazine* made the same point in a rather different way. Commenting upon the flood of commemorative cards that followed within hours of the death of Queen Victoria in 1901, he wrote, '. . . many portrait postcards of Queen Victoria appeared during her life, but none was so good as those published after her death'.

As you collect your cards you will notice that the majority of them have a full-out picture on one side, while the other side is shared by the address and the message. Some that you will see will have the message on the picture side (as in Plate 14), while the other side bears the address only. The cards that share one side between the address and the message are known as 'divided back' cards, because of their dividing line, and they were not made until 1902. An early example is shown below. This is a good pointer when it comes to

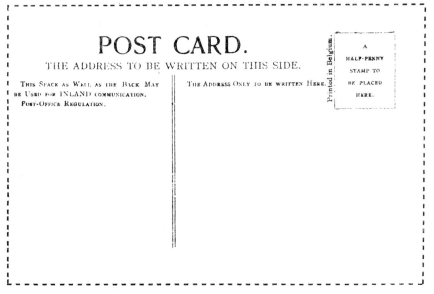

An early divided-back card

dating your cards, yet some authorities on postcards say that writing on the address side was allowed in 1897. Other writers express surprise that anyone could imagine it was allowed in 1897 because the Postal Regulation permitting it was not published until January 1902. We have spent a great deal of time trying to get to the bottom of the divided back business and have come up with our own story of what happened, but if any reader can be more precise then we should like to hear about it.

We start at the beginning in 1870, when it was made clear by the Post Office that one side of their cards was reserved for the address only, and when privately printed cards were allowed from 17 June 1872 the Post Office *Circular* at the time reminded Postmasters '. . . the communication must not extend to the front side' (address side). The first change to this rule was given in a Treasury Warrant of 28 August 1894, which announced that the name and address of the sender of a postcard could now go on the address side, together with any instructions such as 'Immediate, Local, Forward, OHMS,' etc. But as yet no message was allowed on that side. The Member of Parliament for Canterbury, Mr J. Henniker Heaton, asked many questions in the House, from the time of his election in 1895, about the interpretation of the Postal Regulations relating to messages and attachments on the address side of postcards; he even sent cards of his own, designed to flout the regulations, to other MPs, to show how confusing it all was. Eventually in February 1896 the Secretary to the Post Office wrote to the President of the Postage Rates Committee, as follows:

> Mr Hill,
>   You will observe the numerous questions asked in Parliament about what may or may not appear on the address side of a postcard.
>   The maintenance of the existing regulations is hardly worth the time consumed in framing answers to these questions, and I shall be glad if the Postage Rates Committee will consider whether it is possible to sweep away the present restrictions en bloc.

Mr Hill obviously got to work, for the significant change in the regulations was announced in a Post Office Inland Post Warrant of 16 June the following year. The new regulation was:

> . . . nothing shall be written, printed or otherwise impressed upon, or attached to any part of, that side of a postal packet which bears the address at which the packet is to be delivered, which either by tending to prevent the easy and quick reading of the address of the packet by inconvenient proximity to the stamp or stamps used in the payment of postage, or in any other way, is in itself or in the manner in which it is written, printed, impressed or attached, likely in the opinion of the Postmaster General to embarrass the Officers of the Post Office in dealing with a Postal packet.

This was still confusing and open to a wide range of interpretations, but a message was no longer forbidden as such, although no-one seemed to appreciate it at the time. In retrospect, the *Post Office Historical Summary*, published in 1911 by HMSO, says, '. . . in 1897 the prohibition of writing or printing on the address side of a postcard was removed'. But an examination of your cards will show that messages were not written on address sides until 1902.

We have concluded that it did not occur to anyone in 1897 that the regulations could be interpreted in such a way, but as we pointed out when dealing with official cards, the Postage Rates Committee Report of 31 October 1898 recommended that the current card heading, 'THE ADDRESS ONLY TO BE

WRITTEN ON THIS SIDE', should be changed to 'THIS SIDE FOR THE ADDRESS'. They had concluded that the former 'does not correctly represent the present view of the Department'. The mood for the change to having messages on the address side was right, but no-one put it into words.

We believe that it was the pressure of business that brought about the change. F. Hartmann, a German printer, planned to begin as a publisher of postcards in Britain in 1902 and wanted some popular line in order to get off to a good start. After studying the regulations concerning the postcards that he wished to sell, he concluded that there was no reason why a message should not be written on the address side of a card provided it was well clear of the address and the stamp. He decided that a good way to separate the two would be to draw a line down the back of the card and clearly mark the places for the address, the stamp and the message. He probably made some specimen cards and sent them to the Postmaster General for his approval in 1901. The Postmaster General approved of the idea, and asked that the change be announced by the Editor of the *Picture Postcard Magazine* in its January 1902 issue. This is what the Editor said:

> Picture Postcards have at last received official recognition at the hands of the British Postal Authorities and we have been asked by the Postmaster General to call the attention of our readers to an important rule which came into force on the first day of this month. This is to the effect that postcards must bear the stamp on the front, or address, side of the card and unless they do so the cards will be treated as insufficiently paid letters and surcharged accordingly. This has long been the rule on the Continent . . . and we ask those of our readers who cling to this unsportsmanlike custom to give way in this instance. On the other hand, and as showing that the Post Office does not wantonly worry its patrons, the public, postcards may bear on the front, i.e. address side, a continuation of the message, or the name and address of the sender, or even an advertisement, so long as such matter does not interfere in any way with the legibility of the address.

Mr Hartmann soon had his cards on the market and other publishers immediately followed suit. The card illustrated on page 38 claims that: 'This Space as Well as the Back May be Used for INLAND Communication. Post-Office Regulation.' We have been unable to find such a Regulation. The *Post Office Guide* for the quarter before January 1902 had the following to say: 'Nothing may be written or printed on the address side of any postal packet which, either by tending to prevent the easy and quick reading of the address, or by inconvenient proximity to the postage stamp, or in any other way is likely to embarrass the Officers of the Department. . . .' The reference to 'any postal packet' includes the postcard. If a change in the formal regulations had taken place in January 1902 it would have been reflected in the *Post Office Guide* for January 1903. There was no change; the regulation remained word for word as it had been in 1901. Hence our theory about Mr

Hartmann, and the Postmaster General's interpretation of what was basically the 1897 Regulation.

Other countries adopted the divided back slowly, and the Universal Postal Union as a whole did not agree to use it until June 1906. Today these delays are helpful to us. The countries which would accept the divided back were often listed on the card, and this enables the printing date to be fixed quite closely, as explained in Appendix 5.

The great majority of the early cards used in Britain were printed in Germany, either for representatives of German firms operating in this country or for native entrepreneurs who wished for the best in printing. One of the latter was John Evelyn Wrench, who started selling his first twenty-five German-printed views in December 1900, and by 1903 was looking forward to selling 50 million cards a year. As we explain later, he did not.

By 1910 private postcards formed 90 per cent of the cards in the post and it seemed as if the postcard boom would go on for ever. But the boom had reached its peak.

When the postcard had been introduced it had attracted scorn because of the openness of the message. Its image changed slowly with the help of Mr Gladstone and the moneyed classes who travelled to the Continent. By 1900 the *Picture Postcard Magazine*, perhaps partisan, described the Picture Postcard collector as a member of 'an artistic, cultured and wealthy class'. But by 1910, the Editor of *Country Life*, a magazine aimed at that class, said of the halfpenny postcard, '. . . many of us scarcely ever use these means of communication except in urgent cases. The present writer . . . must confess to an unmitigated and prejudicial dislike to postcards in any shape or form.' The picture card was now a product for the masses, and standards began to decline as quantity displaced quality. The reputable firms such as Messrs Tuck and Valentine's maintained their standards, but the quality of design suffered, particularly with imported cards.

In 1914 the start of the First World War stemmed the flow of imported cards, as most of them came from Germany. British manufacturers produced some fine designs during the war years, but despite the remarkable front line photographs published by the *Daily Mail* in their immensely popular 'Battle Picture Series', the Picture Postcard was not a part of public life as it had been during the Boer War. This time the war was too near home to be glorified without regard for reality, and its results more readily measured in dead and wounded soldiers.

The final blow to the picture postcard craze came in 1918 when the Inland postage was raised to 1d. The number of cards in the post dropped to almost a half of the previous year's total. Some cards could still be posted for a halfpenny provided that they carried a 'formula of courtesy' of five words or less and not a message. The Postal Regulations were confusing once again and the newspapers were full of their own interpretations. A representative of the Post Office explained the regulations to a *Daily Mail* reporter: '. . . such phrases as "Love from all, to all", "Kind regards to all", "Wishing you a Happy Birthday", come within the definition of formulas of courtesy . . . but phrases such as "Arrived safely", "Fine weather here", "Having a good time", are in the nature of letters, and the cards should bear a penny stamp.'

We would like to finish this chapter on the history of the postcard in the way we started it, by looking at an official card. In 1918 the 'Pig Control Postcard' was given away free during October to anyone who asked for it. It was already addressed to the 'Livestock Commissioner Area No. – ' and was for the use of owners of small numbers of pigs. We haven't seen one and don't know what information had to be put upon it. Another case to be solved, perhaps, but as far as the picture postcard was concerned the Golden Age was over.

# 2

# The Mechanics of Collecting

What you decide to collect will depend upon your reasons for collecting. In the end you will only be able to rationalize your collecting by deciding why you are anxious to acquire picture postcards. For example, during the years from 1900 to 1910 between 1 and 3 million postcards passed through the post daily. If we suppose that 99 per cent of those cards have been destroyed, then considering those years alone, and doing an elementary and probably highly inaccurate piece of mathematics, we may guess that about 35 million of those cards are still around today. You would be foolish, therefore, if you were to attempt to collect in terms of quantity alone. Of course the drive to own a large collection is a natural one, and the ultimate satisfaction of owning the largest would be euphoric, but in general terms it is impossible. It is not impossible, however, if you have decided that your reason for collecting picture postcards is that you like pictures of, say, old Edwardian and Victorian letter boxes. It seems reasonable to suppose that you could build up the world's largest collection in a fairly short time.

In this chapter we look at the 'what' and 'where' of collecting, and also suggest the sort of cards that might be of interest to those looking for an investment. The postcard has not been the subject of widespread collecting since Edwardian times, and those who have the best collections today have built them up in an atmosphere of calm and insulation from commerce and dealers. Their reaction to the rapidly growing number of new collectors generated by the hundredth birthday of the postcard is an angry one. In response to the public demand for cards many antique shops now sell them, but no-one yet devotes his whole time to it, and most of the trade in postcards is done through the post.

The newcomer to postcards may find that the beginnings of a collection are under his own roof. The first places to look are in the attic, the cellar, the garden shed and in all those old boxes and cases that have been lying around for ages and ages. Grandma and Grandpa may have popped cards between the covers of books or in the family photograph album. They could well have some just lying around the house, so the next thing is to go and see them, as well as all the aunts and uncles that you can remember. Try the family first and you could be very surprised at the result. Follow them up with your friends and neighbours, the local publican and colleagues at work. Then the dustman. He has a marvellous opportunity to see the things that are cleared out of houses, although most of the cards that were made before 1918 have left their houses for the dustbins already. But there were a lot of cards and a fair number are still being thrown away. For a few shillings the dustman could get your collection off to a fair start, but finding cards this way is becoming more and more difficult as interest in them revives, and for some types of card the demand is already beginning to overtake the supply.

The jumble sale and church bazaar can sometimes be good hunting grounds. On these occasions all household stones are turned over by the good-hearted people who stock the stalls. With luck a collection of cards can be had for a few shillings, together with the satisfaction of helping a good cause, a satisfaction well in keeping with the high moral image that the early postcard enthusiasts had of their hobby.

The junk stalls at your local market can be a fine source of postcards. Quite often there will be a complete album for sale, and the average album seldom holds less than three hundred cards. Look at the album carefully and see if many cards are missing. If the album has clearly been only partly filled and the cards stop short at some definite point on the way through, all is well. Count the total number of cards and make an offer, which should not need to be more than one or two new pence per card unless there is something very unusual there. But be careful about the something unusual that is not there. If the gaps in the album are haphazard, then it is almost certain that the junk dealer or another more advanced collector has been through the book and taken out the best cards. In that case, supposing that you still want the cards to get your collection started, make a fuss about it and greatly reduce the offer that you first thought of. Don't remind the dealer that you are getting the album too, but remember the need for somewhere to keep your cards: the album may be worth buying for its own sake.

Buying cards in job lots from market stalls or junk shops is unlikely to appeal to the advanced collector, but as a way of obtaining a representative starting collection it can hardly be improved upon. Later on it will be better to sort through the album for just those cards that you wish to collect.

The more sophisticated antique shops are beginning to notice the picture postcard, particularly since the hundredth anniversary, and the value of some cards has risen to £10 or more each. The high prices for silk and embroidered cards, and cards by particular artists such as Raphael Kirchner, have developed over the last few years, and the long-time collectors are doing their best to discourage monetary trade in cards. They argue that their hobby is not one that should be exploited for profit, and that only true collectors should seek out the cards. Unfortunately, from their point of view, the laws of supply and demand apply, and now that there is such an overwhelming issue of postage stamps from practically every country that can think of an excuse to issue them, disillusioned stamp collectors are beginning to turn to postcards. The antique shop that offers picture postcards for sale generally does so quoting an individual price for each card. The collector must bargain over the quoted price, and for a purchase of twenty or more cards prices should come down by about fifty per cent.

Local house sales often turn up a few postcard albums and a measure of the cards' growing popularity is that they now command their own lot numbers, whereas a few years ago they would probably have come under 'contents of attic'. A sale brings one into open competition with other collectors and it is foolish to bid highly for a collection from which you want only a few cards. We do not suggest that you should form a 'ring' of collectors to the vendor's disadvantage, but there is no harm in approaching the purchaser after the sale. He, like you, will specialize, and may be prepared to exchange some of his cards.

Another way of obtaining cards is to advertise for them. Almost any method, from a notice in the local Post Office to an advertisement in a national journal, should bring results. Local papers often tap a reasonably priced source and the Friday or Saturday editions seem to give the best results – presumably because of Sunday browsing. Beware of collections of postcards offered for sale in that way, however, and always insist upon seeing the cards before parting with your money. We have been burnt by not following this rule and have found no way of getting our money back that would cost less than grinning and bearing it.

We mentioned earlier that most of the trading in postcards is done through the post. There are several small journals, mainly part-time ventures that offer postcards for sale or auction. The largest of these is *International Postcard Market* (*IPM*), run by Mr John Smith, and this also carries small articles and extracts from early issues of the *Picture Postcard Magazine* and readers' own advertisements for wants, sales and exchanges. As far as we know there are no specialized magazines openly displayed for sale at the newsagents, but the circulation lists of the postal subscription magazines cover a staggering number of countries. The magazines provide a good service in sorting and classifying the cards for sale, and in providing a medium through which collectors may contact each other. But the purist frowns upon these magazines and prefers to build up his collection by personal exchanges with other collectors. When the normal sources have begun to run out of uncollected material, personal exchange is probably the only way.

In 1961 Mrs Drene Brennan formed the Postcard Collectors' Club of Great Britain, and the club publishes a monthly magazine, *Postcard World*. The club is non-profit making and members pay a small annual subscription to cover postage and printing costs. Meetings are occasionally held in London at which exchanges, sales and discussions on postcard topics take place. Members do research on specific postcard subjects and prepare check lists of the various publishers' output and of various types of cards. These findings are made freely available to fellow members. Through this club and by associations developed through advertisements in other postal magazines the collector can contact an expert in his or her field.

To help the beginner obtain his cards we had hoped to include a comprehensive list of dealers in this book. We had little response to our various advertisements and perhaps this is an encouraging sign that postcards have not yet been appropriated by the antique dealer at large. Nevertheless, those dealers who did reply are listed in Appendix 8 and they represent a very small fraction of the whole, so the reader should not consider the list even remotely complete. One dealer will recommend a second, and a subscription to one of the postal auction magazines often attracts a free copy of another.

The postal auction magazines offer the best route to a collection for someone who has decided what to collect before actually starting to do so, but it is a more expensive method than tramping the junk shops – and less fun. The magazines, with the exception of the *IPM*, include postcards as one of a number of categories of what may be called postal history or postal stationery. The cards are generally classified by subject and each lot is given an estimated valuation by the editor. Bids for lots have to reach the editor by a certain date, by letter or sometimes by telephone, and the winning bid of, say, £5 will not necessarily mean a payment of £5. The magazine normally specifies an amount by which a winning bid will be assumed to exceed the second highest bid. Thus, if the specified amount is £0.25 and Mr A bids £5 while second highest Mr B bids £3, Mr A will pay only £3.25 for the lot. Some postal auction magazines have been in existence for a long time and have established reputations for dealing with postal history. Magazines of that sort, such as the *Rigby Postal History Auction Catalogue*, tend to deal with postcards only if they have some philatelic interest through stamp or postmark. Most collectors of cards would not be prepared to pay the price premium that a stamp or cancellation attracts to the card. These magazines are, however, a useful outlet for the collector who may come across some of these 'specials' and for whom they may hold no particular interest. For the magazines also need to buy in cards or to accept cards for auction, in which case they usually charge a percentage commission.

Appendix 8 lists some of the magazines that we have found useful, and there will certainly be others, although perhaps the only ones which pretend to be magazines rather than postal auction lists are *Postcard World* and *IPM*. Almost all publishers of such lists will send a complimentary copy on receipt of a name and address.

The auction lists include official postcards among their lots, but at prices that reflect philatelic values. Official postcards are hardly ever found mixed with picture cards in markets or shops. The best place to find officials is in the local stamp shop. Unless they have been through the post officials have little to interest the stamp dealer who usually keeps them in an odd-box among his covers. If the dealer can be persuaded to dig out his odd-boxes, mint officials frequently turn up and can be bought for very little, although as with certain picture cards, prices are beginning to rise rather rapidly.

In order to decide what to collect it is probably wise to acquire a hotch-potch collection first in order to get a feel for the enormous variety of cards that were produced. We would suggest that you aim at around five hundred cards and do not worry about their condition at all. The most difficult aspect of deltiology is the cataloguing of one's collection, because there are so many ways of classifying the cards. As you collect the initial five hundred the first stages will be easy and classification by subject matter is obvious and convenient – rivers, trams, railways, actresses, views and so on. As you acquire more cards the simple classifications begin to overlap, with a tramway shown alongside a railway and a river, for example. This highlights the major lesson that the deltiologist has to learn, that eventually it will be necessary to specialize, although the term 'specialization' could apply to a collection containing one card of each type.

Some publishers produced cards of such individual appeal, like Stengel's beautiful art reproductions or W.H.'s 'Hold-to-Light' cards, that they defy any other classification than their own. Similarly, cards produced during the Boer War period may conveniently be filed under a 'war' heading whatever their content: humour, patriotism or plain view. Some collectors confine themselves to the cards of one manufacturer alone, but this does not reduce the number of possible categories by very much in most cases, as almost all the major producers issued examples of most types of cards. Others collect cards that were produced by named artists, such as Raphaël Kirchner, Louis Wain, C. Dana Gibson and many more whom we introduce later. Therefore we believe that each collector must develop his own classification system and, in doing that, he will come to a decision as to what he should collect. We have a composite system that includes three classifications under manufacturer's name (Tuck, Wrench and Bamforth), many subject headings such as 'humorous' and 'trams', artists such as Gibson and Asti, photographers, like 'L.L.', and periods such as pre-1900.

There is a difference between collecting for pleasure and collecting for profit, but it is very small. As pleasure is a premium commodity, those things that provide it soon become valuable. The most attractive postcards were produced during the period we deal with in this book: 1870–1918. Certain artists had a distinctive style, and where this was coupled with their early death, thus limiting their output, their cards have become sought after and hence valuable. A complete collection of a set or a series increases the card's value, and since condition is more important than postmark to the serious deltiologist, unused cards frequently demand higher prices than used ones. Of used cards, the earlier they were posted the higher their value, and cards stamped on the first day of a publisher's debut would be treasures indeed. The postal auction lists give a good idea of current prices, although they vary surprisingly from one publication to another. Appendix 6 gives a guide to the relative values of different types of cards and suggests the artists whose names add value to the pictures. Specific cards command several pounds – such as copies of the 'Beer and Baccy' card, or first day issues of the first postcard – and parallels can be accurately drawn with the stamp trade in assessing postmarks. Two useful books to have are *British Postmarks: a Short History and*

*Guide* by Alcock and Holland, and *Collect British Stamps* by Stanley Gibbons.

As in any field, a comprehensive and well-documented collection enhances its own intrinsic value: thus the decision as to which cards to collect is an important one in that your choice will determine whether you can build up a 'complete' collection. If you go for views there is no hope of acquiring all of them, but if you go for Chas. E. Flower's churches you could do it. Raphael Tuck produced limited editions of cards which they sold by subscription, as we describe in Chapter 10. These were designed to enable 'complete' collections to be made, and Tuck's believed that their value would increase rapidly. Today they are worth over £1 each, and they are well worth looking for, with the chance of completing a set. In our belief the field that offers the best chance of appreciation is the one that has been most neglected so far – the officials – and with the aid of Appendix 1 a good start can be made in identifying the various types and their issue dates up to 1899. There are catalogues available of British postal stationery, such as those produced by Higgins and Gage in America and Robson Lowe in Britain. They do not agree in detail on postcards, sometimes disagree on issue dates and disagree violently on values. We have compiled our Appendix from near-contemporary documents and Post Office records. We believe it to be accurate. If you should need further details you must adjudicate between the opinions of the two or three main catalogues which most large stamp dealers will possess. The list in Appendix 1 together with Plates 1 and 2 is designed to enable the deltiologist to identify any British officials that he may acquire by first selecting the Plate that shows his card, and then referring to the serial number in Appendix 1 indicated on the Plate. Detailed variations in the cards, such as the presence or absence of various full stops, or chains around the unicorn's neck, are best covered by a specialist work.

Cards often need cleaning. A gently applied soft rubber is frequently the most effective method, although shredded rubber gives the lightest touch. Moist, crumbled bread is good on cards that will resist water, but most are strong enough to withstand a cautiously applied, slightly damp cloth. If you have made a card damp be sure to keep it away from heat and allow it to dry at room temperature – if possible between a couple of heavy books to keep it flat. Water does remove some of the smooth, almost gloss, finish that the earlier cards had, but this can be replaced by gentle rubbing with candle wax.

Storage is difficult. Old albums are hard to obtain and their pages are often so brittle that removing a card tears the slots into which the corners are fitted. In any case the message side of a card is frequently as interesting as the picture side and the old paper albums hide one or the other. Plastic sheet can be cut with slots to form pages that will fit into a normal ring binder, and if a fairly heavy duty polythene of over 65 micron gauge is used, neither the slots for the cards nor the holes for the rings will tear or stretch in normal use. Pages that hold four cards on one side need only cost one or two new pence each if the polythene is bought in rolls. Suitable proprietary albums are available in polythene and PVC, the latter, stronger material being much more expensive than polythene. These albums are for postal stationery and the pockets that usually form the pages are larger than needed for postcards. Thus it is not efficient to use such albums since so much space is wasted and the price per page can be over ten new pence.

The best alternatives to albums are shoe boxes. We use them with protruding index cards to locate the different categories and put all our cards into individual small plastic bags. Much of the pleasure to be derived from postcards comes from handling them, unlike stamps which are one-sided creatures anyway, and yet sometimes handling spoils their condition. The plastic bag is a good solution, and postcard-sized bags are available from a number of manufacturers such as Courtaulds – although not specifically for postcards but as one of a wide range of bags. The bags are relatively inexpensive and £1 should buy about a thousand. If the cards are at all damp, or the place where they are stored is likely to suffer from wide variations in temperature, some spotting may occur, and cellophane bags would be more suitable. They are normally opaque on one side and cost about the same as polythene.

There is little doubt that detailed information about how many cards a publisher made, their numbers, their colours and so on can come only from collectors. Those British firms that publish postcards today have a Postcard Association whose current President is Mr Antony Jarrold of Messrs Jarrold & Sons Ltd, Norwich (one of whose earlier cards is shown in Plate 17), but neither they nor any individual publisher other than Bamforths appear to have records of postcard issues over our period. This lack of detailed information is one more of the attractions of postcard collecting: the chance of being the first to find out is always there.

# 3
# Topographical Cards

Topographical or view cards are the bread and butter cards of deltiology. This is not a disparaging remark; bread and butter alone can be very tasty, and there are many kinds of exciting 'jam' to be found on view cards. They are the staple diet of researchers in an ever-increasing range of study, as we showed in the Preface. You will soon discover after you have been through several batches of unclassified cards that the great bulk of postcards readily available today fall into this category. It is an enormous group and you will obviously have to make many sub-classifications within it or you would never find again any card filed under the general heading 'views'. You will naturally evolve your own system to suit your own collection and tastes, but we offer:

1. England, Scotland, Ireland and Wales. Naturally these general groups will soon become too unwieldy, but even after you have made further sub-divisions, cards of a distinctly national flavour may well fit here.

2. Broad topographical classifications such as 'West Country', 'the Lakes', 'islands', 'the Midlands', etc.

3. Classification by county.

4. Every now and then one acquires a collection of a more localized area, when town or even village headings become necessary. We defy anyone to invent a more practical or economical method of storing such town categories than in a shoe box, with headed divisions on white card between the towns in alphabetical order.

As you begin to specialize the following categories emerge: (a) crested cards; (b) trams, horsedrawn buses, motor cars, etc; (c) canals; (d) swans; (e) boating scenes; (f) stately homes, castles, cathedrals, churches, universities, hospitals, prisons, etc; (g) piers; (h) promenades; (i) post offices; (j) beaches; (k) street markets; (l) mills; (m) lighthouses; (n) costume; (o) framed views; (p) composite views. To name but a few! The list is limitless, and most collectors arrive at their own speciality. As mentioned in Chapter 2 there is very often an overlap in subject. Many cards could easily be filed under several headings. A typical view card of *Blackpool* may show one of its *piers* with a *tram* parked near it and a busy section of *beach* with some figures in the foreground showing good detail of *costume*. It may show Blackpool's town *crest* and be split into two or more pictures, which makes it a *composite* view. Seven possible classifications for one card. Only you can decide where to put it.

One name will crop up repeatedly in this chapter – Tuck's. They are the acknowledged master publishers in this field, producing literally thousands of superb view cards – notably in the 'Oilette' range. 'Oilettes' are reproductions of paintings on a host of subjects, most often specially commissioned by Tuck's for their postcard series.

To attempt to give here a bald list of all Tuck's view cards would be boring reading and an almost impossible task. So Tuck's various types will be discussed as we deal with other cards of their nature. It must be mentioned, however, that at least three dedicated collectors in different parts of the world are currently engaged in compiling check lists of all Tuck's series. It is a monumental task which will surely take several years to complete even if this is possible.

As we described in Chapter 1, the British pictorial card was not born until 1894. Publishers had been quick to take advantage of the new regulations, as in the case of Geo. Stewart and their views of Edinburgh. But the early view cards are poor things when compared to the gorgeous products of the Edwardian publishers after 1902, when the message was moved to the back and the picture was allowed to spread fully over the front. Many of these early cards were court sized, a limiting shape, and often the picture took up less than a third of the card, to allow plenty of space for a message. Typical is a card of Shandon Steeple, Cork which just shows the narrow steeple on the left of the card. It was posted in 1900, and incidentally, you will be extremely fortunate if you find many British picture cards posted before this date. The craze for collecting was still in its early stages. Most albums seem to start in 1903, when there was a larger choice of more interesting cards available.

Before they launched into colour many firms brightened the appearance of their pictures by printing them on blue or green card. Blum & Degen produced blue vignetted views taking up only a small portion of the cards of places as far apart as Glen Rosa and Cheltenham in 1901. But colour was creeping in. The most popular of Tuck's early series were the 'Rough Seas'. The earliest were black and white, but soon many were hand tinted and in August 1901 Tuck's issued 'Rough Seas' on blue card. Series 147, tinted views of Ilfracombe, Land's End, Lynmouth and district, and Series 113 of Scarborough, Giant's Causeway and district bear the strange statement 'Photographed in Saxony'. This is even more curious when one notices the signature of an artist, G. E. Newton, and realizes that they aren't even photographs at all. The more believable 'Phototyped in Austria' appears on the backs of most of these series. Some were printed only in green, but much later Tuck's repeated this popular line in their 'Oilette' series, also painted by G. E. Newton. It is rather difficult for us to understand the enormous success these series enjoyed. One 'Rough Sea' looks remarkably like all the others, but they were hugely popular and were imitated by other envious firms, including Valentine's (who even cribbed the name of the series), W. McKenzie in their 'Artistic Series', W. Brooker and C. W. Faulkner.

In 1900 Tuck's put out a large advert for their postcards listing 100 series, numbered from Series 1 to Series 100. With the exception of a few 'Colotype' series, they were all coloured and sold at 6d per packet of six and 1s per packet of twelve. The list includes 'London Views', 'Old Edinburgh', Glasgow, Manchester, Newcastle-on-Tyne, 'Seaside Series' of Margate, Ramsgate, Broadstairs, Westgate, Dover and Folkestone, and two 'Gem Scenery' series by Wedworth Wadsworth and Albert Bowes.

Moonlight effects were very popular. For one thing, a photograph taken by moonlight was still a novelty and a great technical achievement. For some firms it was too technical an undertaking and they achieved their moonlight effects by faking. In 1901 these 'sad perversions of taste' were denounced in the *Picture Postcard Magazine*. It was obvious, claimed the Editor, that many so-called 'moonlight views' had been taken in bright sunshine, as such clear photographs couldn't possibly have been taken 'by the pale moonlight'. In many cases the deep shadows *faced* the moon's rays. Such faked pictures were 'an insult to one's commonsense and an injury to one's artistic perception'. Frequently the streets were crowded with midday traffic and ladies carried sunshades. This 'misleading, inartistic and untruthful style' was hit upon by publishers who discovered that a view printed in a dark neutral tone on a blue board, or in a sepia tone, sometimes gave a moonlight effect which could be completed by painting a big white disc in the sky, often quite haphazardly and with no thought to the direction of the shadows.

Delittle, Fenwick & Co. seem to have been the worst offenders. It is a most amusing exercise to take a pile of their 'Moonlight Views' and go through them spotting the fakes. A great deal of effort went into making them look genuine – too much at times, for every window would be lit up brightly, whether in shops, banks, offices or houses. The 'moons' in these pictures look a little too perfectly round and bland for credibility as you can see from the 'Moonlight View' shown in Plate 6.

Moonlight pictures are far more effective when there are no people or shadows in sight. D.F. & Co's series of Gloucester Cathedral and Bristol look most attractive – but we still believe they are fakes. Woolstone Bros. ('Milton Moonlight Series') are a little more subtle in their touching up. In a picture of Briggate, Leeds the odd window has been left dark, but scrutiny with a magnifying glass reveals that two rather indistinct figures are ladies in un-doubted day dress. Valentine's were the most meticulous in trying to simulate accurate moonlight conditions.

Tuck's, in their series 'Moonlight Effects', achieve the most credible cards of this type. If one did not know that moonlight conditions were so widely faked they would be absolutely acceptable as what they claim to be. After a minute examination of several series we still don't know if they are genuine or not. They certainly avoid one obvious pitfall by not showing the actual moon at all. It is either behind clouds or shining from somewhere beyond the portion of sky shown on the card. Sea and canal views with few or no figures are favoured. Some have appropriate couplets underneath the picture:

*Soon as the evening shadows prevail*
*The moon takes up the wondrous tale*

Tuck's 'Moonlit Sea' series were drawn by G. E. Newton and are printed in a neutralizing green tinge. A far more attractive and more sought-after Tuck's series, 'London by Night', is also above suspicion because the views are painted, not photographed. They are realistic and attentive to detail. Men are illustrated wearing evening dress, silk hats, long black coats and white silk mufflers. Any more plebeian types strolling along the gas-lit London streets wear warm coats or shawls to protect them from the chill night air. It is a most beautiful series. Many provincial towns and beauty spots are treated in this way by Tuck's, including Worcester and the 'Fishermen's Quarters, Hastings'.

Cards that combined another hobby with that of deltiology were assured of success. In December 1900 *Girls' Realm* recommended to its readers who were students of heraldry and crests Tuck's new black and white series of old English towns with the town crest embossed in colour. And what beautiful cards they are. The black and white vignette of an outstanding feature of the town occupies about one-third of the card and is placed at the top right. As you can see in Plate 5 there is room for the message beneath this as the card has a undivided back. To the left is the embossed crest circled in gold or silver and picked out in colour. As is the case with so many of these early attempts at colour, the card has a delicate charm which was somehow lost in the later, brighter cards despite advances in the technique of reproducing colour.

Soon most of the large publishers and many local ones were producing crested views. By far the most prolific and widely collected cards of this type are those produced by JaJa in their 'Heraldic Series'. A typical example is shown in Plate 5. The upright card has no view of the town, the crest occupying the whole central portion of the card, with an ornate gold border incorporating the trademark 'JaJa' in the bottom left-hand corner. Besides towns, JaJa also show the crests of the United Kingdom and England, Scotland, Ireland and Wales. They also produced series of 'Clan Tartan' cards on a tartan background, the clan's crest in a circular thistle-bordered inset with its name on a scroll at the bottom.

C. W. Faulkner made some extremely beautiful and elegant crested cards, printed lengthwise. The crests, which are larger than those on JaJa cards, have no border and seem even more striking without the ornate distraction. They also did a series of ships' crests, printed on upright cards, the crest encircled by an ornate gold frame. Yet another of their series, also on upright cards, has a buff frame and includes the arms of such personalities as Lord Nelson.

Scott, Russell & Co. later produced several series of cards remarkably similar to the JaJa 'Heraldic' series. The crest is slightly smaller and the words 'The Coat of Arms of . . .' are added to the town name. The ornate gold border, so like that of the JaJa cards, is itself enclosed in a plain gold border. Incidentally, all the JaJa cards and those of their close imitators are printed on upright cards.

JaJa were not alone in producing tartan crested cards. Tuck's produced a colourful 'Scottish Clans' series on a tartan background with a gold-bordered view, the crest and any other appropriate symbols. On the back is a short historical note about the particular clan.

The 'Highland Clan' postcard shows a vignetted picture of a Scottish warrior wearing the appropriate tartan, which is also spread along the top of the card, with the crest in the upper right-hand corner. The lower right-hand quarter has a space for the message. There are also details of the clan badge and slogan. On the back of every card is the same Highland gentleman, printed in green. The B & R series and Langlands of Dumbarton both had views set in many-sectioned tartan frames. Each section contained a different named tartan.

In 1902 W. & A. K. Johnston Ltd produced an ambitious series of Scottish clans. There were sixteen sets of six cards, selling at six for 6d or twenty-five for 2s. The cards (one for every clan in Scotland) show the national dress, tartan, badge, war cry and the names of all the families allied to each clan. They are printed in colour.

The arms of the different colleges of Oxford University were favourite illustrations for postcards. Valentine's produced an attractive card with small shields showing the coats of arms of twenty-one colleges, with the name above each and the date when the college was founded below. We have an identical card, complete to the last silver scroll, made by an anonymous firm. The PRPC series issued a set of three cards showing not only the arms but also the oars and flags of each of the Oxford colleges. A set published by Oxford Varsity City for Millar & Lang has a different card for each college.

Another way of combining two interests is to collect map postcards. The best were produced by John Walker and engraved by J. Bartholomew & Co. These most attractive, detailed and accurate maps are printed in green with water shown in blue, and have a small inset view of the location. They were first produced about 1903. By April 1904 400 had already been produced and Walker intended to cover every town and environs of any importance in the British Isles. The East Reading Library issued an interesting reproduction of Speed's *Map of Reading Three Centuries Ago* in 1910, and the 'Garden Isle' series printed detailed maps of the Isle of Wight. These also have a small inset photograph of interesting features of the island such as Osborne House.

One method of compiling a comprehensive collection of British views is to concentrate on 'framed' cards. A framed card is shown at Plate 11. There is tremendous scope in this type of card. From about 1907 most of the major and many of the minor firms produced at least one framed series and great ingenuity has gone into simulating different finishes and decorations.

Valentine's appear to lead the field. Looking through our topographical section we find we have about a dozen different types of their frames. Tuck's were also prolific, with many named series such as 'Framed Granite', 'Framed Gem Morocco', 'Framed Plate Photo' and 'Bordered Sepia', and they were posted between 1910 and 1918. Their 'Platemarked' series have tasteful, plain white borders.

The dark simulated wood frame seems far and away the most popular with grained green of various hues coming second. A colourful 'picture gallery' can be built up with these delightful miniature framed scenes.

Another interesting kind of topographical card is the kind which combines several small views of a town on one card in a composite view. This technique was first used, with vignettes, on the early 'Gruss Aus . . .' cards. Jackson & Son of Grimsby (Jay Em Jay) specialized in this type and produced many combinations and permutations of different sized and shaped views as illustrated below.

Often several different arrangements are used on a series of cards of the same town. The same pictures are used in different shapes. They differ from the 'Gruss Aus . . .' cards in that each picture is sharply bordered, usually in

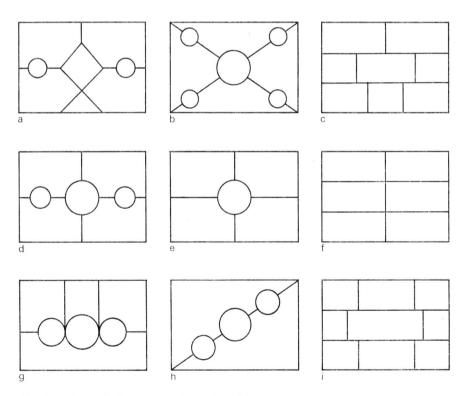

Combinations of views on cards produced by
Jackson & Son of Grimsby (Jay Em Jay)

green, and the patterns symmetrical and regular. The Jay Em Jay cards were in use up to the beginning of World War I, but this was by no means a new idea. A court-sized B. & R. & Co. card of around 1900 uses the same technique, having small overlapping vignetted views of Bournemouth with the bottom right-hand corner left free for the message. Hartmann's 'Miniature Series' appeared in the early 1900s and there were many such cards around 1905 and 1906. Most of the seaside resorts sold series of composite views, from Rhyl, Blackpool and Llandudno to Brighton, Bournemouth and St Anne's on Sea.

A curious phenomenon in this composite group is that what appears to be exactly the same type of card with slight variations in colour is used by several different publishers, including Valentine's, R. Sneath of Sheffield, J. Welch and an anonymous printer. This card has a very matt finish and the shapes of the inset views are impressed, edged with small raised dots.

And so to the most numerous series under the heading 'Topographical': Tuck's 'Oilette' series. The term is defined on the original packets containing sets of Tuck's cards: ' "Oilettes", well termed "THE ARISTOCRATS OF PICTURE POSTCARDS", are reproduced in colours direct from the Original Paintings, the subjects embracing practically every range.' Of course not all 'Oilettes' are views, and many are mentioned elsewhere in this book, but the great majority were indeed scenes of town and country, and not only British. Tuck's did several series of Cairo and French towns, not to mention their American views, but we are concerned here only with the British. The range is vast – seascapes, landscapes, seaside resorts, town series, country series, lake series – we cannot possibly describe all the types of 'Oilettes' you are likely to find. We will compromise by listing some of their named artists and a selection of the series they painted.

*Harry Payne.* Perhaps Tuck's most famous postcard artist, but not exclusively contracted to Tuck's. In 1900 he drew the first of 'The Amewsing Write Away' series and 'The Game of Golf'. More successful are his military pictures, as described in Chapter 5, but he also drew views, with human or equine figures always to the fore – 'The Poor Man's Friend' (donkey); 'Devonshire Lanes' (cart horses); 'Our Country Cousins' (the squire's daughter); the 'Coaching' series.

*Arthur C. Payne* (Harry's brother). Specialized in drawing buildings, especially cathedrals, of which he did several series, and castles; some general views. Also not exclusively contracted to Tuck's.

Both Harry and Arthur started working for Tuck's in the 1880s, designing Christmas cards. With the advent of the full-out picture card, they graduated to postcards and one postcard is signed by both Harry and Arthur, with Harry presumably having drawn the military figures and Arthur the castellated background.

*G. Gretty.* Lovely green tones, good trees, as in 'Country Charms'.

*Henry B. Wimbush.* Versatile: town views, e.g. Bournemouth, Dartmouth;

lovely, busy scenes of London; lakes – 'Picturesque English Lakes'; Scottish views; 'Kingsley's Country'.

*Edwin E. Penley.* Lovely purplish tones, as in 'Scotch Lochs'.

*Walter Severn.* Similar to Penley; not quite so detailed.

*T. Smith.* More impressionistic 'Bonnie Scotland' views.

*E. D. Percival.* Sea views, as 'Ilfracombe'.

*E. H. Vaughan.* Very Turnerish, as in 'Turneresque' series.

*M. Morris.* Rough sea type, as 'Blackpool'. Also sunsets, as in 'Connoisseur' series.

*G. E. Newton.* Rough seas par excellence. Many series under this title – foamy breakers, seagulls, lighthouses etc.

*P. Fletcher-Watson.* Responsible for charming series 'In Dickens Land'.

*J. Fulleylove.* Characters and views, especially 'Holy Land' series, also probably responsible for colourful series of Red Indians.

*F. W. Hayes.* Good mountains in 'North Wales' views.

*Hadfield Cubley.* Town views, usually with figures as in 'Chester', 'Shrewsbury', etc.

*Charles E. Flower.* Superb London views, great detail of buildings, figures, traffic etc. Notable series: 'Inns of Court and Chancery', 'Westminster Abbey', 'Houses of Parliament', 'Old London Churches'.

*W. Mathison.* London views.

*Henry Stannard, RBA.* Landscapes, as 'The Countryside'.

*Ellen Warrington.* Pretty country scenes with flowers predominating, as 'The Time of Flowers'.

*Prof. Van Hier.* Reproductions of his paintings are always clearly attributed to him. Very Turneresque in style, as 'Sunsets', seascapes, many wintry scenes, country scenes, each picture named in the 'Connoisseur' series.

*Helen Jackson.* Charming country scenes, as 'Home from School'.

*F. Esdaile Richardson.* 'Tennyson's Country'.

*R. F. McIntyre.* 'The Picturesque Thames'.

*John A. Heyermans.* Domestic scenes, 'English Cottage Homes' in series with very realistic oil paint finishes.

*A. R. Quinton.* A few town series.

*Jotter.* This is the signature which appears on more facsimile postcards than any other. It is the pseudonym of Walter Hayward Young, a prolific postcard artist who occasionally signed his cards with his real name. Jotter was a freelance artist and worked for many postcard publishers, including Jarrolds, but the bulk of his work was for Tuck's. He had an arrangement with this firm to cover the beauty spots of the British Isles county by county, in series with titles like 'Derbyshire Dales', 'Picturesque Cornwall', 'Cornish Coves'. Perhaps his finest work, however, is to be seen in the set commemorating Robert Burns' centenary.

When preparing one of his county series Jotter would set out on his bicycle from his home in Isleworth into the surrounding countryside. Having found a suitable base, he would spend a week making sketches, colour notes and photographs until he had decided on the six beauty spots which would make up a set of postcards. Back at his studio he would develop the photographs, study his notes and sketches and make his final paintings. Jotter always retained the originals of his postcard designs for private re-sale.

Jotter's postcard output spanned the years from the turn of the century up to the period of the First World War. Of his six children, three of his daughters were competent artists and one of them, Gwendoline, produced many sets of postcards under her own name. Gwendoline worked with her father in his studio, and together they produced two or three sets of postcards entitled 'Cute Kiddies'.

Poster design was another medium in which Walter Hayward Young excelled. He produced many designs for theatrical and railway posters. A sociable person, he was a monthly diner at the Savage Club and a founder member of the Aldwych Club. He also wrote, produced and acted the title role in the silent film 'Romney'.

There are invariably some figures to be seen in a Jotter landscape, showing his love of, and interest in, Britain's inhabitants as well as its beautiful country-side. This common interest led to a friendship with Cecil Sharp, the collector of folk songs.

Walter Hayward Young died in Isleworth in 1920, aged fifty-one.

Almost indistinguishable from the 'Oilette' cards are the 'Aquarette' series. These 'facsimile' reproductions of oil and water colour paintings are generally known as 'facsims'. The term is now used to describe oil or water colour reproductions. Tuck's themselves used the abbreviation when describing their very realistic reproductions of oil paintings. 'Oilfacsims' are veritable minia-ture oil paintings. Here the charming 'Oilette' principle is extended by adding the actual grain of the canvas and the brush marks of the oil painting.

A close examination of Tuck's facsims in comparison with any other firm's shows that they are not always appreciably better cards. There are certainly far more of them—the average collector will probably find two 'Oilettes' to one of any other facsim – and the series are well and clearly numbered.

Of the other publishers, J. Salmon of Sevenoaks is the most helpful to the collector. Each card clearly states on the back, 'From an original Water Colour by . . .'. Salmon's best-known artist was A. R. Quinton who occasionally drew for Tuck's. Quinton's views are quite unmistakable. The characteristic pale blue skies and fantastic detail give them the distinct atmosphere of 'Celesque' cards by Photochrom. From 1912 Quinton worked exclusively for Salmon until his death in 1934, during which time he covered most of the principal resorts in the country. His minute detail of costume and transport is of enormous help in dating an unposted Quinton card.

Another Salmon artist was C. Essenhigh Corke FRPS, painter of the first coloured facsim view to be published by Salmon, dating around 1904. It was of Knole, Sevenoaks, with the co-operation of Lady Sackville-West, and was followed by Kent and Sussex series and Warwickshire Castle. A. L. Pressland drew land and seascapes for Salmon and W. W. Quatremain drew town views, Anne Hathaway's cottage etc.

C. W. Faulkner published several different series of facsimile views. Unfortunately many of them are completely anonymous as to artist and sometimes even location. Of the artists whose names can be distinguished are Ernest Welbourne, country views; S. Clarke, wintry scenes; A. de Bréamski, seascapes; and A. Young, Scottish views.

Hildesheimer name some of their series but not others, and few of their artists. Among those distinguishable are R. Gaston, 'Thames Lock Series'; E. Longstaffe, 'Scottish Lochs'; Harry and Arthur Payne (see Tuck's), cathedrals.

The Regal Art Co. productions (Rapco) are most reminiscent of Tuck's in presentation, especially of the Tuck's 'Jotter' views. All series are clearly named and numbered, and each artist credited. Their series included 'Picturesque Oxfordshire' by Alex Austen, who also drew 'Picturesque Surrey' and 'Picturesque Hampshire'. The 'Delightful Devonshire' series was painted by E. D. Percival.

J. W. Ruddock of Lincoln in their 'Artist' series clearly state, 'Each picture is a facsimile of an original water colour drawing.' Among their artists are Tom Boyne, landscapes; F. M. Minns, seascapes; and Baness, town views. Arthur C. Payne also drew for them.

There was even a Water Colour Post Card Co. The only cards of theirs we have seen are from water colour drawings by W. H. Borrow of views in the Sussex area. W. H. Borrow also drew for the 'B. & W.' series of Sussex views.

Most of the large publishers whose specialities lay elsewhere produced at least a few series of facsims as if to show that they could if they wanted to. Boots (Cash Chemist) published some charming facsims; Photochrom, Philco, Wrench, Davidson Bros., Dennis, Valentine's, Jarrolds and, rather surprisingly, Cynicus all entered the field.

Quite distinctive are the views drawn and published by R. P. Phillimore at his works in North Berwick, until paralysis stopped his artistic output. Most delicate in character, printed on creamy tinted card, they usually bear a short explanatory note by the artist, such as: 'A picturesque view of Bridgnorth from the Railway Station showing the Railway Tunnel that penetrates the rock on which the town is built.'

*Oxford, Painted by John Fulleylove RI, Described by Edward Thomas* was the title of a book published by A. & C. Black in 1903. A series of cards was produced by 'P.R.P.C.' of the illustrations in the book. By comparison with the illustrations in the actual book, the colours of the postcards are poorly reproduced.

A most attractive series of photographic views is the Photochrom Co.'s 'Celesque' series, with predominating tones of grey and blue. They were printed on good, heavy quality board, and for serious collectors they are clearly numbered and named. Another distinctive Photochrom style is the 'Wedgwood' series, printed, as the title suggests, in shades of blue. Fewer of these blue cards are to be found, the coloured 'Celesque' series being far more popular.

Of the photographed view cards, Valentine's produced far more than any other publisher. In 1904 the editorial of the *Postcard Connoisseur* eulogized them:

> Messrs Valentine & Sons have for years been one of the largest publishers of photographed views in the world. When the rapid growth of the picture postcard imported from the Continent destroyed the original trade in photographic views, Messrs Valentine & Sons were the first to realise the future which lay before their competitors, and with an energy which speaks well for the recuperative force of the British manufacturers, they at once boarded the very vessel which threatened their own craft and, utilising their immense collection of negatives, issued series after series of postcards which met with wide appreciation. A style of view cards in which a notable success has been achieved is the series produced by the three colour process which includes all the favourite and most beautiful seaside and holiday resorts in the United Kingdom. These cards are almost perfect examples of this process and in the set of Swanage, for example, the collector will find some striking and uncommon effects of views in colour . . . Really wonderful value for 1d.

High praise indeed; but it was typical of the encouragement the postcard magazines of the period unanimously gave to British manufacturers. The campaign to 'Back Britain' and 'Buy British' was vigorously supported.

Institutions and public buildings were favourite subjects for the postcard photographers, forming an ephemeral monument to Victorian architecture. Schools, medical establishments of all kinds, orphanages, seats of higher learning, shire halls, town halls, almshouses all appear regularly, as do stations, from the quiet country ones, like Colwall, Herefordshire, to the New Street Station, Birmingham, showing platform after platform with its waiting train. There are countless series of prisons, especially Dartmoor, some showing the guards in their American Civil War type uniforms, others some of the prisoners (see Plate 6). Buildings associated with a famous person abound, such as Dickens' birthplace at Portsmouth; Holbech House, Kingswinford where several of the gunpowder plot conspirators were captured; or Dr Jenner's hut in the Chantry Gardens at Berkeley, where he kept a cow for vaccination experiments. There are war memorials, statues, castles, romantic ruins like Peveril Castle or Barnard Castle, natural formations like the Old Harry Rocks near Bournemouth, or man-made formations like Stonehenge or the Avebury Stones – and, of course, literally thousands of churches and cathedrals.

As a contrast to the man-made edifices, the natural charms of famous beauty spots were a well-loved subject for the postcard. Mountains in Wales (especially Snowdon) and Scotland, the Lakes, restful scenes of Easedale Tarn or Dovedale Spires were guaranteed to make the recipient wish he were there. Waterfalls gave an opportunity for the photographer to demonstrate his technical skill, as in the 'Woodbury' series card of the Upper Falls at Devil's Bridge. River and canal scenes are often crowded with gay boating parties, parasols much in evidence, at Henley, Marlow, Hampton and other fashionable riverside resorts.

The most fascinating view cards are the crowded ones: beach scenes showing sands populated with over-dressed sunbathers and rows of bathing machines, promenades thronged with gaily dressed strollers, and town scenes showing Edwardian traffic jams and busy shoppers. One such scene is shown in Plate 7.

With all these cards, a good magnifying glass, or even better, a patent Edwardian postcard magnifying viewer, is vital to extract the maximum information from these detailed views.

When cards are unposted many clues to their age may be gleaned from a careful examination of the picture. Where views show clear details of costume, some knowledge of the trends in fashion is essential as the frequently changing whims of fashion were scrupulously followed by those who could afford this indulgence. Magazines like *The Queen* and *Myra's Journal, the Leader of Fashion* often included supplements showing the latest Paris fashions. Those sold with *The Queen* from the 1880s to about 1900 are beautifully drawn, exquisitely coloured prints by A. Sandoz of Paris. The picture would be taken to the purchaser's dressmaker and rapidly translated into a dress, so every Paris change in fashion was quickly copied by wealthy British ladies of taste. Simpler adaptations were constructed with equal speed by those of more modest means, for the sewing machine was by this time a vital and treasured possession in many British homes. Most views seem to have been deliberately photographed at times when people were parading in their Sunday best, and therefore show a high proportion of fashionably dressed subjects.

Here are some distinctive points to look for. Around the turn of the century the fashionable lady's body was contorted to form a backward sloping S curve; waists were tightly pinched and corseted (anything over an 18 in. waist was considered gross) with a resultant generous bulge of bust and hips (padded if necessary). Hats, after a period of tiny, perched nonsenses, were becoming more substantial. Buttoned boots became fashionable. The sporting and daring wore knickerbockers for bicycling. Children were also booted at this stage and sailor suits and tam o'shanters were in. The men were wearing Norfolk jackets and knee breeches for sporting and country wear, while in town the silk (top) hat, dark coat and striped trousers were worn. Trousers were still generally uncreased and were long, almost covering the heel and instep.

Between 1900 and 1905 the blouse and skirt were gaining in popularity.

Cascades of lace on the blouse emphasized the top curve of the still compulsory S. Day outfits were tailored, with tight sleeves, and lace, beading, buttons and braid were profusely used as trimming. Hair was piled high on the head and hats were either flat, rather like pancakes, or toques. Navy serge was becoming popular for children; sailor suits were still worn and boys were dressed in Eton suits for school and town and Norfolk suits for leisure and the country. Men's trousers were becoming narrower, occasionally with turn-ups. Two distinct forms of evening dress had evolved: the tail coat and the more informal dinner jacket. The straw boater was worn by ladies, children and men.

From 1905 to 1910 hats became wider and wider. The S had unbent into a straight line; hems were shorter and skirts narrower. The favourite trimming was Irish crochet, a substitute for expensive lace; blouses and skirts were more tailored and the corset was let out a few inches. More colour now crept into children's clothes, with full sleeves, three-quarter socks and miles of ribbon.

1910 to 1914 saw one of the most ridiculous phenomena of fashion – the hobble skirt – often derided on the postcard. The desirable outline was now that of an inverted triangle, tapering from an enormous cartwheel hat to a narrow hem. Children's clothes were becoming more sensible, looser and shorter. Turn-ups were universal for men by the outbreak of war.

During the First World War hats shrank dramatically and were usually trimmed with an upright feather. Skirts widened, often with a tunic overskirt. Gradually the tunic became the whole dress, the underskirt abandoned, making dresses altogether shorter. Pleats crept in. V-necks 'dangerous to health and morals' were fashionable. Clothes were altogether looser and less restricting. Only now did the boots worn throughout the period cease to be fashionable. Children blossomed forth in bright colours, with the gymslip coming into its own. Around 1917 children's waists dropped exaggeratedly and the low, low belt had an extremely hampering effect. The town gentleman was still very formally attired, even to spats, with one concession in that the morning coat replaced the frock coat for town wear.

Now let us see what was happening to transport during the same two decades. At the beginning of our period the horse was supreme. Carriages were the wealthy families' means of transport, with broughams and victorias the height of fashion. Every manner of horse or pony drawn trap was used in the country by poorer folk. But the motor car was gradually evolving and in 1895 the need to legislate for it was felt. In this year every mechanically-propelled vehicle on British roads was restricted to 4 m.p.h., with a minimum crew of three, one of whom had to walk twenty yards ahead to warn of the vehicle's approach. It was in this year that Austin designed the first Wolseley – a three-wheeler. In 1896 the 'Locomotives on the Highway' act raised this restricting speed limit to 14 m.p.h., and Daimler started production in Coventry. Daimler was granted the Royal Warrant and attempted to create a monopoly in the motor industry, but his efforts failed in a legal battle in 1901.

Also in 1896, Lanchesters were being manufactured, and before 1900 Sunbeams, Rileys and Humbers were being produced. In 1900 Austin designed the first four-wheeled Wolseley. More and more postcards with a motoring theme started to be issued in the following few years, many of them humorous in nature.

In January 1904 the Motor Car Act raised the speed limit to 20 m.p.h. and required every motorized vehicle to be licensed and registered, whereupon 8,465 private cars, 5,345 hackney carriages and 4,000 trucks were duly registered. Rolls Royce was founded in this year and there was also an Automobile Show from 12–24 February at the Crystal Palace.

Despite the enthusiasm of the growing number of motorists, this was a period of intense persecution of the motor car by the large reactionary section of the general public. As local Justices tended to be 'horsey' people, penalties for the most minor infringements tended to be stiff! But enthusiasm was not easily dampened, as we show in the next chapter, judging by the number of popular rallies and races that were held.

In 1905 the Automobile Association was formally founded, and in 1906 Austin formed his own motor company at Longbridge, Birmingham. There was an Automobile Show at Olympia from 15–24 November and foreign cars such as Mercedes and Panhards were exhibited. Peugeots were also being imported. In 1907 Liverpool held a Motor Show from 25 February to 2 March, and from this time on the motor car went from strength to strength and was an increasingly evident feature of the view card.

Public transport followed much the same pattern. At the end of the century the hansom cab was the major form of hired transport for local journeys for the wealthy, the 28-seater horsedrawn omnibus for the general populace, with the four horse brake still being used in the country. Motorized buses were surprisingly slow in developing, especially in London, when compared with foreign capitals. Liverpool experimented with them in 1898, and for a short period in 1899 two Daimler-engined omnibuses plied from Kennington to Victoria. The century turned, however, in a London that was without one motorized bus, and by 1905 there were still only twenty operating in the metropolis. The next three years saw a phenomenal growth, and in 1908 there were 1,066 motor buses in operation, owned by a handful of private companies. In 1910 the famous 'B' type of open-topped, open-cabbed bus, with its outside spiral staircase, made its debut in the London streets for the London General Co. The last horsedrawn bus was still in operation when the Great War broke out.

The tardy development of the motorized bus was due to the correspondingly rapid expansion in tram development. At the start of our period trams in all but a few go-ahead towns were pulled by horses. London lagged behind, for in 1891 Leeds, in 1892 Bradford, 1893 Walsall, 1894 the Isle of Man, 1895 Bristol and Coventry, 1896 Dublin and Blackpool, 1897 Dover, 1898 Cork, Glasgow and Liverpool, 1899 Aberdeen, Blackburn, the Potteries and Sheffield, and in 1900 Darwen, Dundee, Southampton, Sunderland and Swansea all electrified their tram systems. Meanwhile London used 13,954 horses to pull 1,451 trams on 147 miles of tram lines. Only in 1901 did electrification begin, and by 1914 325 miles of electrified tram lines had been laid.

By 1870 the railways had almost completely taken over from the stage coach and the mail coach as the method for long distance travel and transporting mail. Until the Railways Act of 1921 some 123 separate railways were running in four main groups: London, Midland and Scottish; London and North Eastern; Great Western and Southern Railways. It is interesting to look for the smaller companies who used, or advertised on, their own printed cards, like the Cambrian Railway; the Highland Railway; the London, Chatham and Dover Railway, the Talyllyn Railway, etc. and some of their magnificent engines, like the Cornishman, the Highland Mail and the Flying Dutchman.

It is easy to overlook the informative value of the view card. The editorial of the first edition of the *Picture Postcard Magazine* in July 1900 expressed our sentiments exactly in these words: 'Ostensibly but a mere miniature view of some town or place of interest to the passing traveller, a picture postcard is yet capable of possessing an interest and significance undreamed of by those who have not yet troubled to look into the matter.'

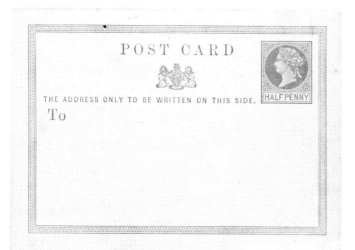

PLATE 1

*Above*—The world's first postcard; Austria, 1869

*Left*—Britain's first postcard, 1 October 1870 *(see Appendix 1 Serial 1)*

*Below*—Britain's first foreign postcard, 1 July 1875 *(See Appendix 1, Serial 6)*

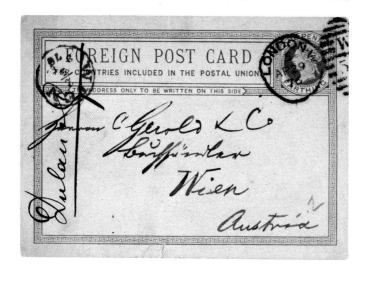

PLATE 2 British 'Officials'. *From top*—1878 *(See Appendix 1 Serial 7).* 1879 *(See Appendix 1 Serial 9).* 1879 *(See Appendix 1 Serial 11).* 1883 *(See Appendix 1 Serial 15).* 1889 *(See Appendix 1 Serial 25).* 1890 *(See Appendix 1 Serial 26).* 1892 *(See Appendix 1 Serial 28).* 1899 *(see Appendix 1 Serial 35).*

PLATE 3  Foreign and Empire 'Officials'. *From top*—1871 type: Belgium; black on buff. 1889 type; British North Borneo; green on white. 1891 type; Republic of Honduras; red on white. 1897 type; Republic of Guatemala; reply-paid; black on white. 1897 type; Hungary; multi-coloured on white. Republic of Guatemala; violet and black on white, 1896 type.

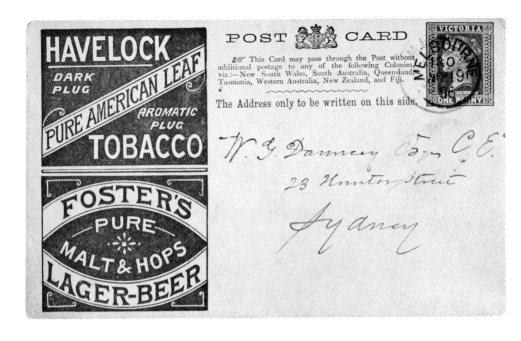

PLATE 4  *Above*—Victoria State: 'Beer and Baccy', 1895. *Below*—Red-brown aerial postcard flown from London to Windsor, 9 September 1911

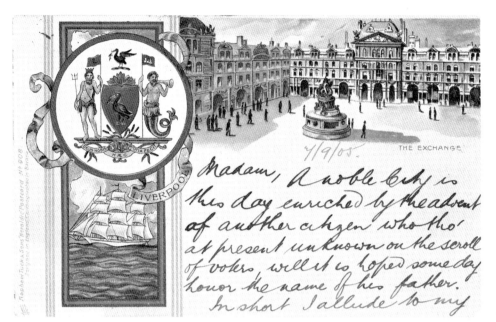

THE EXCHANGE

*7/9/05.*

*Madam, A noble City is this day enriched by the advent of another citizen who tho' at present unknown on the scroll of voters, will it is hoped some day honor the name of his father. In short I allude to my*

PLATE 5

*Above*—Tuck: 'Heraldic' card of Liverpool, c. 1901

*Right*—'Ja-Ja' Heraldic Series: Liverpool, c. 1905

PLATE 6 *Above*—Valentine's: 'Convicts proceeding to work, Dartmoor', c. 1903. *Below*—D. F. & Co: Moonlight view of Tramway Centre, Bristol, c. 1904

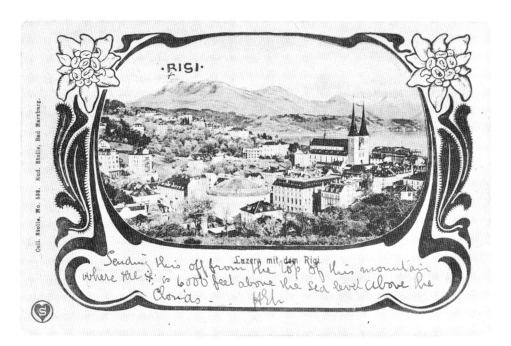

·RIGI·

Luzern mit dem Rigi

*Sending this off from the top of this mountain where the X is 6000 feet above the sea level above the clouds —* H.S.M.

PLATE 7 *Above*—Card posted from the top of the Rigi, Switzerland, c. 1904. *Below*—LL: Broadstairs, c. 1909

13 BROADSTAIRS. — *View of the Sands, showing Bleak House* — LL.

RUSSIAN OUTRAGE ON HULL FISHING FLEET.
22.10.1904.

Published at

THE ILLUSTRATED
Daily Post-card

39 & 40. Shoe Lane, E.C.

No. 13.     Nov. 4.  1905.     Price ½d.

*Photo Press.*

The Gladstone Statue, which Mr. John Morley unveils to-day in the Strand, is the work of Mr. Hamo Thornycroft, R.A.

Mr. Gladstone was born December 9th. 1809, died May 19th, 1898.  Was Prime Minister 1868-74, 1880-85, 1886, 1892-94.

PLATE 8

*Above*—Valentine's: 'Russian outrage on Hull fishing fleet, 22.10.1904'

*Left*—'The Illustrated Daily Post-card' (publisher anon.), 4 November 1905

# 4

# Topical and Commemorative Cards

'Great Fire at Gloucester Docks', 'SS *Mahratta* Wrecked on Goodwins', 'Accident to Goods Train, SE Railway' – newspaper headlines you may think. But no, these are from picture postcards specially photographed and issued to commemorate these tragedies. With no radio or television to present the news in an easily digestible form, and a large proportion of the populace still partly or wholly illiterate, the newsy picture postcard fulfilled an important function in recording and broadcasting (in the literal sense) events of local and national importance. No happening seemed too small – or too great – to find its way onto a postcard, but the greatest non-event ever celebrated by a postcard was the coronation of King Edward VII, set for 26 June 1902. Thousands of postcards were printed and issued with captions such as 'Souvenir of the Coronation of HM King Edward VII, June 1902', and cards incorporating portraits of Edward and Alexandra with the words 'Long May They Reign. Coronation June 1902'. Tuck's had prepared forty different series of sets of four to twelve cards and had even produced a beautiful coloured reproduction of a portrait of Edward, shown (in black and white) in Plate 9. You will notice that in the shield in the top left-hand corner, which gives Edward's pertinent dates, the bottom two lines, giving the coronation date, have been carefully erased. On the back is printed, 'To the King's Guest July 5th 1902'. Tuck's issued 100,000 of these cards free as a charitable gesture to celebrate the coronation, choosing a date in July.

In fact, owing to Edward's indisposition immediately prior to the appointed day, after most of the distinguished guests had arrived in London, the coronation did not take place until 9 August.

The King's illness was sudden and serious. For a while the worst was feared and the coronation cards that were actually posted around 26 June were described at the time as a 'ghastly mockery'. Wrench had the contract to publish the official souvenirs for the coronation as well as printing many commemorative postcards. He was actually supervising the delivery of the cards when the terrible news of the King's illness reached him. But this enterprising young man had had the foresight to take out a £50 policy with Lloyd's which would provide him with £1,000 if for any reason the coronation did not take place on the appointed day.

Naturally cards posted for the actual coronation on 9 August have more curiosity value and are rarer than the earlier premature cards.

During Edward's reign, which was so happy and popular that it earned him the title of 'The Peacemaker', every Royal event was celebrated by commemorative postcards. Towns, delighted at a Royal visit for no matter what purpose, quickly issued postcards to record the proud event.

Many Royal events involving foreign monarchs were recorded on postcards during Edward's reign. In 1904 the King and Queen of Portugal paid a visit to England. As you will see in Plate 9 they and their entourage posed for a commemorative photograph at Windsor Castle. On 15 June 1905 there was the wedding of TRH Prince and Princess Gustavus Adolphus of Sweden. An unusual card to commemorate the marriage of Princess Ena of Battenberg to the King of Spain shows her magnificent wedding cake.

November 1907 saw a splendid Royal Occasion, fully recorded on countless series of postcards, notably by W. & D. Downey. It was 'An Historic Gathering of Crowned Heads. Windsor Castle, 17 November 1907'. Besides our own Royal Family, including the Prince and Princess of Wales, there were the Emperor and Empress of Germany, the Queen of Portugal, the King and Queen of Spain and the Queen of Norway. During her stay the Queen of Portugal visited Evesham Hospital on 13 November with HRM Princess Louise of France. A local photographer was on hand to record the event for a postcard.

The next year saw a visit from the King and Queen of Sweden, with appropriate postcards. Another magnificent Royal occasion was well documented on British cards – the christening of the Heir to the Spanish throne, including the impressive ceremony of the King of Spain presenting the Heir to the grandees and dignitaries at the Spanish court.

The Royal ceremony which perhaps occasioned more postcards than any other was a sad and deeply felt one: the funeral of King Edward VII. There were the memorial cards, bordered in black or purple, and several versions of Queen Alexandra's moving letter to the nation:

> From the depth of my poor broken heart I wish to express to the whole Nation, and our kind People whom we love so well, my deep felt thanks for all their touching sympathy in my overwhelming sorrow and unspeakable anguish.
>
> Not alone have I lost everything in Him, my beloved husband, but the Nation too has suffered an irreparable loss by their best friend, father and Sovereign thus suddenly called away . . . I confide my dear son into your care, who I know will follow in his dear father's footsteps. . . .

The new King also addressed a message to the nation which was printed on many postcards.

Photographs by all the main publishers showed the funeral procession at various points along the route to Westminster Abbey and back to Buckingham Palace, the lying in state at Westminster, the gun carriage, Albert Memorial Chapel with hundreds of wreaths and the scenes outside St George's Chapel, Windsor. Reporters were no more respectful of private grief (if Royal grief can ever be private) in those days than they are now. Every endeavour was made to take clear close-ups of the veiled face of Queen Alexandra as she passed along the route in the Royal carriage.

Then there were portraits of the Royal mourners. One card might show many of the principal characters who were to feature in the complex and bloody affairs of Europe in the years to come. How many of them, we wonder, at this sad, peaceful, dignified and yet splendid Royal occasion had any inkling of the horrors to come? Our own King George was to lead the nation against Wilhelm II and Germany in the costliest struggle – in terms of lives, destruction and materials – that the world had ever known: the First World War. The holocaust was to be sparked off when another guest at the funeral, Francis Ferdinand, Archduke of Austria, was assassinated at Sarajevo on 28 June 1914. Nor did Wilhelm keep his empire much longer. On 10 November 1918 he was forced to flee Germany, and spent the rest of his life interned at Doorn in Holland, where he died in 1941. Meanwhile George I of Greece had also been assassinated, in March 1913 at Salonika, and the dethroned Manoel II of Portugal was soon back in England. After the revolution in his country on 4 October 1910 (the funeral was in May) he fled to Twickenham, where he lived until his death in 1932. Alfonso, King of Spain, managed to hold on to his throne in the face of great civil unrest until 14 April 1931, when he finally abdicated. In 1936 he was to see his country torn apart by the cruel Civil War.

Perhaps the most tragic story of all was that of Maria Feodorovna, Dowager Empress of Russia. She survived the horror of the butchery of her son Nicholas and his family at Ekaterinburg on the night of 16 July 1918, and was permitted to live in the Crimea under close guard. She left the Crimea in 1919 and lived until her death in 1928 in her native capital of Copenhagen.

The previous Royal death, that of Queen Victoria on 22 January 1901, was the first great home event that the publishers had had a chance to exploit since the advent of the truly pictorial card. It was also a test of the speed with which they could deal with current events. C. W. Faulkner rose to the challenge by producing 'In Memoriam' cards within fifteen hours of the Queen's death, whereas Wrench's commemorative postcards were a week late in coming out.

But on to happier Royal events. The funeral of Edward VII meant that the country was soon rejoicing at the coronation of King George V. 'The King is Dead: Long Live the King' and, as ever, the picture postcard recorded the celebrations.

The most original and enterprising celebration of the Coronation was the First Great Britain Aerial Post. It was, moreover, Britain's only official air mail service from the advent of the aeroplane in 1903 until after the First World War.

A committee was set up to organize this exciting and novel postal event and the 'net proceeds' were 'devoted to Public Charity'. The enterprise was sanctioned by the Postmaster General, but the committee ran into difficulties with postal regulations. Naturally it would cost more to deliver mail by air, and as the proceeds were promised to charity a profit had to be made. Yet the Post Office could only charge their normal rates for any official postal stationery. The problem was overcome by designing special cards and envelopes, already stamped with the regular $\frac{1}{2}$d or 1d stamps, and these alone would be carried by the aerial post. One or two 'special designs', however, crept into circulation. The cards cost 6$\frac{1}{2}$d and the envelopes 1/1d. They were printed in the following colours.

### London to Windsor

1. Violet: not available to the public, 'privileged mail' bearing greetings to important persons at home and abroad, on 'stout' card.
2. Red brown: available to the public, franked with $\frac{1}{2}$d stamp on limp card.
3. Dark brown: as 2.
4. Olive green: as 2.

### Windsor to London

5. Violet: as 1.
6. Olive green: as 2.

It is probable that there were also red brown and dark brown cards as 2. sent in this direction, but we have been unable to find any official listing of them.

The designs, apart from the colour, are the same for all the cards. The right half is white, bears the ordinary green George V $\frac{1}{2}$d stamp and is stamped with a special postmark reading 'First United Kingdom Aerial Post', with the date and location of the postmark. Then there are the words '(Address only to be written here)'. Some cards, we have noticed, omit the opening parenthesis, an accident in printing to look out for. On the left, coloured half of the card are the words 'AD Coronation 1911. First UK Aerial Post. By Sanction of HM Postmaster General'. Beneath is a picture of Windsor Castle with a hazardous-looking aeroplane flying over it. The London to Windsor cards state, 'For conveyance by AEROPLANE from LONDON to WINDSOR', and the cards flown in the opposite direction, 'For conveyance by AEROPLANE from WINDSOR to LONDON', this being the only difference in the two cards. This is followed by the words, 'No responsibility in respect of loss, damage or delay is undertaken by the Postmaster General'. In Plate 4 we show a red-brown card flown from London to Windsor.

The cards could be purchased and posted at the following places: Army & Navy Stores, Arding & Hobbs, John Barker, John Barnes, Benetfinks, D. H. Evans, Gamages, Harrods, London Aerodrome, Selfridges, Whiteley's and General Buildings, Aldwych. Cards posted in any other boxes would 'NOT be conveyed by Aerial Post'.

Many firms took advantage of the Aerial Post as a unique method of advertising. Black & White Whisky sent a thousand cards, Wright's Coal Tar Soap five hundred, and General Accident, Schweppes, Colmans, the Gramophone Co., Punch, Remington Typewriters, the Worcestershire *Advertiser* and Nobell's Explosive Co. Ltd were among others who sent advertising cards by air. Some of the stores who sold them, such as D. H. Evans, marked the cards with their own rubber stamp.

It is estimated that 87,345 postcards were flown from London to Windsor and 9,772 from Windsor to London. In terms of value the special violet cards from Windsor were worth £10 each in the 1930s, the lowest valuation of 12s 6d being given at that time to the red-brown cards flown from London on 9 September.

The planes used for Aerial Post were flimsy open monoplane Bleriots, and the principal pilots were Greswell and Hamel.

We have battled our way through many contemporary and later reports of this flight, and have found most of them to be annoyingly conflicting and even self-contradictory when it comes to the actual dates and numbers of flights in each direction. We have spent much time and thought attempting to sort out the facts, and the following summary is as accurate as we believe possible.

The first flight from London to Windsor was scheduled for 8 September 1911, but with the possible exception of the special violet cards and envelopes no mail was actually flown on this day. The mail collected for delivery on the 8th was actually flown and date stamped on the 9th, and twenty-three sacks were delivered to Windsor. Again, as far as we can establish, there were sixteen flights in this direction, the majority taking place between 11 and 15 September, some sources maintaining that the last flight in this direction, flown by Hamel, took place on the 16th. The four flights in the opposite direction appear to have taken place on 17 and 18 September, with all the violet cards being carried by Greswell on the 17th. But there is considerable confusion about the dates of the cards flown from Windsor as some cards were back stamped at Cricklewood Post Office and some Windsor cards, including violet ones, bear the date 16 September.

This historic event naturally provoked much interest and excitement. There was even the added drama of one of the pilots, Charles Hubert, breaking both legs while attempting a flight. Many were extremely dubious about the success of the whole project, and one card which actually made the flight bears the message, 'If you get this, which is doubtful, keep it, as it will no doubt be a curiosity in years to come.'

Other more conventional cards celebrated George's accession to the throne. A beautiful Harry Payne portrait for Tuck's shows 'King George V holding his first court, 7 May 1910'. About this time a postcard celebrating a much earlier event was published for the first time by W. & D. Downey. It is 'The only authentic photograph of the Christening of the Prince of Wales' and shows 'Four Generations. His Majesty King George V, Queen Victoria, King Edward and HRH the Prince of Wales.' And soon there was the Investiture of the Prince of Wales at Caernarvon Castle in 1911, duly recorded on postcards.

Current event and topical postcards initially caught the public imagination in 1897, when Geo. Stewart produced the first cards of this nature. They illustrated the Nile Expedition, with portraits of Gordon and Lord Kitchener, and the words, 'I have done my best for the honour of our Country. Goodbye,' the last entry in Gordon's diary. The cards are court sized, with the illustrations occupying only about half of the front.

In July 1900 the PMG selected a design for the Commonwealth Commemorative Card, which was to celebrate the formation of the Commonwealth of Australia, and 250,000 copies were printed, to sell at 1d each. The design incorporates an arrangement of the various Australian coats of arms, and on half of the address side – a unique innovation at this time – are portraits of Queen Victoria, the Duke of York and Lord Hopetoun, with the message, 'One People, One Empire, One Destiny'. In the same month Tuck's produced a card to celebrate the Relief of Ladysmith.

But 1901 was the year when the topical card really came into its own. It was an eventful year, with many fascinating topics for the publishers to commemorate.

Wrench and Henry Stead both produced 'Current Event' cards on a subscription basis. Wrench called his 'Links of the Empire' and in March 1901 he invited people to subscribe for the ten cards in the Australian Commonwealth Commemoration Set, which were mementoes of the Duke and Duchess of Cornwall and York's journey to open the First Parliament in Australia. Each card was to be stamped and posted on the day the Royal party arrived at the principal ports of call. They cost three shillings, including postage, and had to be ordered in advance. The cards illustrate: 1. the Goodbye from Portsmouth. 2. view of Gibraltar. 3. view of Malta. 4. view of Port Said. 5. a map of the route from England to Australia. 6. a picture of a kangaroo. 7. Adelaide Town Hall. 8. Sydney and the harbour. 9. Brisbane. 10. view of the Exhibition Buildings in which the First Parliament sat.

In June, also as part of the 'Links of the Empire' series, Wrench published a set of cards to commemorate the Royal Return Journey and the Visit to Canada. The ten cards show: 1. Durban. 2. a panoramic view of Capetown. 3. the Island of Ascension. 4. a picture of the Royal vessel *Ophir*. 5. Quebec. 6. Montreal. 7. Niagara Falls. 8. the Parliament at Ottawa. 9. St John's Newfoundland. 10. the Port of Landing in England, 'subject to slight modification'.

In the New Year Wrench had started negotiations with Captain Scott for a most exciting set for the 'Links of the Empire' series. In June 1901 Wrench advertised for subscribers to the 'National Expedition to the South Pole' cards. With 'the courteous cooperation of Captain Scott,' Wrench published four cards, showing: 1. a view of SS *Discovery* and a portrait of Captain Scott, especially 'autographed' for the series: to be posted from London on the day of the expedition's departure. 2. a map of the proposed route of the *Discovery*. 3. an appropriate design dealing with the departure of the expedition in search of the South Pole. 4. taken aboard the SS *Discovery*, accompanying her in her wanderings, to be posted at a foreign port of call on the expedition's return.

The advertisement added, 'By the further kindness of Captain Scott, it has been arranged that the card will be stamped with the postmark of the SS *Discovery*, so that any cards sold without this postmark are not genuine Links of the Empire Postcards.'

All subscribers had to have their names in by 20 July, and in August the *Discovery* was on her way, bearing 'thousands of postcards'.

In October a mirthful uproar was provoked in scientific circles by one of the Antarctic Expedition cards. The *Westminster Gazette* reported,

> Scientists are never tired of scoffing at the errors into which superficial knowledge betrays the general reader of popular science. The general reader will be delighted to have the laugh back at the scientists for once as he may certainly do over the series of illustrated postcards prepared for use of the Staff of the *Discovery* on her Antarctic journey. One represents the ship surrounded by icebergs and upon one of the heights a great polar bear is depicted looking down upon the human intruders into his realms. This is certainly a discovery, for, as the proverbial schoolboy knows, there are no polar bears in the Antarctic. The great beast is confined to the North!

Undeterred, Wrench promptly produced another commemorative card in October. With a mourning border, and printed in black, it recorded the assassination of President McKinley, who was 'laid to rest on Thursday, 19 September'.

Meanwhile, Henry Stead had been enjoying great success with his 'Current Event' subscription cards. Both he and Tuck's issued cards to celebrate the news of the peace in South Africa. They were both out on Monday 2 June, within twenty-four hours of the announcement in Parliament. Stead's card had the added distinction of being posted to, and in some cases received by, subscribers on the same day.

In November Stead was advertising his 'Current Event' cards as recording the chief events of the year, pictorially, at 5s for fifteen cards. In January 1902 he produced fifteen cards to commemorate the opening of Parliament by Edward VII, and they also cost 5s for the set.

The Collectors' Publishing Co. published topical cards too. In August 1901 they produced one to commemorate the 'pathetic passing' of 'the wife of the President of the late Transvaal Republic defeated in the recent War.' Mrs Kruger's mourning card cost 2d.

Postcards commemorating events of national importance and interest continued to be published throughout our period, although no successive year contained quite the concentration of drama of that vintage year of 1901 for the topical postcard. The most famous commemorative cards are those issued in France in 1897–1898 in connection with the Dreyfus affair, but our concern here is with Britain, and we shall now offer a selection of events thought worthy of postcard recognition in the following years – events typical of those shown on the postcards that most collectors can expect to find.

1905 saw national disaster, the death of 'England's greatest actor', Sir Henry Irving. Rotary's splendid memorial card shows a portrait of the actor wreathed in laurel leaves, the house in which he was born at Keinton Mandeville – 'Sir Henry was born in the room marked with a X' – and 'Irving's Resting Place', Westminster Abbey. 'Into Thy hands, O Lord (Becket)' is the appropriate caption.

A card posted in January 1911 shows a dramatic development in the 'Battle of Stepney' – the anarchists' house on fire. Groups of helmeted policemen, strategically placed, peep out from behind corners as the fire blazes merrily. A curious crowd watches from a respectful distance.

The Sinn Fein Rebellion in Dublin in 1916 was the subject of cards by Valentine's and Rotary, and they show the terrible wreckage of the Post Office and the Hotel Metropole on 28 April. 'What a lot has happened since last week – good and bad,' comments a Dubliner, sending a card illustrating the event to a friend in London.

Not only national, but local happenings too, found their way onto postcards. On 30 May 1906 a thrush built a nest in the wheel shaft of a railway truck that arrived at Colwall station, Hereford the day before. No-one had the heart to disturb the new tenant by moving the truck and the next day their kindness was rewarded by an egg appearing in the nest. By Tuesday 5 June there were four eggs and a local photographer recorded the domestic event for posterity!

The laying of foundation stones was another popular ceremony. We have cards of two such ceremonies in Malvern: the foundation stones of the Free Library on 9 December 1905 and the Christchurch Hall. Both ceremonies drew large crowds and the scaffolding of the emergent buildings is strewn with bunting.

Exhibitions always drew great crowds, and cards commemorating them are numerous. From the turn of the century until the outbreak of the First World War, exhibitions seem to have been held more frequently and were wider ranging in their themes and better attended than today. The halls, displays, exhibits, amusements and special structures built for each exhibition give a fascinating insight into the Edwardian way of life.

The first major exhibition in our period was the Glasgow International Exhibition in 1901. This was the period of the undivided back on postcards, so most illustrations take up only a small proportion of the front to leave room for a message. Interesting exceptions are the cards designed by the Belgian artist H. Cassiers, contemporary and stylistically similar to Mucha and Kirchner. One of his exhibition cards shows a view of shipyards on the Clyde, and leaves only enough space for a signature in the bottom left-hand corner. There are twelve cards in the series, showing views of the exhibition and of Glasgow itself. Four cards are upright and eight lengthwise, and the set sold for 1s. They were published by Dietrich of Brussels. More typical of 1901 are the cards which show the Royal Bungalow in black and white and the Industrial Hall in pretty colours – the pictures only occupy a small portion of the front. Alexander Baird & Sons also produced cards for this exhibition: an attractively embossed set of illustrations of various parts of it.

The next important British exhibition was the Wolverhampton Art and Industrial Exhibition in 1902, and again the cards commemorating it have undivided backs. The water chute was the most novel attraction here and in 1904 at Earls Court the Flying Machine was the biggest draw. Gale & Polden were the official printers to the I.R. Austrian Exhibition at Earl's Court in 1906, and one of their most attractive cards shows the Emperor of Austria and Edward VII with their respective coats of arms. The same publishers printed the official cards for the Balkan States Exhibition of 1908, also held at Earls Court.

1908 saw the most fully documented and photographed exhibition of all, the first to be held at the White City. It was the Franco-British Exhibition. Valentine's were the official photographers and in their coloured series are some of the most exquisite view cards issued during our whole period. The ephemeral beauty of the white plaster buildings makes a perfect background for the elegant ladies in their lovely gowns. The predominant colour is white against deep blue skies, and the fairytale theatricality recalls a sumptuous Cecil Beaton stage set. Besides the normal coloured views, Valentine's issued 'Giant' versions of the same views, $7\frac{1}{2}$ in. by $5\frac{1}{2}$ in. cards framed with patriotic emblems of the two exhibiting nations, with the words 'Entente Cordiale' in pride of place, and black and white views. Tuck's, Wildt & Kray, Davidson Bros., Gale & Polden, the Rapid Photo Co. and several other publishers also issued cards to commemorate the exhibition. The great novelty here was the 'Flip-Flap' – a frightening looking machine with two giant arms with a platform for passengers at the top of each, which gave visitors a bird's eye view over the exhibition and offered a good vantage point for the photographers. There were even cartoons, like the one by Crombie, showing a cosmopolitan crowd gaping at the Flip-Flap, whose arms disappear into the clouds. 'The Flip-Flap is IMMENSE,' is the caption. On the back, the sender writes, 'Imagine us up in this. We are going after dinner as it is not safe to go before.'

The Irish village of Ballymaclinton, erected by the makers of M'Clinton's soap, was another popular attraction. It even had its own postal facilities for postmarking and posting cards.

Endeavour, progress and achievement in artistic and industrial fields alike were all represented at this vast exhibition, including several commonwealth halls. The Taj Mahal style structures of the many exhibits and places of amusement or rest were a joy to the eye and provided an almost indigestible feast of culture and amusement for the thousands of fascinated visitors.

The main buildings in the White City were intended for future exhibitions, such as the Japan-British Exhibition in 1910, and Earls Court continued to be the site of many exhibitions. Nor were exhibitions confined to London. Inverness, Bradford, Caernarvon and Glasgow were but a few of the towns to hold regional, national and international exhibitions, congresses and various shows during our period.

A selection of such events and pageants is listed in Appendix 7. Remember that any of these cards is more interesting and more valuable if posted at the actual site.

Pageants gave another opportunity to put on splendid traditional and historical displays, and a postcard record of them was always made. There are postcards of the Chester Pageant, the Sherborne Pageant, the Festival of Empire at the Crystal Palace in June 1911 and the Annual Feast at Ripon. There is a colourful Tuck's set, 'Official Postcards of the Oxford Pageant 1907', from original pictures by artists such as A. Ludovici, J. W. King, Adolf Thiede, Byam Shaw, Howard Davie and J. Finnemore. On the back of each card is a short historical note on the scene portrayed on the front. G. G. Walmsley of Liverpool printed the equally colourful commemorative 'Official Postcards of the Liverpool Pageant'. The Colchester Pageant is commemorated in the Jarrolds 'Pageant Series' of matt sepia photographs of the picturesque scenes, and by Rogers of Colchester in glossy photographs in black and white showing individual actors as well as tableaux.

But life was not always so happy: more unpleasant events occurred as well as these entertaining events and, of course, were commemorated on postcards. These disasters are one of the most fascinating groups in this category. Some have to be taken with a pinch of salt, as the card which announces dramatically 'AWFUL CALAMITY. A Liver (Rara Avis) was found on the border of *Bootle* swollen to an enormous size having swallowed a tramway route. Although large doses of community of interest were administered, the bird died on Tuesday the 7th of July 1903. Funeral procession tonight at 6.30 headed by the Mayor and Corporation of *Bootle*.'

In more serious vein is the card showing the 'Vanguard Motor Accident' at Handscross, 12 July 1906. The London Motor Omnibus Co.'s Vanguard looks to be a complete write-off. Wreckage from a derailed goods train of the South Eastern Railway is shown on a 'Real Photo Series' card by Harold H. Camburn of Tunbridge Wells. The line is being cleared by some railway officials.

Many disasters to ships are illustrated on postcards. In 1904 the Hampton Court steamboat *Queen Elizabeth* sank off Kew on 5 September. On the back of the card commemorating the event, which was posted on 10 September, the sender writes, 'I have read in the papers of this.' There are both black and white and coloured cards showing the 'Wreck of HMS *Montagu*' at Lundy Island in 1906; 'A Wreck at Crosby', and many pictures of stranded ships, such as the *Alford* in Bude Harbour, 23 September 1908, and the *Scotia* at Northcot Mouth, 11 May 1909.

Even more interesting and far more unusual in those days were aeroplane accidents. On a card posted 8 May 1911, of a frighteningly fragile craft perched ignominiously in some tree tops, the sender writes, 'This is a photograph of the first aeroplane I have seen in flight. This mishap took place the day after I saw it about a mile and half from where I am staying. It was Morison's machine.'

Just as unusual, and far more frightening, were the Zeppelin air raids that took place during the First World War. 'Bombardment of Scarborough. House struck in Gladstone Road, Scarborough' is shown on a card posted on 11 May 1915. 'I bought this card *just now*,' writes the sender. 'Hope Mr Frisby will in time get the use of his arm again, poor fellow. This war is really too awful.'

Flying in happier circumstances is commemorated on many postcards. M. Louis Bleriot is seen standing by his aeroplane after landing in Dover after his historic flight from Calais at 5.30 a.m. on 25 July 1909. A card posted in Blackpool on 22 October of the same year reads, 'Have just seen Latham up. He went twice round the course. Very strong.' The picture shows 'M. Latham's flying machine' with a circular inset portrait of the aviator. The Blackpool Aviation Meeting drew many famous international names in the world of Aviation such as Grace, Drexel, Grahame-White, McArdle, Duray, Chavez, Champel, Mons, Cattanes and Roe. The meeting was commemorated by cards published by E.R.G. & Co., Times, Gale & Polden, Rotary and many others. The aviators were portrayed singly, in groups, sitting in their stationary machines and in flight. One magnificent view of Blackpool has seven weird flying machines zooming round the tower. Well done though the faking is, it is made quite apparent by the fact that not one person on the crowded pier is looking up into the air, as you can see in Plate 30.

Many cards illustrate aviators in the *Daily Mail* Aeroplane Circuit of 1912 and the *Daily Mail* Water Circuit, especially M. H. Salmet who in his 50 h.p. Bleriot monoplane took the 'British record for height, 9,000ft, London to Paris in 3 hrs 12 mins. Crossed the Channel Eastbourne to Dieppe.' Before his tragically early death in an air disaster, Gustav Hamel made several flights which, unofficially, carried mail. One card, posted at Stone on 18 October 1913, is stamped besides the official date stamp 'Staffs Aerial Post'. The sender writes, 'This P.C. is going by the aerial mail from Stone to Stafford.' On the front is a picture of 'Gustav Hamel. England's Daring Aviator.'

Rallies and races in another fast growing field – motoring – were also commemorated on postcards. Among the most fully documented meetings were the race meetings on the Isle of Man in 1904 and 1905. Photographs of the racers 'weighing in', incidents along the route and, of course, the finish and the triumphal winners appear on the cards. Interest in motor racing and even in motoring in general was growing every year, and a large, enthusiastic crowd can be seen in many of these pictures.

Many other sporting occasions are illustrated, such as the Grasmere Sports and the ever popular game of golf. The 'eights' at Oxford are the subject of an interesting series of cards published in 1907, showing the procession of the boats, the different college crews and action shots of the races. A most amusing cartoon of 'Eights Week in the Stone Age' by E. T. Reed was first published in 1903, but continued to be sold at Eights Weeks for many years after.

Fires were frequently recorded on postcards. We have one card showing pictures of three different fires. An engraving of 'The Disastrous Fire at Mr Somerville's House, Harrow School, 3 April 1908' is the subject of another card, showing firemen's hoses playing on the blazing building.

Locally produced cards show record waves, lightning, crashing chimneys, wrecked piers and so on. One of the more unusual pictures is of some whales lined up pathetically on the beach on a 'John o' Groat Series' card. The caption reads 'A remarkable Capture of Whales was made at Thurso on the Pentland Firth, on 19 June 1899. Half a dozen Fishing Boats fought them from noon till six o'clock before they were driven into shallow water and speared. The school numbered 104.' On a national scale, there are many cards recording the smallest house in England, the oldest lifeboat in the world (the *Zetland* of Redcar), and many other 'record' breakers in different fields.

*Greetings Cards*

Greetings postcards to commemorate Christmas, New Year, Easter, birthdays and other auspicious occasions include some of the most elaborate and lavishly decorated postcards in any category.

Embossing was a popular embellishment for greetings cards, and many of the heavily embossed cards were imported from Germany. From the turn of the century, and especially after 1902 when a full-out design was adopted, cards flooded into this country from the Continent, mainly from Germany, and the German printers excelled at the embossing process. Heavy embossing naturally indents the back of the card, making it very difficult to write on, but some German cards have a smooth layer of card glued on the back. 'Silver' cards that simulate aluminium were also popular as Christmas cards. Wildt & Kray produced many series for the festive season in this finish, mostly incorporating holly in the design, with others composed mainly of flowers. Davidson Bros used 'silver' for Christmas too, either as a frame or as the background to the whole card, often with embossing as well. Tuck's produced one of their 'Christmas Series' with embossed Christmas emblems, such as bells, on a silver background.

The 'Popular Series' produced some magnificently elaborate Christmas cards in pretty colours with embossing, jewelling and gilding. Some extremely pretty German cards painted by Mailick are artistically highlighted in gold. These are early cards, with undivided backs, but reach an advanced technical standard of printing.

As was the case with advertisement cards, many publishers re-issued standard series, suitably inscribed for the festive season, including many portrait cards, especially of famous beauties.

Of the postcards made specifically as Christmas cards, Tuck's produced a great many 'Christmas Series', including 'Picturesque Natives of Norway', a charming series of Florence K. Upton's Golliwogs, various wintry scenes and some of the few Christmas postcards made during our period that make any reference at all to the religious origins of the festival. One card, showing Mary and the baby Jesus, prints some verses from 'Hark the Herald Angels Sing' and wishes us a 'Happy Christmastide'. Watkins and Kracke, who produced very glossy domestic Christmas scenes, F. W. Woolworth, Wildt & Kray, Valentine's, Birn Bros., Mische & Co., Stiebel, Davidson Bros., as well as many anonymous German exporters made postcard designs specially for Christmas. Some are in humorous vein, like the series of cards drawn by Tom Browne for Davidson Bros.

An interesting bonus to look for in this group are cards actually postmarked 25 December. It seems there was no need to 'post early for Christmas' in those days.

The distinction of being the first British publisher of New Year postcards is attributed to Rotary in January 1902. In general New Year cards are very similar in decoration and design to the Christmas cards described above, and some cards, one feels, were probably issued for either occasion by simply altering the caption. Of the cards specifically designed for the New Year, those bearing the date 'January 1' were most common. A postmark of the same date again adds interest and value to a New Year card.

Moving on to Easter, one finds that the majority of cards for this festival seem to have been specially designed. The religious aspect of Easter is stressed far more frequently than is the case at Christmas, a cross being the usual symbol. Tuck's, Valentine's, Wildt & Kray, Philco and many other British and German publishers issued Easter cards bearing crosses. They were often embossed, silvered or gilded. Chicks and eggs are the secular symbols of Easter, and these too abound, published by, among others, Tuck's, Wildt & Kray, Ettlinger, Schwerdtfeger, Excelsior and, of course, the German exporters. Again, regular series were re-issued as Easter cards, including many actress portraits.

The Christmas cards of the period seem a perfect vehicle for the display of exuberant Edwardian sentimentality, but they are often eclipsed by the lavish use of decoration on the birthday cards. It's flowers, flowers all the way on the large majority – jewelled flowers and embossed flowers, glossy flowers and matt flowers, beribboned flowers, gold or silver bordered flowers and hand-painted flowers. There are actresses with flowers and children and appealing animals. In most cases, the later in the period the glossier the cards become, until they are quite brittle. As we mention in Chapter 9, many birthday cards are appliquéd.

Valentine cards were not in our period the works of art they had been in Victorian times. Hearts and cupids, with some pretty embossed designs, still featured, but equally popular were the humorous cards by artists in the Phil May style, or homely humour like Donald McGill's.

Elaborate greetings from towns were available, such as 'Best Wishes from Statham' in jewelled letters, or 'A Loving Wish from Harringay' on a flower-strewn card, and there were many all-purpose general greetings cards simply saying 'Greetings' or 'Best Wishes', or even 'Love and Best Wishes'.

An extremely popular type of greetings card that seems to have gone entirely out of fashion now is the 'Hands Across the Sea' card. They almost invariably incorporate a picture of two hands clasping, sometimes an obvious male and female hand, or female and female, or male and male, with captions like 'Though Seas Divide' and 'Greetings Oversea'.

Millar & Lang ('National Series') produced a dazzling array of variations on the theme. They are absolutely splendid cards, incorporating ships and trains, motor cars and motor bikes, aeroplanes and airships, and birds carrying letters in their mouths, telegraph wires, flowers and flags, globes and maps, shields and tartans, horseshoes and anchors and flowers. Many were designed to be sent from a specific part of the United Kingdom to a specific country abroad: tartan and thistles from Scotland; maps showing England alone; maple leaves, canoes and log cabins to send to Canada; pyramids and camels to Egypt; topless native ladies and palm trees to Africa; kangaroos and cowboys to Australia. A colourful example is shown on the jacket of this book.

The cards bear poignant messages to indicate how much the faraway friend is missed.

> *Though you're far across the ocean*
> *And your face we cannot see,*
> *In your dear old native Homeland*
> *Kindly hearts still think of thee.*

or

> *Not to be measured by time*
> *Is the love that I bear for thee :*
> *And I feel that no fortune nor clime*
> *Can alter your thoughts of me.*

The immense vogue of the commemorative or topical postcard is demonstrated by the fact that in 1905 a news postcard that was published every day came out. It was called the 'Illustrated Daily Postcard' and no. 13 for 4 November 1905 may be seen at Plate 8. It shows the statue of Mr Gladstone unveiled that day by John Morley.

# 5

## Pictures from the War

Before the postcard was a year old it was involved in war. At the end of July 1870 war broke out between France and Prussia, and by September Paris was surrounded and under siege. Only the balloon could get in and out of the city and special light postcards were produced for the balloon post. The post wasn't totally reliable, however, for one particular balloon carrying an important message about a possible breakout from the city landed not in France, but in Norway, which delayed things a little. In the same year M. Besnardeau put pictures onto his cards at Conlie and there must be many other occasions when cards were used during the conflict, waiting to be discovered by the inquisitive collector.

The British and Indian forces stationed in India soon made use of the postcard. Official, thin, buff quarter-anna cards, overprinted with the name of the state in which they were to be used, appeared in 1879, and a year later whiter cards with a blue stamp were introduced. Some of these carried a quarter-anna Queen's head stamp, while others were entitled 'Quarter-Anna Post Card(s)' and carried a stamp-sized blue square reading 'On H.M.'s Service'. Regiments frequently turned postcards into forms for short communications.

By the start of the Boer War in October 1899 the idea of putting pictures onto postcards was becoming firmly established, and the mood of Britain was one of patriotic enthusiasm for the conflict. The picture postcard was an ideal vehicle to express and encourage this enthusiasm.

The early cards of the war were mainly idealized coloured drawings with bravely flying flags, well-groomed horses, immaculate uniforms and officers leading men in acts of derring-do. Richard Caton Woodville, the British son of an American father, who had served in Egypt in the 1880s, drew striking war pictures which were in great demand by the illustrated papers. A Royal Academician who died in 1927, aged 71, his originals were much sought after, and Queen Victoria is known to have bought some. The Picture Postcard Co. issued cards in 1900 showing some of his drawings, one of which, 'A Gentleman in Khaki', was drawn to illustrate Rudyard Kipling's poem. Rudyard Kipling's stories and poems had been partly responsible for the growth of imperialistic feeling in Britain at the end of the nineteenth century, and it was natural that such a card should be one of the earliest of the war. Strangely, however, Kipling came under heavy criticism in 1902, towards the end of the war, for his poem 'The Islanders'. In it he used two descriptive phrases which upset cricketers and footballers alike. The offending phrases were, 'the flannelled fools at the wicket' and 'the muddied oafs at the goal'. Some post-cards were produced by a firm called Messrs Beeching of the Strand which reflected the nation's anger with Kipling. Beechings attempted to show that these sporting asses were good enough to die for their country. The football card shows 'the muddied oafs' kicking a football on half of the front, and on the other half the same men are pictured charging up a hill at the Boers and one is shot dead. A similar treatment is given to the 'flannelled fools'.

The range of cards produced was prodigious. In August 1901 the Editor of the *Picture Postcard Magazine* wrote, '. . . so great has been the outburst of national and imperial feeling consequent upon the South African War, that series after series of patriotic and imperialistic cards are being issued.'

Raphael Tuck & Sons, who had only begun to issue picture postcards on 1 November 1899, had ten continuous series devoted to military subjects out of their first thirty. Most of these cards were from originals drawn by Harry Payne who, with R. C. Woodville, drew the best of the idealized pictures. One of Payne's early cards is shown in Plate 14. Since it was printed in 1900 both the picture and the message space had to occupy the same side.

The realities of the war did not come through to the public as they were to fourteen years later. There were photographic studies of camp life, em-barkation, and the leaders of both sides in the war, but equally popular were cards showing the uniforms of the regiments of the Army. F. O. Beinne pro-duced a fine chromolithographed set towards the end of 1900 for Blum & Degen, but such cards were not only concerned with the current period: they were just as likely to show the 'King's Army' of 1415 as of 1900.

At the turn of the century, the mass communication media were not estab-lished as they are today. Literacy was not high and radio did not exist. The picture postcard may well have commanded more readers than the newspapers, and publishers of cards anticipated the emergence of national personalities in the present sense, featuring Lords Roberts and Kitchener prominently on many war cards. Lord Roberts, or 'Bobs' as he was popularly known, had lost his only son in the war and had earlier served with great distinction in India. Lord Kitchener, who took over from Bobs in South Africa, was to play a part in the bigger war which then lay in the future.

One of the card types that emerged from the war was the topical card. These were usually produced in black and white as this was quicker than colour work, and thus the cards could be issued soon after the events depicted upon them. Henry Stead issued his 'Current Event' series and Wrench his 'Links of the Empire' series. The series sometimes tried to tell a story in themselves: the fighting forces in South Africa had to be reinforced by intensive recruiting at home, as there was no conscription, and locally raised battalions inspired locally produced postcards; even the national centre, London, was no excep-tion. The CIVs, the City of London Volunteers, marched through London to the Guildhall when they returned from South Africa on 29 October 1900. Tuck's issued coloured and monochrome commemorative cards for the occasion, giving details of when the CIVs went to war and what the cards were commemorating. Special arrangements were made for the whole regiment to post its cards en route to the Guildhall, where they were to receive the Freedom of the City, so cards dated the 29th should be available today – but not easily.

Both Tuck's and George Stewart issued war cards in khaki envelopes early on in the campaign. The word 'khaki', derived from the Urdu word for dust, had originated as a name for a uniform colour in India in the 1850s. The Boers who made much of concealment and camouflage, forced the British to do the same, and to adopt khaki uniforms for combat. Thus the word became synonymous with 'things military'. Commemorative cards were popular too, and Mr Adolph Tuck said that his firm's most popular cards, after one showing a picture of the Queen, were those commemorating the relief of Mafeking, and then Ladysmith, respectively. These cards were issued very quickly and with perseverance the collector might find one dated within a few days of the event. There are semi-official cards too that commemorate these events; on 6 January 1900 the Boers nearly took Ladysmith, but were repulsed in fighting at localities known as Caesar's Camp and Wagon Hill, and the garrison printed their own postcard to celebrate the victory.

The collector who concentrates upon the period of the Boer War will find in it cards representative of every style, from humorous to macabre, patriotic to advertising. However, cards from this period are not easy to obtain, and the more desirable items could cost a pound or two. Of course a card bearing a postmark such as 2 June 1902 and showing a picture of a Briton and a Boer shaking hands, might be worth more, as this would be a first day issue. The war ended on Saturday 31 May, and both Tuck's, whose card is described above, and Henry Stead had cards out on the Monday.

The Boer War offers the collector a chance to find valuable cards, but often the monetary value is philatelic, and sieges and set piece battles produced many opportunities for first day issues.

The South African War made military subjects popular, and the details and colours of the dress uniforms of the different regiments were ideal challenges for the new colour printing techniques. Harry Payne, who drew the early Tuck's military cards, was increasing in popularity and was soon the 'in' artist in this field. Stewart & Woolf and Gale & Polden now published his military pictures and Tuck's put out series after series of 'History and Tradition', 'Grenadier Guards', 'The Golden Highlanders', 'Scotch Pipes' and the like, usually with a résumé of the regiment's history on the back. Harry Payne was the principal artist in these series, but other artists such as N. Drummond were also featured. C. W. Faulkner were in the market too with distinctly 'Payne-like' pictures, although they do not credit the artist.

The most famous military series were produced by Gale & Polden. The firm, based at Aldershot, 'the home of the British Army', had strong military associations, and adopted the name 'Wellington Series' as their trademark.

Their largest and most ambitious series covers all the British regiments. On the left of each card is a coloured vignette showing the uniform of the particular regiment. The illustrations were drawn by J. McNeil in 1908 and Ernest Ibbotson in 1909. On the right is the name of the regiment, its crest, battle honours and a short 'History and Traditions'.

HM Stationery Office commissioned Gale & Polden to print some cards of this series as recruiting cards. We have one on which the address portion on the back is hopefully rubber-stamped to 'Nearest Recruiting Office'. The picture side shows the uniform of the Duke of Cambridge's Own (Middlesex Regiment). But instead of the usual regimental history, details of soldiers' pay are printed on the right (the infantry soldiers' starting rate was 6s 8½d a week).

Once the war was over, the leading postcard personalities could no longer be generals, and it wasn't long before stage stars, politicians and even clergymen usurped their role. But war was never far out of sight, and relations between Russia and Japan were very strained, even during the Boer War. In January 1902, before the end of that war, Japan and Britain formed an alliance, and once the Boer War was over the postcard manufacturers took advantage of the new subject possibilities.

By 1904 almost every manufacturer had made cards with an oriental flavour, subtle or blatant, and when the Russo-Japanese War began on 8 February the public was ready for cards depicting 'Our New Allies', 'Our Gallant Allies' and scenes from the 'England of the East'. The most interesting postcard innovation of the war was the issue of Japanese government cards showing coloured pictures of the conflict as well as pictures of their generals.

These cards often found their way to this country, and one of them, depicting General Kuroki, is shown in Plate 17. Kuroki had led the First Army to victory in Japan's first battle against the Russians – also their first against a white nation – on the River Yalu in Korea, and was one of Japan's most distinguished soldiers. Another interesting card of the period is shown in Plate 8 and is a Valentine's issue, but other manufacturers depicted the incident. The Russian navy had not done well against the Japanese, and the Russian Baltic Fleet steaming gingerly through the North Sea were in fear of night attacks by torpedo boats – though it is difficult to see where these might have been based – and on the night of 21 October 1904, thinking they had seen such boats, opened fire.

Unfortunately their target was actually a fleet of trawlers from Hull, fishing on the Dogger Bank. Several fishermen were killed and for a short time there was a possibility of war between Britain and Russia. The Royal Navy put a fleet to sea and followed the Russians until they were well out of British waters. The Valentine's card is black and white, and the copy we show was posted on 31 October. It was obviously produced very quickly after the event occurred, as indicated by the lack of colour and also the message on the back: 'This is the last they had in. I got it yesterday. I will try and get Mags one also . . .' The event provoked a national stir and cards commemorating it were sold throughout the country. This particular copy was posted from the Isle of Man.

The influence of 'Our New Ally' was apparent in the production of cards until about 1910. The East was indeed mysterious to most people in Britain, for there was little public knowledge about a country that had only opened her ports to foreign trade less than half a century before. But at the end of that decade events in Europe were assuming greater importance, and the unrest beneath the surface showed consecutively in the Portuguese Revolution, the Italo-Turkish War and the Balkan Wars of 1912 and 1913, so that by 1914 the chain of events following the assassination of Archduke Franz Ferdinand at Sarajevo was of little surprise to anyone.

The cards of the First World War are the easiest war cards of our period to obtain, but the collector must not shun them on that account. Indeed the techniques and machines of war have advanced so far since that time that, by their availability, the cards offer a chance to assemble a unique photographic record of an age that might be a thousand years past in the light of the scientific achievements that have followed it.

The cards reflect the mood of the country as it changed from the early conviction that the war would be over in a few months – by 1915 – to an uneasy feeling that it could go on for ever. Early cards of the 1914 period were little different in design from those of the Boer War, save that the picture could cover the whole of one side of the card. War was thought of as a grand adventure, despite the experiences of twelve years before in South Africa, and the pictures of flags and uniforms, soldiers and generals, were soon back in circulation. Jarrolds produced several series of cards entitled 'The Great War', and a card from the first series, issued in 1914, is shown in Plate 17. Jarrolds had probably anticipated the war, for the card was posted only one month after Britain had entered the conflict.

R. Caton Woodville is usually associated with the Boer War, but postcards reproduced from his paintings were also issued during the First World War. Typical are a series of paintings of blinded soldiers. On the back of each card in the series is a message describing the work done for blind soldiers at St Dunstan's, with an appeal for contributions.

Photography played a much more important part in this war, for by now the professional photographer who got out and about had evolved, and newspapers carried far more pictures than they had in Queen Victoria's time. The postcard makers seized on the war as they had before, but at first the camera had to be content with preparations for war, and home based photographers had no choice but to print pictures of army camps, canteens, bands, church parades and any assembly of soldiers they could persuade to pose for them. The existing army camps in the country expanded and many other tented camps were established. Local photographers in the areas concerned produced their own postcards, and these glossy sepia creations, now generally cracked at the edges, are among some of the most fascinating cards. They often have a

philatelic value, too, for to cater for the new and expanded army camps Field
Post Offices (FPOs) were often established, and their postmarks are sought
after by collectors of postal history.

Lords Roberts and Kitchener, heroes of the Boer War, were soon back on
the Picture Postcard. The former featured with Lord Nelson and the Duke
of Wellington on cards published by C. W. Faulkner in 1914, bearing stirring
messages from the great men. A card with Lord Roberts is shown at Plate 12.
The advertising aspect of these three cards is described in Chapter 8. Only the
Union Jack is in colour, and the very white board has a fine pale blue edge.

The message from Lord Roberts printed on the top card illustrated in
Plate 12 must have been one of his last public pronouncements, for during his
visit to France in November 1914 he caught pneumonia and died. It is possible,
therefore, that the Roberts card, at least, had a limited issue.

Lord Kitchener, who became Secretary of State for War at the outbreak of
hostilities, immediately undertook to raise seventy new divisions, and his
famous 'Your Country Needs You' poster with pointing finger is known to
most people. He featured too on postcards as a symbol of courage, as a leader
to be trusted. It is said that Rudyard Kipling's 'If' was a favourite poem of his.
The public certainly considered that Kitchener personified the qualities
described by Kipling in the poem, and an anonymous publisher produced a
magnificent card, only the flag of which is coloured, shown in Plate 12. The
only word on the card is 'If', a trigger to any British-educated memory to
continue ' . . . you can keep your head when all about you are losing theirs . . .'.

Lord Kitchener was drowned when the ship taking him to Russia struck
a mine and sank on 5 June 1916. He was sixty-six years old. The card illustrated does not show a man of sixty, and its sombre black background leads
us to believe it is a mourning card. The reference to the poem is a message
to the nation, saying in effect, 'you know what he would do'.

Personalities, generals, admirals, and politicians figured on cards throughout
the war, different publishers frequently using the same picture when it was
particularly impressive. These cards are stylistically quite different from those
issued during the South African War. The reality introduced by the camera
and the growing acceptance that its use was an 'art' led to less stilted portraits
than those that followed the formality of the Victorian era. Many of the cards
are in black and white, and while formal by today's standards, in comparison
with the Victorian cabinet studies they were considered very natural at the
time. Tuck's and Photochrom produced excellent photogravure cards, the
former in their 'Notabilities' series and the latter in their 'Photogravure'
series. Rotary published their usual photographic prints with a high gloss
finish, and F. W. Woolworth produced some fine photographic studies by
Reginald Haines.

So high was the esteem in which the war leaders were held that some were
even reproduced on cards in bas-relief. Sir John French, for instance, is
shown in all the glory of three dimensions on a card published by Scopes & Co.

It is a good likeness of the Field Marshal and Photochrom reproduce the same photograph on a plain card in their sepia 'Photogravure' series.

Not all the personalities, however, were of the sort to be believed in as leaders through whom morale developed by confidence. One in particular raised morale by laughter. That was 'Old Bill'.

'Old Bill' was the creation of Bruce Bairnsfather, a humorous artist who drew for the *Bystander*. Bairnsfather had gone to France in 1914 with the Royal Warwicks, and for two years had lived through the appalling conditions of trench warfare. His cartoons, featuring from one to three characters, were later collected and published as 'Fragments from France'. The *Bystander* issued many of these cartoons as postcards, and Old Bill was the name by which the principal character became known. Old Bill and two of his companions came to the stage in August 1917 when Bairnsfather co-operated in writing a play entitled 'The Better 'Ole', the name coming from one of his best-known cartoons where Old Bill, hiding in a shell crater, is saying, 'Well if you knows of a better 'ole, go to it!' This too became a postcard and is shown in Plate 13.

The war introduced its own type of humour. The women at home were rapidly breaking out from the restrictions that had stifled them in Victorian times, and now were to be found in uniform and in jobs that had once been done exclusively by men. A woman was no longer an adjunct to a man, but a separate, identifiable human being. In the years leading up to the war, the Suffragette movement had campaigned strongly to gain women the right to vote, culminating in 1913 when Emily Davidson threw herself to death under the hooves of the Derby runners. The war stopped the militant activities of the women's organizations, but the male awareness of woman's changing role is apparent in the postcard. Generally it is clearer in humorous cards: perhaps a male attempt to laugh off a growing unease at women's determination to play an independent role. Fred Spurgin's card for the 'Art and Humour Publishing Co.' in 1916 shown in Plate 21 makes the point.

Of the new weapons that appeared in the First World War, the Zeppelin and the submarine in particular had the effect of making the war truly a national experience, and not something that could be left by civilians at home to the soldiers at the front. In January 1915 Zeppelin airships began to drop bombs on England and the picture postcard pictured the huge machines, the damage they caused, and the people who shot them down. Today a card showing a Zeppelin is greatly sought after and something of their fascination and size can be seen in the card shown in Plate 24. The card is a German one published some years before the war. As far as we know there were few, if any, British photographic cards showing Zeppelins; they are certainly very hard to find. The public at home reacted to the new menace with a foretaste of the resolution that the country was to show under the Nazi air bombardment in the Second World War, and this is reflected in cards like Tuck's 'The Zeppelin Raider' shown in Plate 20.

A card which brings out another of the war's weapons – the tank, is shown on the jacket of this book. On 15 September 1916, on the Somme, the British-invented tank was used for the first time. It owed its deployment in part to Winston Churchill's foresight, yet the morale-boosting card shown in this card shows almost as much foresight on the part of the artist. The censor who passed the drawing less than a month after the tank had been revealed could not have realized that the idealized drawing on the card looked more like the tank that would be used at the end of the war than the real thing!

The censor clamped down on the postcard very soon after the war broke out. Postcards continued to be sent to neutral countries though, and surprisingly it was not until 6 June 1916 that a formal announcement was made that no further picture cards showing HM ships could be issued. The Admiralty authorized some exceptions for morale purposes, the first of which were published by Photochrom in June/July 1916. These show scenes from an official cinema film of the fleet, 'Britain Prepared!'

At home, pictures showing any activity that could be connected with the war effort – like a card which shows 'Making Bessemer Steel' – had to be authorized. This particular card bears the words 'Passed by the Censor 24/4/17'.

The idea that war was glorious and ennobling, still prevalent in 1914, soon disappeared. This too was reflected in the postcard. The dramatic heroics of Boer War cards were displaced by both a more realistic approach and a compensating wealth of sentiment. One manufacturer in particular catered for this sentiment, and that was Bamforth & Co. of Holmfirth in Lancashire. James Bamforth, the founder of the firm, started in 1870 by producing lantern slides. He used life models, often members of his family, the firm or just friends, and illustrated popular songs or stories, some of which we discuss in Chapter 10. When the divided back card was introduced in 1902 Bamforth's joined in the manufacture of postcards, using photographic studies just as they had on their slides and often employing the same negatives. Their early cards were humorous, but they rapidly widened their scope to include the song cards, repeating and then outstripping the success that they had had with their slides. By the time war broke out they were a limited company and had augmented their range with artist-drawn sketches. In our own collection we have come to associate the name 'Bamforth' with a particular type of card that was produced during the war. Any collector, having seen one of this type, will easily recognize another, for only Bamforth really found an acceptable and distinctive method of loading a card with oversentimentality. Frederick Alderson in his book *The Comic Postcard in English Life*, written to celebrate Bamforth's centenary year, groups the cards issued by the company during the war into three classes: 'rallying to the flag', 'comic relief' and 'remembering'. It is the 'remembering' sort that we discuss now.

The cards, printed in distinctive, somewhat off-beat colours, generally pictured verses from a popular song or hymn, many with obvious associations for those fighting at the front or those left behind. At the time they were very popular with both audiences, expressing feelings that senders and recipients were often too inarticulate to put into words themselves. It is difficult today to imagine why anyone should want to send a card to a loved soldier telling him that he would soon be dead! For one card shows a wounded soldier and a nurse, with the happy lines, 'I'll whisper soft while dying. Farewell, farewell my own true love.'

Bamforth's did not have a monopoly of sentiment, and all the major publishers produced cards that helped to bridge the gaps between husbands and wives, lovers and sweethearts, fathers and children. But Bamforth's had the right formula, and what might be called 'mock Bamforths' were issued by some firms in an attempt to cash in on their popularity.

This war, like the Boer War before it, had its share of regimental uniforms and artistic interpretations of the meaning of battle. As we said earlier, this tendency decreased as the war progressed, and the cards began more and more to reflect reality. A transitional stage between idealized artists' impressions and the impartiality of the camera was demonstrated by the cards sketched by Herbert Ward. He toured the battlefields in 1915 and sent back sketches from life that were produced as coloured postcards by C. W. Faulkner. All these cards are signed and dated. But it is the camera which is responsible for one of the most interesting groups of cards that the collector could search for in this category.

The camera had been used in war almost from its birth. Matthew Brady had recorded the American Civil War in considerable detail in the 1860s, and the Boer War was reported by camera. Now the photograph could be printed in its full tonal range, thanks to the half-tone process (see Appendix 4), and reprinted in large quantities, owing to the development of mechanical printing equipment. The camera was portable, and film readily changed and processed, so that with a cameraman at the front line it was possible for the first time for large numbers of the population to see real action scenes within a short time of their occurrence.

In 1916 the Press Bureau asked for tenders for the exclusive right to reproduce as postcards pictures taken by official photographers of the fighting on the Western Front. The *Daily Mail* tender was accepted, half the net profits to go to military charities, with a minimum payment of £5,000.

The collecting craze now surged to its highest peak, and these cards were probably more in demand than any cards had been before. It is likely that the intensity of the demand for the war cards contributed in a major way to the demise of card collecting once the war was over, for after the battle pictures everything else must have seemed dull and uninteresting. We cannot portray the public response better than the contemporary accounts published in that newspaper:

*8 August 1916*. First Forty Official Pictures. Four of the largest and most eminent firms in the postcard printing trade are already engaged on the first edition of the cards. The number of cards turned out will be numbered in millions. The work is highly skilled and takes time, but the *Daily Mail* is determined that the postcards shall be the best that can be made. The first selection of pictures numbers forty and these represent all phases of the new warfare. They are up to date for they depict scenes in the great Battle of the Somme which began on July 1st. They will form a precious record of the gallantry and devotion of our soldiers in the great advance . . .

*22 August 1916*. Rush for War Pictures. *Daily Mail* Battle Postcards in Millions. World wide interest has been aroused in the forthcoming issue of the *Daily Mail* battle postcards made from official photographs. Already the demand is extraordinary. Although the postcards are not yet issued, millions have been ordered from the War Picture Department at Carmelite House. Yesterday one important organisation sent a first order for 250,000 cards. All tastes are suited in the production of the cards. They will be in three styles, photogravure, three-colour and silver print style (photographic facsimile). Some are printed in the two styles and some in all three. For the convenience of collectors every card is numbered . . .

Seven sets of cards, numbers IV to X, were put on sale on 6 September. The *Daily Mail* told the story the following day.

*7 September 1916*. Amazing Demand for *Daily Mail* Battle Postcards. At 11 o'clock yesterday morning the *Daily Mail* branch offices were an astonishing spectacle of high-tide work. The vans of the printers were delivering postcards as fast as they could unload, but they were unable to feed fast enough the vans that came to take the postcards away. The wholesale dealers had already been cleaned out by the retailers, the retailers were bombarding the wholesalers with repeat orders and for their own repeat orders the wholesalers were sending not only vans, but carts of all kinds, motor cars of all kinds, trucks of all kinds, hand barrows, box cycles, cyclists with sacks and even boys who went away bent under emergency parcels almost as big as themselves. The routine of ordinary business had to be abandoned . . . There were other searchers too, among the show sets of the war postcards. They were the buyers who looked for the face of their own man.

The cards were sold in sets or series of eight in one packet for 6d, and in October the *Daily Mail* produced special albums at 2s 6d each to hold 240 cards. The three-coloured sets in packets, Series I, II and III, were issued about a fortnight after the first sets and caused some comment when it was seen that the same picture appeared in different packets. For example, card no. 1 in Series I is entitled, 'Wounded Tommy to the photographer, "I'm not a German." ' The same picture appears as no. 44 in Series IV and no. 57 in Series VIII. The *Mail* explained that the first eighty cards were made up from forty different photographs, and the repeated pictures were always in different types of printing in order 'to satisfy all tastes'.

At the end of September the censor allowed the war cards to be sent abroad, even to the soldiers at the front who, as a result, found out more about what was going on around them than ever before. The *Daily Mail* encouraged the process and went on to suggest that stories could be made up by selecting different cards – although it would be necessary to own all ten sets to do so properly.

Sets were issued frequently and the *Mail* announced that, although it had to order millions of cards, it had had to increase some of its original printing orders sevenfold. We were unable to find out how many sets were issued altogether, or when the issues stopped, but there were at least twenty-two, for set XXII, which depicts the stages of an attack, was issued on 3 April 1917. Details of the first three sets are given in Appendix 3 under the *Daily Mail* entry.

A nice story connected with the war cards concerns card no 16 (Plate 13). On the back of the card is printed, 'A gallant act of self-sacrifice is shown in the photograph, for the man who is carrying a wounded comrade on his back is actually under fire.' On 7 October, under the heading 'Postcard Hero,' the *Mail* published the following report:

'Much interest has been aroused in postcard Number 16 . . . It now turns out that the gallant rescuer is Driver Tom Spencer, who enlisted shortly after war broke out . . .'. It seems that Tom's mother recognized his picture on the postcard and told the newspaper. Whether the authorities in turn recognized Tom's bravery and gave him a medal, we do not know.

The *Daily Mail* cards are fascinating in the detailed record of trench warfare and its implications that they provide. They are not too difficult to find, although because they are growing in popularity their value is rising. Nevertheless they are worth collecting, particularly since they are one of the few series of cards that is well documented – up to set XXII at any rate.

There were many issues of cards by other publishers, including Raphael Tuck & Sons, whose trade was hit by the popularity of the *Daily Mail* cards, that aped the official pictures; but they had to be passed by the censor and the Associated Newspapers had an exclusive contract, so that none was a serious challenge. Interesting issues showing war scenes were made by various charitable or governmental agencies to raise money, including the British Ambulance Committee and the National War Savings Committee. But perhaps the most revealing of the semi-official or official cards was the Field Post Card, Army Form A2042. The frustration of the writer at having to use what might be Huxley's idea of a 'Write Away' card can be imagined. The German prisoners of war in the Alexandra Palace were a little more fortunate. Although their cards could not be sent home they did have pictures on them – 'Gruss Aus Alexandra Palace!' (Plate 24).

When the war came to an end the postcard designers managed to forget the realities that had beset them for the last four years and burst into splendid colours and fanciful designs. The Philco card in bright colours shown in Plate 19 was a throwback to the ideas of 1914, and the soldier's message on the back to his wife says, 'I am come home tonight' [sic]. It was all over for him, but alas, it was also pretty well over for the picture postcard too.

# 6

## Humour and Politics

When Henry Mayhew started *Punch* in 1841 he confirmed the public's interest in satire through cartoons. From the beginning the magazine drew much of its material from politics and political figures, and the writers and cartoonists who contributed to its pages were the best of their kind. *Punch*'s readers belonged to the educated classes, not to the masses, and when the picture postcard evolved around 1900 with aficionados, as Richardson put it, 'of a wealthy educated class,' the earliest attempts at humour were transplants from the pages of *Punch* and its rival, *Vanity Fair*.

The postcard proved so popular that contemporary, up-to-date humour was needed, and so, in addition to reproduced cartoons original drawings were commissioned for the market. *Punch* and *Vanity Fair* contributors were the natural names to choose and Sir Leslie Ward, Tom Browne, Will Owen, John Hassall, Phil May and many others may be collected on cards today. They did not confine themselves to political cartoons in this new medium, but offered comment on the bicycle, the motor car and any events of interest.

The picture postcard trade developed at an incredible speed and spread to all classes, so that by about 1901 the majority of the people who used them were unlikely to appreciate the sophistication of *Punch* humour. Some of the artists adapted their style early, like Tom Browne, who concentrated on the seaside and domestic humour, and may even have been the originator of the topical seaside postcard – though not the blatant sexual double entendre card. New artists appeared and humour became coarser and more popular. Political satire still had a place, and the *Punch* artists were in demand throughout the whole of our period.

There are three broad streams of humour that can be followed through the pictures on old postcards: political, sophisticated and comic. Although these frequently blend and are indistinguishable, we will try to identify each one in the hope that in so doing we can give the reader a general idea of what is available, should he look assiduously enough. Since the humour of the cards lies mainly in their pictures, and we can only show a few, we will concentrate on those artists who, in our opinion, merit individual attention. We will start with a comic artist who died in 1962, who is believed to have designed more than three thousand cards, and whose sales of one design alone were over three million at the time of his death. His name was Donald McGill, and when some of his original drawings were auctioned in 1967 and 1968 they fetched a total of almost £3,000.

We have begun with McGill because cards that bear his signature are known to millions as the crudely drawn, brightly coloured souvenirs that festoon the seaside holiday resorts. Their double entendre jokes are frequently considered to be in bad taste, and have been the cause of concern to Watch Committees all around the coast. McGill always denied that his cards were in poor taste and George Orwell was outspoken in their defence. It may be that in the years following the First World War his successful style, and perhaps even his signature, was copied by others.

McGill began his postcard career well within our period, in 1904 when, to cheer up his nephew who was in hospital, he sketched a humorous picture on the back of a postcard. Through his brother he was introduced to the Pictorial Postcard Co., and by December 1905 the *Picture Postcard Magazine* had picked him out as a designer whose cards would become 'widely popular'. In a letter to the *International Postcard Market* in 1969, a reader asked if anyone had an earlier McGill card than his – no. 1140 in the 'Woodbury' series, postmarked 7 December 1904. No-one appeared to have an earlier example.

The collector could well build up a specialized McGill collection, aiming, perhaps, at finding the earliest cards and one example of each basic cartoon design. McGill did not draw for one publisher only; his cartoons were published by many firms including, later, his own company, and frequently there are different versions of one basic joke.

In addition to the Pictorial Postcard Co., Joseph Asher & Co., the Inter-Art Co. and Eyre & Spottiswoode were among publishers of his cards, and prior to the First World War many were anonymously published and printed in Holland. One of these latter cards is shown in Plate 25, and while the words forecast the way in which his cards were to develop, the picture is well drawn, unlike those that appeared after the war, when the postcard was no longer a medium for artistic expression but purely a commercial product.

The card that sold over three million copies was no. 1772, which he designed in 1916. It shows a puppy tugging at a small girl's nightdress and the caption reads, 'Please Lord, excuse me a minute while I kick Fido!'

The crudely-pictured, doubtfully captioned seaside card, of which McGill became the major exponent, did not dominate the popular market until after the First World War. Indecent and risqué cards were probably produced as early as any other sort, and by 1913, following correspondence in its columns on the subject, *The Times* reported,

. . . attempts to check the trade in vulgar and semi-indecent postcards by police action have already been made at Manchester, Hastings and some of the manufacturing districts of Lancashire and Yorkshire. Sir Adolph Tuck, of Raphael Tuck & Sons Ltd, stated to a representative of *The Times* that he had often been amazed at the inactivity of the police because the machinery for putting down the sale of these undesirable publications exists, and has been made use of, in a large number of towns.

By 1918 dealers in several seaside towns had formed their own local committees to keep the vulgarity on locally sold postcards within limits, but regular outbursts of protest continued and still continue today.

The category that we have called 'comic' is the one that truly applies to McGill, and it is, with the general view card, the only type that has a popular identity today. The reason is that it has adapted itself to changing times, but in so doing it has lost all those attributes of artistic innovation, fine printing, attention to detail and quality that make the early cards so appealing. To some collectors who go beyond our period, the cards reflect the age in which we live, to others they are evidence of a degradation of deltiological standards. Whichever view one takes, the study of the development of Donald McGill's cards from 1904 to 1918 will provide a complete definition of comic cards and a fascinating story of change.

Sophisticated humour in our classification lies between McGill and the satire of the political postcard. There were many publishers of such cards, and many artists, so that today there is a good supply of the genre available in postcard circles. One publisher, Davidson Bros., seems to have specialized in these cards shortly after 1901, when they first began to appear in quantity. The artists that Davidson's used are mostly those whose work is sought today, and the firm's cards are considered characteristic of the artist. By 1903 Phil May, his friend Louis Wain, Anthony Ludovici, John Hassall, Tom Browne and Dudley Hardy had all drawn for the company. Artists did not seem tied to one publisher, although few appeared to be quite as mobile as Reg Carter, whose signature appears on cards from around 1904 published by Wildt & Kray, Tuck's, Millar & Lang, Alfred Stiebel, Ettlinger and later himself. In April of that year Tuck's were issuing as 'Write Away' cards the well drawn, comical 'chinamen' at which Carter excelled. Towards the end of the year Carter's 'John Chinaman' appeared on Ettlinger cards of the 'Royal' series, portraying various 'Winter Sports'.

Phil May died in August 1903, in London, aged thirty-nine, but cards bearing his name can be found dated up to about 1910, although his cards are much collected and tend to be difficult to obtain and relatively expensive. He was a *Punch* artist and one of the best satirical cartoonists of the time, and after his death collections of his sketches from *Punch* were published as books. Tuck's 'Write Away' series, with its part-completed messages, had been a great success, and it is a measure of Phil May's ability that Tuck's did not just commission May to draw for that series, but produced a similar series of his drawings entitled the 'Phil May Series'. A card of the 'Phil May Series' 1294, posted in December 1903, is shown in Plate 16, and unlike the majority of his cards, the original in our possession is coloured.

The tragic story of Louis Wain is mentioned in Chapter 7, and a card of his is shown in Plate 15. Wain's humour generally derives from the spectacle of cats humanized in situations that most people have experienced themselves. His cards reveal a superb artistry, especially his early work. The collector of

Wain cats will find the cards quite expensive in postcard terms, as Appendix 6 shows, and they are also very difficult to obtain. Wain made very little money out of his cats. The story of his life and fortunes is excellently told by Rodney Dale in his book *Louis Wain: the Man who Drew Cats*.

John Hassall was another *Punch* artist whose work can be found throughout our period, some of his earlier cards being for Davidson Bros.' version of Tuck's 'Write Away' series. He was born in Manitoba in 1868 and graduated from farming to drawing posters, then book covers and children's books. Like most of the artists of note who came to the postcard in the early 1900s, he has his signature on all his cards. Although his cards are well drawn and are definitely 'sophisticated' by our scale, they are as yet not too expensive. Hassall died in March 1948 and although we are not certain that he did continue to produce cards up to 1918, from the number of cards we have seen it seems probable that he did.

The man who covered the whole range of the sophisticated humorous postcard category is Tom Browne, or Tom B., as he usually signed his cards (beware of the deliberate confusion caused by the artist who signed himself 'Tom P'), who commented, quite often through proverbs or well-known sayings, on events of everyday life – telephones, boats, motor cars and bicycles. He was drawing on Davidson's cards in the year 1901, offering his pictorial interpretation of such phrases as 'two heads are better than one'. He is popular with collectors and his cards are well drawn. They have a style distinctive enough to have imitators, and often made a play on the husband/wife or master/servant situation, as in the card shown on the jacket of this book. This is funny today, despite the fact that it is one of a Davidson's series called 'Our Servants', not a title that would have much contemporary appeal now. Any woman who has been a 'daily' or employed as a 'daily' will understand Tom's joke. Another card in the same series is captioned, 'The Master and Mistress Return Home Unexpectedly from their Holidays'. Master and mistress loom large in a doorway, through which they glare at the two surprised maids, one policeman and one soldier caught in the middle of a hearty meal, with fruit and wine, and clearly in the 'upstairs' dining-room. The humour is a relic from an age when a significant proportion of the population was engaged in domestic service. But Tom B did not stay in the towns or in the country; he also got to the seaside where increasing numbers of people went for their holidays. By the end of the nineteenth century the fear that outdoor bathing might lead to epidemic diseases had disappeared, and a trip to the seaside became a popular and much recorded activity.

Thomas Arthur Browne was born in Nottingham in 1870, and after having run away from school when he was eleven, became apprenticed to a firm of lithographers until he was twenty-one. It was during this time that he mastered the art of line drawing that was to ensure the clarity and style of his cartoons. His first humorous drawings appeared in the magazine *Scraps*, and he went on to draw for many others including the *Tatler* and *Punch*. He was also a gifted water colour artist and exhibited at the Royal Academy in 1897. He had many friends and his genial personality comes through in many of his cards and his books – such as *Tom Browne's Comic Annual* of 1904. It is believed that he was the creator of those two famous comic characters, Weary Willie and Tired Tim, but we have been unable to establish this definitely. He produced a large number of cards and they are readily available today.

The other two Davidson's artists we have mentioned, Ludovici and Hardy, both had clear, distinctive styles. The former, however, had a more relaxed pen than the other cartoonists and commented upon the political scene more by the subject matter of his pictures than their draughtsmanship. After being secretary to Rodin, Anthony Ludovici turned from art to literature, and how long his postcard career extended we do not know. The card illustrating his style (Plate 20), c. 1903, is particularly apt for the 1970s. After the support that Britain had received from her colonies in the Boer War Joseph Chamberlain felt that the Empire as a whole should be brought closer together to form a united and powerful unit. The only way that such an aim could be accomplished was through trade, and he proposed that the existing principle of free trade be modified to 'imperial preference'. This was heavily opposed in Parliament and claims were made that the price of bread would rise if Chamberlain's plans went through. The public reacted strongly against imperial preference, and Ludovici's card shows Chamberlain and the colonies trying to force public opinion (John Bull) over to their side, while America, and presumably France and Germany representing Europe, watch with interest. Little modification would be needed to make the card an up-to-date comment on Britain's entry into the Common Market.

Dudley Hardy was best known as an illustrator of periodicals and also worked on books and posters. He was born in Sheffield in 1867 and was an accomplished water colour artist. Since his death in August 1922 his pictures have increased in popularity and certainly his postcards are hard to find. He signed his cards, usually in script, and like other Davidson's artists, used sayings or proverbs as captions for his cards; he was a humorist in the way that Tom Browne was, but his figures and compositions have the fluency of the true artist.

Every publisher of any size produced humorous cards, often using the same artists, but it was Davidson's who seem to have used most of the major names. The Pictorial Stationery Co. published cards by Lawson Wood around 1902, and these too are signed by the artist. His cards are well drawn, as befits a man who studied art at the Slade, and often show an animal in a humorous situation. His postcard work developed from a spell as a staff artist and then freelance contributor to illustrated magazines in England and America. Lawson Wood was an active worker for animal welfare and could well have known Louis Wain. He survived both World Wars, having served with the RFC in France in the first war, and died in October 1957.

There are many other artists and noted series: G. E. Shepheard, who drew the comic adventures of man and horse for Tuck's and Faulkner; Douglas Tempest, who joined Bamforth's in 1911 and stayed with the firm until the 1950s, seems at his best in the war years, his cards as characteristic as a trademark; George Davey commented on telephones and tube trains for Misch & Stock, the firm who produced several series of cards entitled 'Addled Ads'. They used a real advertisement from a newspaper or magazine and made pictorial comment on it. Another contributor to Tuck's 'Write Away' and 'Oilette' series was Lance Thackeray, a painter and illustrator who, besides having had one-man shows of his work in several London galleries, published books about Egypt. Like the other artists whose draughtsmanship adds to the appeal of their cards, his postcard work is sought after today, and his death in August 1916 means that there are relatively few of his cards about. One of them is shown in Plate 16, a 'Write Away' card posted in December 1903 on which the sender only added the five words at the end. There is an interesting similarity in the work of Thackeray and May, which can be seen by comparing their cards at Plate 16.

Another 'Write Away' artist was Will Owen, who had started life as a civil servant with the General Post Office and then went on to produce pictorial humour for posters and magazines, and illustrated some of W. W. Jacobs' short stories – the most famous of which is probably *The Monkey's Paw*. Owen was also a *Punch* artist, and perhaps his best postcard work was for Wrench. Before his death in April 1957 Owen published several books of his own. The *Tatler* of 13 January 1904 reproduced a page of cards with this caption: 'The postcard enthusiasm has extended to literature. The Wrench Postcard Company has just issued a number of exceedingly clever postcards illustrating the titles of well known novels.' Unfortunately, there is no artist's signature on any of these cards. By a careful comparison of the postcard humorists' styles we are led to the conclusion that this series was drawn by Will Owen. We have, however, no tangible proof that he was in fact the artist. The amusing series includes such titles as 'Lady Audley's Secret' (which according to the artist was that she had a wooden leg!) by Miss Braddon, and 'The Descent of Man' (a gay old gentleman sliding down the banisters) by Darwin.

Many fine cards often do not bear the artist's name, and some do not identify the publisher either. Millar & Lang in their 'National Series' rarely name the artist, and one of their best selling ideas does not carry a by-line. This is the 'When Father Says "Turn" We All Turn' cartoon, showing a large family packed into a single bed. There is always another complementary issue showing the disastrous results on family and bed when everybody turns. Many different versions were issued, some with political connotations aimed, yet again, at Chamberlain and his fiscal policies, while others simply make the most of what had become a catch phrase, a thing that radio entertainment later made familiar. The families differ greatly. Some are all male, some have mother wearing a bed cap, and their number varies from seven to thirteen. A medium-

PLATE 9

*Right*–Tuck: 'Kings and Queens of England' Series— Edward VII, 1902

*Below*—Broom: 'Visit of the King and Queen of Portugal to Windsor Castle, 1904'

VISIT OF THE KING AND QUEEN OF PORTUGAL TO WINDSOR CASTLE, 1904.
H.R.H. PRINCESS VICTORIA. H.R.H. PR. OF WALES. H.M. THE QUEEN. M.H.E. MARQ. DE SOVERAL. H.R.H. PR. CHRISTIAN. COL. Hon. H.C. LEGGE.
H.R.H. DUKE OF CONNAUGHT. H.M. THE QUEEN OF PORTUGAL. H.M. THE KING. H.M. THE KING OF PORTUGAL. H.E. SENOR A.E. VILLACA.

PLATE 10  *Above*—Typical 'Gruss Aus . . .' card, c. 1890. *Below*—Card posted from the top of Vesuvius, 1904

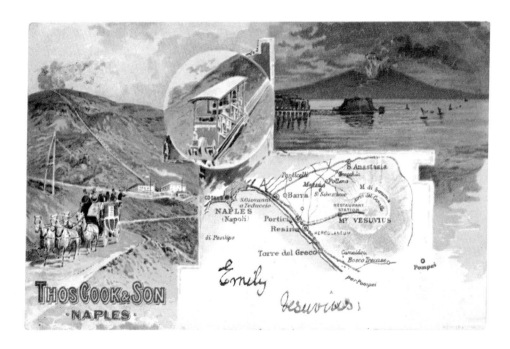

PLATE 11    *Above*—Tuck: 'Oilette'—'Laxey Wheel, I. of Man', c. 1905. *Below*—Valentine's: view of Newport, Mon., c. 1910

Earl Roberts.

"GOD BLESS AND WATCH OVER
YOU ALL."

*Extract from a letter written by Lord Roberts shortly
before he left for France, 1914.*

*I send with pleasure the photograph*

*Yours sincerely*

*Roberts*

LORD ROBERTS' CALL TO ARMS.

"I am proud to be the first to welcome you as brother soldiers
and to congratulate you on the splendid example you are setting
to your fellow-countrymen. You are doing exactly what all able-
bodied men in the kingdom should do, no matter what their rank
or what their station in life may be. I respect and honour you
more than I can say. My feeling towards you is one of intense
admiration. . . .

This is not the time to play games . . . . We are engaged
in a life and death struggle, and you are showing your determination to do your duty as soldiers, and, by all means in your
power to bring this war to a successful result. God bless and
watch over you all!"

PLATE 12

*Left*—C. W. Faulkner: Bovril
Card, 1914

*Below*—Lord Kitchener and
'If', c. 1916

A GALLANT RESCUE UNDER FIRE.
THIS MAN SAVED TWENTY LIVES LIKE THIS. Nº 16

PLATE 13

*Above—Daily Mail :* 'Official
War Photographs', Series II No.
16, 6 September 1916

*Right—*Bystander : 'Fragments
from France', Series I, c. 1916

" Well if you knows of a better 'ole, go to it."

THE BRITISH ARMY. Royal Irish Lancers

PLATE 14

*Above*—Tuck: 'British Army'
Series No. 125 by Harry Payne
—Royal Irish Lancers, 1900

*Right*—Tuck: 'Defenders of
the Empire' Series—Oilette
by Harry Payne, c. 1914

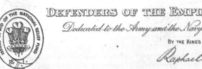

DEFENDERS OF THE EMPIRE.
*Dedicated to the Army and the Navy.*
BY THE KING'S PUBLISHERS.

Punting

PLATE 15
*Left*—C. W. Faulkner:
'Punting' by Louis Wain,
c. 1903

*Below*—C. W. Faulkner:
'Dutch' card by Florence
Hardy, c. 1913

Love lightens labour.

PLATE 16  *Above*—Tuck: 'Phil May' Series No. 1294, c. 1903. *Below*—Tuck: 'Write Away' Series No. 986 by Lance Thackeray (LT), c. 1903

sized family can be seen in Plate 21. This card, which was posted in October 1903, attributes the saying to Austen Chamberlain – or at least that is one interpretation of the cartoon. Joseph Chamberlain, Austen's father, also in the bed, resigned from A. J. Balfour's Government in September 1903 because of their opposition to his tariff reform policy. Austen, however, remained in the Government and was Chancellor of the Exchequer from 1903 to 1905 with his father's approval. During this time Joseph set about persuading the public that his policy was the right one, and that the one being followed by the Government, including his son, was wrong. Gradually support for his policies grew and the card 'When Father says turn . . .' provides apt comment on Austen Chamberlain's position. What is not clear is whether the artist was mimicking what Austen might be saying to his colleagues, or whether he was telling Austen to do what his father told him to. Joseph and Austen looked very much alike, were thin and wore monocles, so that it is sometimes difficult to know which one is being caricatured. It is probable that during and before 1903 Joseph was the main target and that from 1904 onwards Austen was the 'man of the hour'.

The collector of humorous cards is bound to find a considerable number published by the Cynicus Publishing Co. Ltd. of either Tayport, Fife or Leeds. All the cards are signed 'Cynicus' and generally make it clear that their designs are protected by copyright. The earlier cards do not specify their place of origin, but after 1902 they bear the town name Tayport and later Leeds. Cynicus seems to have commented upon everything: babies, weddings, holidays, seasickness and, like most of his contemporaries, motor cars and bicycles. His earlier cards were finely drawn and the standard was generally maintained, although some of the later series are less attractive. In Plate 25 we show a card, posted in February 1907, of the 'Our Local Express' series, a type of which Cynicus produced many versions. The basic drawing could be adapted to apply to any holiday area. In the first issue of the *Postcard Connoisseur* of March 1904 the Editor writes, 'Cynicus is the cognomen of Mr Anderson, that widely popular and clever Scottish caricaturist. So great has been the demand for the work of this artist that a commercial undertaking has been formed with the name of the Cynicus Publishing Company, who print and place on the market the works of this somewhat erratic genius!' As his cognomen implies, Anderson's work is often extremely cynical in flavour and he pokes malicious fun at sacred British institutions like the rainy seaside holiday, maiden aunts and parenthood. One card in particular shows perspicacious foresight on a subject that was not to cause national alarm for another sixty or so years: pollution. It shows a river, on whose bed lie rotting hulks and animal carcasses and a pipe bearing the notice 'Sewage by Order'. On its banks factory chimneys pour out clouds of filthy smoke. But Cynicus can be jollier, and many of his cards are crowded with trippers having a good time. However gay the scene, Cynicus nevertheless implies that this wouldn't be his idea of entertainment.

Another cognomen found on postcards is 'Spy'. In June 1902 Stewart & Woolf advertised two series, nos. 101 and 102, each of twelve cards, being reproductions of cartoons painted by Spy for *Vanity Fair*. The pictures occupied only half of one side of the cards, were framed by a raised gilt border, and represented the most popular personages shown in recent *Vanity Fair* cartoons. The Editor of the magazine in which the advertisement appeared welcomed the cards as a 'new, capital and original idea'. Spy was Sir Leslie Ward, a famous Victorian political caricaturist who specialized in depicting public figures in comical cartoons with big heads. He died, aged sixty-five, in 1922.

Charles Dana Gibson, whose 'girls' are described in Chapter 7, did not just draw pretty pictures. He had a sharp wit and a telling pencil, and produced many fine line drawings for James Henderson & Sons. Almost all of his cards are in black and white, although some sport a coloured border. Strangely, his cards are not enthusiastically collected at the time of writing, except for those that portray his 'Gibson Girl'.

The firm of Wrench & Co, in its short six years from the end of 1900, gained a deserved reputation for high quality cards. This applied also to their humorous issues, which were often line drawings reproduced from *Punch*. Early issues with undivided backs make much of Chamberlain's policies, and on the address sides carry a brown reproduction of *Punch*'s famous cover. These cards come into the political category like those of Ludovici, whom we mentioned earlier, and indeed, most of the *Punch* artists commented on current political issues. The Chamberlains and Lord Rosebery came in for a great deal of attention from the caricaturists.

Political satire in pictures and terse captions seems sharper on cards from the early part of the century. A collection of such cards can stimulate the collector to spend hours in fascinating research through the reference books of his local library. But not all comment was personal in the way that Spy made it, and much humorous comment was made about politicians in general.

There were many cards with a regional flavour, showing Welsh ladies in their tall hats and confused Englishmen breaking their jaws trying to say Llanfairpwllgwyngyllgogerychwyrndrobwllllandyssiliogogogoch. Reg Carter and Valentine's made a meal of Welsh jokes and the cards frequently border on the comic category, unlike the Scottish jokes of Cynicus which are well drawn, particularly his Series 8914 and 8916 of 'Scottish Character Sketches', published at Tayport.

A favourite butt of the cartoonists was the hen-pecked husband, typified in many cartoons by a certain Mr Caudle and his wife. The dictionary definition of 'caudle' is 'a warm drink, sweetened and spiced', and it was often Mr Caudle's over-indulgence that led to one of Mrs Caudle's fierce 'bedtime lectures'. 'A. L.' and Tom B. both used the characters on Davidson's cards around 1906, and later Tuck's produced an amusing series of 'Mrs Caudle's Curtain Lectures'. The Tuck's cards portray Mr and Mrs Caudle as different animals –

a duck and a drake, a cock and a hen or a pair of dogs – but Mrs Caudle's lectures are all too human. 'No – I don't care if you are tired, I *shan't* let you go to sleep. No, and I won't say what I have to say in the morning, I'll say it now,' is a typical example. Their common source was probably a book of the same title as Tuck's series, *Mrs Caudle's Curtain Lectures* by Douglas William Jerrold, 1803–57.

There is much amusement to be found in the pictures on postcards that were not originally intended to be funny. The type of card where this most often occurs is the one which is based on a photograph of real people rather than drawings. The stage beauty photographs that were enormously popular around 1903 are a rich field, not only because photographic techniques have improved so much that old pictures often seem stiff and lifeless, but also because the public image of a seductive woman has changed so much since that time (judge from Plate 32!).

Many publishers used real people in comedy situations, including Davidson's, Valentine's, Beagles and Bamforth's. The latter in particular made use of models and retained the human touch in their cards. Bamforth's made comic capital out of popular songs, whose verses appeared on the cards, and their success attracted imitators who never managed to capture the flair that the Bamforth family had developed from their lantern slide days. The company continued to produce their photographic cards until about 1916, when artist-drawn scenes began to replace live models.

Tuck's 'Write Away' series, mentioned earlier in this chapter, combines a picture, frequently amusing, with a related and partly completed sentence alongside it. This allowed the artist more material to create his humorous situation, and benefited the lazy sender in that most of the message was already written for him. The Phil May card and the Lance Thackeray version shown in Plate 16 are of this type, which was so popular that almost all manufacturers copied it. Tuck's introduced this series early in their postcard career, for Series 42 was called 'The Amewsing Write Away! Series', 58 was called 'The Write Away! Series' and 59 'The Write Away! Series (South African War. Khaki Edition)'. They were advertised in the first issue of the *Picture Postcard* which appeared in July 1900.

We mentioned earlier in the chapter the vulgar seaside cards which caused trouble early in the century. There were, inevitably, erotic and indecent postcards, and Erik Nørgaard has written a book about them called *With Love. The Erotic Postcard*. He points out that the period up to 1918 was one in which public expression of any form of sexuality was strictly forbidden, the embargo reducing in severity from 1900 onwards. Because of the suppression of overt sexual symbols, the symbolic replacements of fountains, pillars and swans' necks feature in many cards. However, the Victorian morality which professed to represent the true character of the British people was titillated by accounts of indecent cards in Paris and then shocked by their sale in London.

In a smug article in the *Picture Postcard*, 'Lex Heinze' wrote in October

1900, 'but "every virtue has its fault" and the picture postcard which in the country of its origin is a harmless thing, dressed in the garb of innocence, has in Paris rapidly degenerated. We are sure that no Post Office would forward such obscenity as is openly exhibited in the arcades of the Rue de Rivoli, or thrust into one's hands by the itinerant newsvendors outside the cafés.' Heinze points out that the Paris Exhibition of 1900 had popularized the post-card in France, although the Germans were the chief buyers. A raid on shops all over Paris as well as near the Exhibition was made by the French police on 22 August and 80,000 objectionable cards were seized. Unfortunately the police let it be known that the raid would take place, 'which indiscretion acted as an advertisement, causing a run on the shops before closing time'. Presumably by the Germans?

Two years later, in August 1902, the Editor of the magazine had had no qualms about pointing the finger at Frenchmen when two men were prosecuted for selling obscene postcards in Tottenham Court Road. They were found guilty and one was sentenced to six weeks' imprisonment with hard labour, while the other was fined £10 with 5 guineas costs. The names of the two were Bordez and Dion, and the Editor concludes, '. . . as the names suggest, both the prisoners were Frenchmen, and we cannot conceal our satisfaction that persons guilty of such a disgusting offence were not English tradesmen . . .'. We haven't any truly obscene vintage postcards, although we have tried to find some. We can offer no advice here as to prices or sources, although a collection of such cards might appeal to some for other than erotic reasons. Our problem is that we find it difficult to say 'Have you any dirty postcards?'

# 7

# Portraits

Literally Everyman and his dog were pictured on cards up to and including the First World War, from Queen Victoria to the newspaper boy. In this chapter we can point out only the commoner types you are likely to come across, and a few of the more unusual subjects you may be interested to look for.

The bizarre is well represented under this heading, for the many freaks of nature that appeared in the travelling circuses and stage shows seemed to have a curious fascination for the Victorians and Edwardians. Even animal freaks were celebrated on postcards, like 'Linus the Wonderful Long Tailed and Double Maned Horse'.

A group of 'Shanghai Chinese Gymnasts, Acrobats and Conjurers' was an even greater draw because it included 'Genuine High Caste Small-footed Ladies'. Major and Mrs Mite, following in the successful tiny footsteps of General and Mrs Tom Thumb, are portrayed on a number of cards. One shows the tiny pair with their minute baby, and on another they stand by their miniature coach pulled by two Shetland ponies, the top of which doesn't reach the waistline of the bowler-hatted gent who is opening the door for them.

At the other extreme is Machnow, the Russian giant, who appeared at the London Hippodrome. He was photographed in bed – or rather in three beds joined together. Sad and gentle faced, he is tenderly holding a baby in his huge hands. Another postcard personality is the 'Nottingham Giant Girl'. Unfortunately no details of her weight and girth are given, but she is 'MASSIVE'!

Perhaps the most spectacular showbiz personalities to be immortalized on the postcard were a group of six Red Indians in tribal dress. On a Gale & Polden card they are described as the 'Sole Survivors of the Black Hawk Massacre Episode. Now taking part in the Red Man Spectacle, Earls Court.'

Of the professional entertainers, actors and actresses are the most common postcard personalities on portrait cards. They range from obscure groups like 'Kitty Denton's Eight Little Rays of Sunshine' and 'Geo. Hall's Merry Japs' to household names like Henry Irving and Vesta Tilley. The majority of the big publishers produced 'Star' series, including Tuck's 'Play Pictorial Series', 'Stage Pictorial Series', 'Stage Favourites' and 'Real Photograph' series, in black and white or sepia, machine coloured and hand tinted. The Rotary Photographic Co. was foremost in the field. They produced photographic studies of individual stars and scenes from current productions in black and white, in sepia and in glossy and matt finishes. Some of their cards were coloured and sold by M. H. Armstrong of Manchester, as were some J. Beagles & Co. cards.

Ettlinger, always on the lookout for a new line, is credited with being the first to publish pictures of stage scenes showing the actors playing their parts on the stage. This new venture started in March 1903 and illustrated *A Chinese Honeymoon*, then playing at the Strand Theatre. Printed on cream tinted board, there are six in the set – five lengthwise and one upright. There were many sets of scenes from the stage available at that time, but the cast normally went to the studio to be photographed.

It was a favourite trick to send a whole set illustrating a certain production to the same person with the message spread over the six cards. A Hartmann set of *Three Little Maids* (1903) bears the message thus:

'1. My dear Belle 2. I hope you 3. like this set, 4. as I know 5. you have seen 6. it. Love Katie.'

They were posted on 10 July 1903.

Some series of star portraits combined several pictures on one card so one got two or more beauties for the price of one. Philco produced a set of glossy white cards with two round coloured portraits of one star inset in embossed frames, showing Phyllis Dare, Gabrielle Ray or Billie Burke. The Rapid Photo Printing Co. had the same idea, but with two different stars and in black and white – Valli Valli and Iris Hoey, Mabel Green and Ethel Oliver, etc. The most elaborate set is by Philco. The card is dark green and glossy and the two oval portraits are framed by pink rosebuds and joined by elaborate swags.

There are many variations on a theme. Davidson Bros used the same picture of Edna May on several cards, some with the words, 'Sole monopoly of Davidson Bros. London'. This applied to the photograph and not to Miss May herself, as other pictures of her were used by all the principal publishers. Rotary showed her in one of the fantasy compositions that were so popular. She stands by an enormous capital E. On the centre bar of the E sits a monkey and a naked little girl, and an inscrutable white cat sits on the ground.

Hartmann's 'Bubbles' is another fantasy series. A small boy dressed as a clown is blowing iridescent bubbles which contain different sized pictures of the stars – Nina Sevening and Pauline Chase, for instance. Still in the realm of fantasy is Tuck's 'Flower and Beauty Silverette Series'. On the 'Bluebell' card Miss Jessie Bateman looks out of a gigantic capital B from two portraits, one full face, the other in profile. The whole composition is strewn with blue-bells.

The actresses were often photographed with members of their families. The sisters Dare, Zena and Phyllis, with their personal brand of alluring youthful purity, were frequently photographed together, but sometimes one finds one or both of the sisters with their father. The sisters Arundel, Grace and Sybil were another much-photographed trio. Rotary produced series after series of that eternal beauty Gladys Cooper, many showing her with her two children, Joan and John. There are also a number of series of Joan and John by themselves, with small inset pictures of their famous mother. Ellaline Terriss (Mrs Seymour Hicks) was often photographed with the photogenic 'Baby Betty' or, as she grew older, 'daughter'. There are many pictures of Baby Betty's celebrated parents, especially in scenes from *The Beauty of Bath*, in which they appeared together.

Even pet animals were photographed with their lovely mistresses. The ruse of depicting the beauty cuddling a child or an animal is the postcard extension of advice offered in the *Kama Sutra* on ways of arousing an intended lover: 'to embrace and kiss a child in her presence'. She is saying, in effect, 'See how tenderly I embrace this child or this puppy.' It is a short step for the male purchaser of the card to imagine how tenderly she would embrace him!

Tremendous thought obviously went into trying to dream up new poses, backgrounds and costumes. Take the case of Miss Marie Studholme – reputed to be the most photographed of the Edwardian stars. Judging from the fact that over the last nine months we have acquired sixty different poses of Miss Studholme without really trying, and that this is a good twenty more than the cards showing her nearest rivals, the Dare sisters, it would seem wholly probable. We have pictures of her with a tennis racquet (and a lovely lacy cartwheel hat); as 'Lady Madcap' in a peaked cap, coyly pointing her right index finger; standing with arms resting lightly on a chair; looking at herself in a mirror; leaning pensively on a desk; just about to enter a door; just about to enter a cab; dressed as a maid; swathed in furs; as Alice in Wonderland; smiling through an elaborate frame; contemplating various flowers on various cards; in Pierrot costume with a peke; in a summer house; in an elaborately carved chair; several in rather unbecoming Japanese costume (of course) – see Plate 32; with a parrot in a cage; working a puppet; absolutely smothered in flowers and holding on to a swing; winding a long case clock; dressed as a farmer's boy; in a man's trilby; dripping with jewellery and artificial flowers in her hair, and even more poses.

The lovelies were natural subjects for the publishers to embellish. Beagles, Rapid Photo Co. and Philco were among those who liberally 'jewelled' their subjects. There were several experiments in colouring – some more successful than others.

It is always fascinating to have two copies of the same photograph, one black and white and one coloured. One of our pairs is of Vesta Tilley, elegant in a superbly-cut frock coat and silk hat. The matt black and white picture is published by the Rotary Photo Co. and the glossy coloured card by Wane & Co. Both acknowledge the photographers Brown, Barnes & Bell. Miss Tilley looks far more dashing in the coloured version, with her pearl grey coat and trousers, green bow tie, pink buttonhole and brown waistcoat with gold buttons.

Another device to add interest was for the stars to 'autograph' the cards. 'Sincerely yours, Queenie Leighton' on a Rotary card; 'Delia Mason' casually written across her skirt on a Milton 'Photolette' card; 'Sincerely yours, Phyllis Dare' on a Philco card; 'Sincerely yours, Daisy le May' on a Tuck's 'Celebrities of the Stage' card.

The gentlemen were not forgotten, either. They were also given a variety of treatments, if not so elaborate as those meted out to the fairer sex. A touch of fantasy creeps into a card showing Forbes-Robertson as a playing card – the King of Hearts, naturally – and on another Rotary card with pictures of galleons and flying swallows.

Occasionally they were coloured, like Fred Terry in cavalier costume on a Rotary card, and again the men appear in a variety of costumes and poses, from Seymour Hicks' melting glance to Sir Henry Irving's aesthetic, intelligent gaze and F. Benson's aquiline profile; in naval uniform, as Regency dandies, as Attila the Hun, etc. The most dramatic poses were undoubtedly struck by Sir Henry in the action pictures from some of his productions, notably as Mathias in *The Bells*. In complete contrast, Little Tich as a soldier carries a rifle that is almost as big as himself.

The male star's family also joined him on postcards, but usually in staid family groups far removed from the calculatedly stimulating poses of some of the female groups. George Robey personified the upright Edwardian family father when photographed on a Philco card with Mrs Robey and the two little Robeys.

We cannot leave the stars without discussing a phenomenon of the early Edwardian period – the Gibson Girl. Charles Dana Gibson, an American artist born in 1867, was on one of his frequent visits to England. On a long train journey his train halted at a small country station and Gibson's eye was caught by a vivacious group of young people. Reputedly crying 'I must draw those girls', he dashed off the train and onto the platform. Not only did he draw the girls, he married one of them – Irene, one of the five beautiful Langhorne sisters of whom Nancy, Lady Astor, was another. He continued to draw Irene in a variety of poses until she became known as the Gibson Girl, and the tag, irrevocably fixed to her from that first sketch in 1895, clung to her for the rest of her life. The personality that emerged from the drawings was so consistent and so strong, that, from being drawings of one girl, they became drawings of a complete type or genre, immediately recognizable. Sometimes pert, sometimes haughty, always alluring, she was described as 'something between the Anglo-Saxon Amazon and the Parisian, being of chic and frills and fascination'. Soon the Gibson Girl was recognizable to the whole world, but her success was redoubled and immortalized by a British actress, Camille Clifford. Camille met Gibson on a trip to America and was so taken with his 'girl' that on her return to London, she copied the Gibson Girl style in her next show, *The Prince of Pilsen*. It was an instant success and in her show in 1904, *The Catch of the Season*, she wedded herself irrevocably to the Gibson Girl image by creating the Gibson walk with a sexy swing of the hips, and the smash hit song 'Why Do They Call Me the Gibson Girl?' Camille, of the incredibly tiny waist in that age of small waists (she was said to have had her lower pair of ribs removed to enable her to lace up tighter), became the toast of London and her photograph on postcards sold by the thousand. So did postcards of Gibson's sketches. You can compare Camille's picture with an original Gibson in Plate 26. They were published by James Henderson in the 'Pictorial Comedy' series on fine quality dark cream tinted cards and also on shiny white cards by the same publisher, and are always signed by the artist. The 'Pictorial Comedy' series also included girls by Allan Gilbert, drawn in 1900, which are superficially very similar in style. But the Gilbert Girls appear like Vestal Virgins beside the languorous Gibson Girls.

By far the most fascinating and often amusing portrait cards are the personal ones. Many were made by the do-it-yourself method described in Chapter 9, on Kodak, Mallandain, Velox or Rotary sensitized cards. Those who hadn't the time or the skill to produce cards from their own negatives could take advantage of offers such as that appearing in a photographer's advertisement in 1902: 'Your Own Pictorial Postcards While You Wait'. They cost 4s 6d per dozen – rather expensive. The previous year, in plenty of time for the festive season, Mr Noel Hammond of Battle, Sussex was advertising 'Private Portrait Cards'. He offered samples in brown tint with 'appropriate wintry border for Christmas or the new Year'.

These studio-produced cards tended to result in rather stilted studies. Earnest family groups stare as if hypnotized by the camera's mesmeric lens. Young ladies in their very, very best pose obviously and unnaturally by the inevitable potted plant.

One advantage the professional photographer had over the amateur card maker was that he could vary the size, shape and background of the actual picture. Most towns soon had their own card-producing photographer. Many had amusing figures with a hole for clients to put their heads through and so be photographed in the guise of a 'toff', a Dutch girl, a parson or a footballer. Often the bodies were completely out of proportion to the heads (usually much smaller), which added to the comic effect.

The professional photographer was out and about too, taking pictures of local events. The results were eagerly bought by anyone recognizing the top of a head or their own left eye in the picture. What a rich source of historical information these personal cards are. The picture they give of life in the first twenty years of this century would be even more complete if only the printer had always added a few vital details on where the photograph was taken, whom it portrayed and when it was taken. So often one finds enigmatic pictures of inscrutable groups of people who give no clue as to what they are doing to warrant being photographed.

Sometimes one can piece together the story. Costume can be one indication of date, as shown in Chapter 3, but sometimes we have to look for other clues. A typical photograph taken, we know, in Worcester shows a group of adults seated in front of a brick building. The ladies all wear extravagantly decorated straw cartwheel hats; the men, happily beaming, sport a mixture of boaters, cloth caps and bowlers. Probably it was taken between 1908 and 1910, deducing from the clothes, and surely they are proud parents, for in front of them on the grass sit some smiling little boys, clutching certificates. We assume it was the school sports day. But then it may have been an open air speech day, and which school was it?

The popularity of bicycling as a sport is shown by the number of cards that illustrate the craze. A picture of the 'QVPO Gymkhana Holford' in 1909 shows some athletic young ladies hastily dismounting, not from their horses but from their bicycles, to pick up an apple in their teeth from a bucket. A picture of the 'Waterloo Cycling Club' in 1905 shows five young ladies and three young men posing in front of their machines.

Posters and advertisements in the background often supply what the caption omits. A picture dated 11 September 1905 shows a crowded coach pulled by two horses. Behind them is a poster which reads, 'Book here for Sam Colwill's Excursions. Daily to Lynton.' The message on the back can be equally informative. A card posted in 1904 at Portishead shows elegant groups strolling between gay marquees strewn with bunting. On the back is written, 'I send you a Photo of the Bazaar. Can you recognize anyone? They took £400 but of course there are some expenses.'

One of our favourite cards in this category shows an al fresco below stairs tea party. Round a typical Edwardian table complete with starched cloth, silver teapot and vase of flowers sit what are obviously the butler, frock-coated and moustached; the housekeeper, respectability personified; the parlour maid, with stiff white apron; and two younger men whose occupations one can only guess at. Such scenes are the crystallization of an era on a small card.

The new arrival was, of course, a popular subject for cards to be sent to all members of the family. He or she was often portrayed surrounded by half a dozen bored-looking elder brothers and sisters. 'Kenneth. 5 weeks old,' writes proud Mamma on the back of one such portrait. 'Baby is perfect. He is very different from the others,' she adds in relief.

Bridal groups abound, with serious grooms contemplating the responsibilities they have assumed on this auspicious day. And then there are the houses – unnamed and featureless, but Home Sweet Home to someone.

The amateur photographers were, naturally enough, not always so successful as the professionals. 'Papa will write to you soon and he says that photo you want is not quite a success and sends this one instead. Will it do?' writes Willie Wallie West in 1905. He is pictured on the other side with his sister and younger brother.

'Do you think this is any better?' asks Fanny in July 1915. On the other side one can just distinguish a rather blurred Fanny having a picnic tea with the rest of her equally fuzzy family.

The greatest advantage of the DIY cards was that one wasn't confined by the four walls of the photographer's studio, nor at outside functions did one have to rely on the presence of a professional photographer to record the event. Any interesting situation could be photographed and shared with one's friends wherever and whenever it had occurred.

A group of six globe-trotters recorded their trip round the world for their friends at home on Kodak cards. We see them sitting in rickshaws or under palm trees, on board ship, wearing pith helmets, photographing the photographer, taking tea at an open air café, with an Australian aborigine, on sandy beaches and rocky beaches, perched in tree houses, or with some Indian natives. How much more interesting and personal a record this is of their great adventure than if they had merely popped into the studios of the local photographer at each port of call, or had simply bought view cards wherever they stopped.

The star of amateur dramatics shines nearly as brightly on postcards as does the professional. Certain themes emerge as favourites. Around 1904–5 the Japanese influence was strong. The Russo-Japanese war was drawing to an end and the whole country, it seemed, was preoccupied with 'our new Ally'. So kimonos and obis, parasols and fans were de rigueur for amateur productions at this time. Red Indians and Spanish señoritas, pirates and pierrots, were close runners up and a Patriotic Tableau, with Britannia much in evidence, was the finale to many a variety show.

Cards of school productions, with bewhiskered young ladies in the male lead and 'Sleeping Beauties' trying hard to repress a smile, were eagerly bought by admiring friends and relations. The T. H. Everitt Studios of Upper Norwood took a whole series of school plays around 1913 and advertised that 'Further copies can be obtained at any time.'

Sporting personalities and teams, both local and national, made popular postcards. Again, the schools were much photographed. The girls of a Wimbledon school's hockey team all wear sporting two-toned caps and a team of girls was photographed in 1910 outside the local Wesleyan Church. The minister proudly escorts them, but what, one wonders, did they play? Another anonymous girls' team display what looks like a football, with the words 1908 on it.

Beauty and sport are combined in a set of Rotary postcards of about 1912. 'This is a hand painted real photograph of a British Beauty,' we are told, and the set includes Miss Kathleen Vincent in green velvet cap with a set of golf clubs casually slung over her shoulder. Look closely at the next photograph in the series and you will get a feeling of déjà vu, although Miss Vincent is facing the opposite way and this time is wearing a purple hat. The same feeling of slight puzzlement will be experienced on scrutinizing the next pair in the series, but on examining the last pair (sets nearly always came in sixes) you will have spotted what was an habitual stratagem of the Rotary Photo Co. In the set of six only three photographs were actually taken, but each has been printed not only the right way around but back to front, and every card has been hand tinted in different colours.

Among the most photographed sporting heroes of the day were the aviators – Salmet and Hamel, Latham and Bleriot. Many cards were published to commemorate trail-blazing flights, and these are examined in Chapter 4. Those intrepid early motorists often crop up on cards. DIY portraits show whole families perched jauntily in a horseless carriage, complete with goggles and motoring veils. Motor racing was gaining enthusiastic support and a card captioned 'Winner of the Race. 1905' shows two serious gentlemen at the wheel of their magnificent, long-bonneted motor.

Pioneers in yet another dangerous field were the Antarctic explorers. Ernest Shackleton's 1907–9 expedition is illustrated by a series of postcards. First we see Shackleton in a studio portrait before he set out, immaculately groomed and handsome. Later all the members of the party are shown, bearded and rotund with layers of clothes and fur-lined boots: Dr Forbes McKay, Joyce *et al*, singly and in groups. The animals of the party take pride of place in many photographs.

One of the most beautiful dog series is that painted by F. T. Daws for Spratt's 'Portrait Postcards of Champion Dogs'. There is a huge range of breeds and sizes, from the massive Newfoundland Champion Gypsy Duke to the tiny Yorkshire terrier Champion Shanton Amethyst. Stanley Berkeley drew a black and white series of dogs of various breeds for Hildesheimer in 1903. A. Muller was another dog artist. In 1903 he painted a fine series for Hildesheimer. At about this time Wrench produced a black and white series of photographs of dogs at work. Another of Wrench's dog series includes a sepia 'Autotype' photograph of six curly poodle puppies. It is entitled 'The Black Watch'. Reproductions of Landseer's animal portraits were published by several different firms. Eyre & Spottiswoode ('Woodbury Series') reproduce his portrait of a St Bernard, 'A distinguished member of the Royal Humane Society', and the Photochrom Co. in their 'Gallery Reproduction' series show his picture of 'Spaniels'. The card gives a potted biography of Sir Edwin on the back. 'In his late years he was subject to lengthy and severe fits of depression and died in 1873,' it tells us. The influence of Landseer's paintings shows in the many photographs and drawings of animals which were directly inspired by his subjects and composition, not only of dogs but also of the 'Monarch of the Glen' genre. A direct crib is 'The Lord of the Lake', a stag perched on a rocky crag, painted for the 'Opalette Series' in 1910 by Henry Whitroy.

Another very reminiscent card, posted in 1906, is of a white terrier with ears cocked. It was photographed by F. A. Bourne of Eastbourne and the caption reads 'Its Master's Voice'. The faint outlines of a gramophone can be discerned in the background and altogether it shows a marked resemblance to the famous HMV trademark, first used in 1899.

Photographs of dogs in all sorts of contrived situations, with appropriate captions, often with children, were most popular, and nearly all the leading publishers produced them. 'Dignity and Impudence', 'Dear Old Pals', 'Climb up Doggie' are typical titles. Cats were also treated in this way. The most prolific and successful cat photographer was Landor. Hartmann, Wrench and Tuck's were amongst those to issue Landor series, and again they were mostly entitled 'One Summer's Day', 'Out for an Outing', etc.

The gimmick of depicting animals in human clothes and situations was largely due to the influence of one man – Louis Wain. His cats, which first appeared in his animal books, were to be seen on postcards soon after the turn of the century. His studies were immensely popular then, and today are avidly sought and, as a result, command a high price. As you can see from the Louis Wain card in Plate 15 his postcards are all clearly signed. His earlier Tuck's cards have undivided backs and he was among the first artists to draw for the ragingly successful 'Write Away' series. 'Just a line . . .' are the printed words on one of these cards, and an extremely top cat type with silk hat, monocle and cane is just about to trip over a line held out by two mischievous kittens in bright collars. As time went on Wain's cats became more and more human-ized and more completely dressed. By 1909, when one card he drew for David-son Bros was posted, his cat people were fully clothed and more people than cat. A lady customer, her only feline characteristic being her furry face, demands of an astonished cat-faced assistant, 'Give me my farthing change' as she buys some ribbon advertised as 'cheap – $2\frac{3}{4}$d'.

Between these two phases of the cat-people's development was the Tuck's series 'Louis Wain's Cats'. On the surface these are simply beautiful portraits of cats, but a disconcertingly strong personality emerges. The portrait of 'A Persian Prince' has eyes of such deep, piercing amber that they seem to be penetrating one's thoughts in an uncanny way. The latent human quality was seen, too, by the sender of this particular card, who jokingly laughs off the extraordinary feeling that he recognizes a person in this handsome cat, 'My fourth cousin five times removed.'

It somehow comes as no surprise to learn that Wain, beset by financial problems largely brought on by his own business incompetence, spent the last fifteen years of his life in a mental hospital. During this last period he continued to draw cats; but the charming appealing animals sometimes degenerated, as his mind relinquished its links with reality, into horrific, nightmare caricatures more like patterns than figures. This artistic disinte-gration has a curious parallel with the voluntary experiments recently con-ducted by a group of Austrian artists. Under the influence of scientifically controlled doses of LSD their work, notably the animal studies, deteriorated as disorientated intellect tried vainly to express the vivid hallucinatory images it had produced. So it was with Louis Wain, although he continued to pro-duce well drawn, saleable work in his more lucid moments; he died, still in the mental hospital, in 1939.

Horses, especially in hunting scenes, mice, geese, rabbits, sheep, chicks, donkeys, birds – all find their place on postcards. Many collectors specialize in one animal and the range of treatments, processes and backgrounds given to

any one animal can make a varied and fairly comprehensive collection of
different types of cards. Swans are a good choice, as the angle of many a view
card was specially chosen to include some of these picturesque birds. By
collecting swans, one can acquire a good range of rivers, canals, boating lakes,
public parks and stately home view cards.

Countless series of un-named beauties were published – photographs,
paintings and sketches. Perhaps the most sought after are those painted by
Raphaël Kirchner, and all clearly bear his signature. Kirchner was born in
Vienna in 1876 and is credited with being the creator of the pin-up. In 1905
he moved to Paris and *la vie bohême*. Here he drew for the popular illustrated
papers like *La Vie Parisienne* seductive girls in various stages of déshabillé.
His work, like that of his contemporary, Mucha (who also created postcard
designs), developed in the distinctive art nouveau style, which seemed so
fresh and new, and which owed much to Aubrey Beardsley's innovations.

By 1901 his postcards were selling in England and the public, confirming the
publishers' high-minded hopes that the postcard was an art form attracting
the discerning appreciation of art lovers, eagerly bought Kirchner's and
Mucha's designs in this contemporary style. Kirchner's first postcards were
in the fashionable Japanese idiom that we see in practically all categories of
postcard at this time. They illustrated 'Japanese' shows currently running in
London.

Amongst the series produced by British publishers were Tuck's set in
September 1902 of girls in monochrome 'enriched in gold' at 1s per set. In the
summer of 1903 Henry Moss produced a new set of Kirchner girls, beautiful
designs that were also to appear as Christmas cards and calendars for 1904.

Like Gibson, Kirchner's inspiration and constant model was his wife, 'the
lovely Nina', and the Kirchner Girl is as distinctive as the Gibson Girl.
Slender, immature, with a tender eroticism far subtler than the blatant
seduction of the bosomy Asti girl (Plate 27), she evolved by 1914 into the
alluring, partly dressed girl who was pinned up in barracks and trenches all
over the front and avidly bought by Allied soldiers throughout the war years
(Plate 26).

As Camille Clifford in the guise of the Gibson Girl helped to sell ever-more
tightly constricting corsets, so Nina, as the Kirchner Girl, her slender natural
curves undistorted by whalebone, sparked off a craze for dieting and a boom
in the sale of black silk stockings. The Kirchner Girl is sometimes a blonde,
sometimes a redhead, but Kirchner always drew her from the blue-eyed,
brunette Nina, varying her hair style and colouring. Her perpetual air of
innocent youthfulness robbed even the most seductive poses of vulgarity.
Again, as the stage version of the Gibson Girl was such a roaring success at
the height of her popularity, so no later stage revue was complete without its
Kirchner Girl scene.

At the height of his success in 1913 Raphaël and Nina paid an extended
visit to the United States. Here the pair were fêted and acclaimed. Great

wealth was surely just around the corner when, in 1917, Kirchner died, suddenly and surprisingly for such a comparatively young and healthy man, after an emergency operation to remove his appendix.

There is a tragically prophetic note about some of his most popular studies, such as the famous 'Cigarettes du Monde' series and later drawings like the best-selling 'Opium Eater'. They depict Nina inhaling with an almost mystical, yet highly sensual, satisfaction. Shattered by her husband's death, Nina tried to commit suicide. She was prescribed mild drugs as a sedative, but in a desperate attempt to numb her grief she managed to get hold of large doses of opium and hashish. Eventually she was certified as incurably insane and, sadly, spent the last years of her life as a mental patient in the tight cocoon of the dream world which her 'Raphie' alone shared with her.

Next to Kirchner Girls in popularity are the luscious, Rembrandtesque, full-breasted beauties of Asti. Angelo Asti was born in Paris in 1847. He was famous for his female portraits and his work was exhibited at le Salon between 1890 and 1901. He died at Mantua on 23 March 1903. Tuck's reproduced some of them with a clear Asti signature in their 'Connoisseur' series about 1906–7. Tuck's made full use of their purchase of Asti originals. They used the same trick as Rotary with their photographed stage beauties – printing the same picture twice, the right way and back to front, using different colourings. So Asti's 'Gladys' (Plate 27) is a looking-glass version of 'Rosalind' (series 2731), and 'Helena' a looking-glass version of 'Portia' (series 2743). At the same time other publishers were producing not only the same pictures but Asti style portraits of curvaceous, rosy-cheeked seductresses, usually with a red flower in the hair. Birn Bros were the most successful. We have several printed by them which are difficult to distinguish from the signed Astis of Tuck's.

Later beauties were drawn by Charles Morell and F. Aveline for James Henderson during the First World War period. Morrell's girls are the sweet girl-next-door type and are portrayed hugging dogs of different breeds. Aveline's 'Head Studies' are of more sophisticated types with elegant hats. During the same period 'A.E.' drew an elegant set of lovelies for the 'National Series'. They each clutch a posy of flowers and a poetical message shows that they were probably destined for our gallant lads in the trenches:

*I send these fragrant roses*
*Token of love sincere*
*To one who though so far away*
*In thoughts is ever near.*

And then there are the photographs – thousands upon thousands of them by Rotary, Schwerdtfeger, Philco and a host of other publishers from the turn of the century to the end of our period. Girls in evening dress, in day dress, in sports dress, in bathing costumes; girls with children and cats and dogs and most of all, flowers. There are black and white girls and sepia girls, delicately tinted girls and jewelled girls, embossed girls and bordered girls. There are standing girls and seated girls and girls lying down invitingly; smiling girls and pensive girls, haughty girls and coy girls. There are studio portraits and very false outdoor backgrounds of sands and rocks, mountains and lakes. Some have captions and others poems. Some are even *nude*!

It wasn't all play and lying about in exotic clothes in languorous poses, however. Britain was proud of her industrious working man and he was celebrated in many forms on postcards.

Our traditional links with the sea are shown in countless series of fishing occupations. The Pictorial Stationery Co. produced their coloured 'Auto-chrom' cards of Cornish fishwives and fishermen with captions like 'A Weather-beaten Veteran'. Hartmann also illustrated 'Cornish Fisher Folk' in picturesque costume, loading their catch on to a donkey cart and doing other fishy tasks. Paul's of Penzance showed 'Blanche Fishwife' – who must have been a professional 'character' for she is the subject of many cards by different pub-lishers.

Round the coast we come to 'Welsh Fisherwomen', in shawls and aprons like the Cornish fishwives, but wearing a sort of battered trilby in place of the Cornish bonnet. If the cards are to be believed as an accurate record of con-temporary life, it would seem that most of their fellow countrywomen sat around all day in their national costumes taking Welsh afternoon teas, as is shown on many of Valentine's and local photographers' cards.

The 'Scotch Fisher Girls' at Scarborough, photographed by the Advance Publishing Co. in 1908 and by Valentine's in 1910, worked hatless as they packed the fish in barrels, but the 'Newhaven Fishwives' wore lacy bonnets covered by woollen shawls and suspended the heavy baskets of fish from a strap around their heads, as is shown in Valentine's 'Scottish Studies'.

Should the fishing boats get into trouble, our gallant lifeboat men were always at the ready. A. Martyn of Hoylake produced a card, posted in 1905, of the Hoylake lifeboat, 'Off to the Rescue', pulled at top speed by a team of eight horses. In the same year the Hilbre Island crew are pictured standing by their lifeboat on a Wrench card.

Now that machines have replaced human labour in the hop fields, pictures of hop picking are an invaluable record of a bygone occupation. Young & Cooper of Maidstone show Londoners picking in the Kentish hop fields, filling the large bins, loading the horse-drawn cart, delivering a load to the oast house for drying, and in their encampment of gypsy-like caravans, with children of all ages.

Herefordshire and Worcestershire are Britain's other hop-growing districts, and Tilley's of Ledbury, Herefordshire produced black and white and coloured series of hop picking around their town. Again all the family pitches in to help. In one photograph Granny has stopped work to look at the camera, clay pipe clenched between her teeth.

The idealization of rural life and occupations as a contrast to the hurly-burly of town life, with trams, motor cars, trains and telephones, resulted in the glamorization of pastoral pursuits on the postcard. 'And hill and valley rang with glee' is the caption on a Hartmann card of 1906. It shows a merry ploughboy behind his team of two majestic horses. The haymakers on a card posted in 1908 are colourful young people wielding rakes in a languorous and quite ineffectual way. Tuck's produced some very attractive portraits of simple, earthy folk in their 'Firelight Effects' series.

There are many series which show the contrasting bustle of work in the towns. Several publishers, notably Tuck's, produced series of London life pictures, such as flower sellers and barrow boys. The 'E.F.A.' series includes such cards as 'The Shoeblack', 'The News Boy' and 'The Postman'. They are attractive sketches printed in white, red, dark blue and black on a sort of khaki background. Another effective series is Tuck's 'The District Messengers of London' in the 'Oilette' range. One shows a uniformed boy in a pillbox hat delivering a turkey on Christmas morn.

In this age of the postcard the postman was one of the most popular figures in the daily scene. He is pictured on his rounds: leaving the Post Office, arriving back at the Post Office, and emptying boxes. A popular idea in collecting today is to display together a picture of a village Post Office, a portrait of the Postmaster or Mistress and the local postman, and a card showing the postmark of the particular Post Office. The difficulty of obtaining all four types of card from the same location adds spice to the search, but it is possible with perseverance, as these are all quite common subjects.

Cultural and artistic occupations are commonly represented. In 1900 Blum & Degen produced a series of 'Eminent Writers' and 'Composers'. Wrench, C. W. Faulkner, Rotary and Valentine's were among the many to use great men of the arts as illustrations for their postcards.

Tuck's issued several portrait series of great men in different fields, including the 'Eventful Nelson' series, by the artist Robert H. Smith. A single card issue, 'A Hundred Years Ago – Nelson', shows a modern sailor looking reverently at a portrait of Nelson. 'England! What thou wert, thou art' is the caption.

In December 1900 Mr Tuck, of the publishing firm, announced that, 'Of all the cards that we have published, the portrait of the Queen in black and white with the Great British Standard floating above her head has been most popular.' Sales of this card, the first in Tuck's 'Empire Series', reached the hundreds of thousands mark. It was a foretaste of the tremendous success that all Royal portrait cards would enjoy, reaching the peak of their popularity in the Edwardian era. One set of cards of Victoria, however, was not so popular. In 1900 some 'foul caricatures of the Royal Family' were produced. *The Times* maintained that this view of Royalty 'never corresponded with the real popular sentiment'.

At the same time as they produced their 'Empire' postcards, Tuck's produced 'Political' postcards, celebrating famous men of the day. The Lord Rosebery card of the series quotes George S. Hillard, 'A great man, living for high ends.' Also contemporary are Tuck's 'Royal Postcard' series, and all three series are very similar, printed on smooth, cream card with an oval portrait of the subject surmounted by an embossed Royal Standard and Union Jack. The 'Empire' postcards usually incorporate an embossed rose of England, thistle of Scotland and shamrock of Ireland. These three series typify all that was best in taste, design and printing techniques at that time – truly exquisite cards.

Queen Victoria was the first British monarch whose every stage of growth was documented on picture postcards. The process was repeated, with far greater numbers of cards, with Edward VII and George V.

Edward VII was pictured in all kinds of dress, formal and informal, and in all kinds of places, at state functions, yachting at Cowes, at Doncaster races or weekending at Hove, as well as in numerous studio portraits. Perhaps the most attractive portraits are the reproductions of contemporary paintings in which he is shown in the full glory of his regalia as in Tuck's superb 'Kings and Queens of England' series of 1902 (Plate 9). Queen Alexandra, of the tiny waist, tightly curled fringe that was her trademark and slightly wistful expression, appears with her husband in many portraits, but is just as frequently pictured alone. The 'Ducal' series produced a most magnificent card of Alexandra in deep bas-relief.

Edward's death in 1910 produced a spate of cards of 'The Late King Edward VII', and even his dog Caesar, who was much photographed with his master during his lifetime, had a special card in 1910 titled 'Caesar – the late King Edward's favourite dog'.

Group portraits had a special appeal. A Beagles card, circa 1902, shows 'Four Generations: Her late Majesty Queen Victoria, HM King Edward, HRH Prince of Wales, HRH Prince Edward of Wales.' A later Rotary card shows 'Three Generations: HM King George V, the late King Edward VII and the Duke of Cornwall.' All are in immaculate Naval uniform.

Not only was our own beloved Royal Family of such fascination but also the many crowned heads of Europe and their families. British publishers like Rotary, Philco and Beagles produced portraits of the late Crown Prince of Portugal, an earnest teenager who was assassinated on 1 February 1908; HM King Manoel of Portugal, who was proclaimed on 2 February 1908; the King of Spain and his fiancée Princess Ena of Battenberg, and later, in 1907, the King and Queen of Spain and Infant; HM the King of the Belgians and Astrid, his beautiful bride; King George and Queen Olga of Greece, and until the First World War, the German Royal Family.

Clergymen, in this age when religious sentiment was sincere and fervent, frequently found their way onto postcards. Indeed, special facilities were offered to them by the publishers. In 1900 the *Picture Postcard* advertised 'Clergymen's cards' at 100 for 18s 6d, with an Oxford border round one's own portrait and an appropriate message of one's own choice printed in red. In October 1902 Rotary came up with what they thought was a new idea which 'breaks new ground' – ecclesiastical postcards. They were 'bromide pictures' of clergymen, ministers, and priests; upright portraits 'superior to ordinary cabinet pictures'. The set sold at 1s and included such prominent churchmen as the Archbishop of Canterbury, the Bishop of London and the Reverend Mark Guy Pearse.

Though Anglican dignitaries are in the majority, more unusual cults were catered for. A card posted in 1906 shows Mr Josephy Salomonson of Amsterdam (ex-Consul) latterly known as 'Meva, The Apostle of Natural Life'. Meva appears in John the Baptist-like clothes and stance. He was obviously on tour, for the sender writes on the back of the card, 'Meva is Brighton's latest visitor.' Another curious religious personality is Mrs Schor, pictured in somewhat Biblical dress. The caption tells us she belongs to the 'London Society for promoting Christianity among the Jews.'

In direct contrast to the calm that emanated from the benign ecclesiastical portraits, the suffragettes and their shocking activities were illustrated on cards. There are portraits of the leading lights in the feminist movement like Mrs Emily Pankhurst and her daughter Christabel, organizing secretary of the Women's Social and Political Union. Their more outrageous protests – chainings to railings, hunger strikes in prison and other demonstrations – are also recorded on the postcard. Some unconscious humour is shown on a card reporting Mrs Pankhurst's address to suffragettes at St James' Hall. It reads, 'Ladies. We have met tonight to pass the following Resolution: that we mean to have all that the men have got, we are willing to take it quietly and smoothly, but if they want Friction, they can have it, we should not take it lying down, but with our backs to the wall. If we cannot have it through our organizations we will have it through our combinations. Loud cheers.'

Their opponents, the politicians, were almost as popular as the Royal Family as postcard subjects, from aspirants like Mr Harold Elveston, who was beaten in February 1908 by a majority of 1,292 in Worcester, to a group portrait of the members of the Cabinet of the new Liberal Government of 1912, which included Mr Gladstone, Mr Asquith, Mr Lloyd George, Sir H. Campbell-Bannerman and Earl Carrington. As early as December 1900 Tuck's produced a series of 'Our New Parliament' less than a week after the general election.

Mr Gladstone would seem to top the popularity polls as far as postcards are concerned. There are reproductions of paintings of him, photographs at various ages and in various poses, pictures of the lovely Mrs Gladstone and the Hawarden home, church and village, their children and grandchildren, produced by all the principal publishers and some local ones.

In 1904, however, Mr Chamberlain had his day. Described as 'The Man of the Hour' for his deft handling of the fiscal crisis and controversy, Rotary produced in March 1904 a series of 'machine printed photographs' of him and 'his clever wife'. At the same time Delittle, Fenwick & Co. produced a 'Chamberlains at Home' series of carbon gravure portraits containing views of his stately home at Highbury. Also in March 1904, Eyre & Spottiswoode produced a set of 'Twelve Great Men' including Chamberlain, Balfour and Lord Rosebery, from original paintings by F. Carruthers-Gould. Tuck's produced a most effective series of 'Political Leaders', bold black and white sketches on a red background with a black border. It includes Lord Rosebery and Sir Henry Campbell-Bannerman.

From the portrait card we can build up a comprehensive gallery of the heroes and anti-heroes of late Victorian and Edwardian times. We learn whom the public loved, whom they admired, their leaders of fashion and government, and what is perhaps most engrossing, the faces and costumes of the ordinary man, woman and child and dog in the streets. The immense popularity of this type of card is demonstrated by a game called 'Who are They?' described in an Edwardian booklet called 'Drawing Room Games'. The instructions read,

Purchase beforehand thirty or forty picture postcards of celebrated authors, actors, musicians, clergymen, politicians, etc. Number them, and cut off or obliterate the names. Hang these picture cards round the room, and when the guests have arrived give them each paper and pencil and ask them to write down the name of each celebrity opposite their respective numbers. The one whose list contains the greatest number of correct names is the winner of the game. As a rule a small prize is given to the winner of this game.

# 8

# Advertisements

By October 1900 the picture postcard was established as a vehicle for advertisements. Firms had been quick to 'take advantage in reaching an artistic, cultured and wealthy class, utterly unapproachable by the ordinary, vulgar and frequently repulsive forms of modern advertisements,' to quote a postcard collectors' magazine editorial of the time. In many cases the postcard was a dual blessing to the businessman. It was a cheap, convenient way of corresponding with clients and, at the same time, it could advertise his services and wares. For not only did the person to whom the card was addressed see the card, but also any Post Office officials who handled it, not to mention the servants and other members of the household.

In pre-pictorial days many firms printed messages on the permitted private cards or marked them with their own rubber stamp. In the 1880s for example, the Oriental Tea Agency had had cards printed addressed to themselves. On the back were columns to fill in for the quantity, price and description of tea required, with the name and address of the client and 'mode of conveyance'. The versatile John Preston, of Christchurch, had the same idea in the 1890s. On the back the following services and commodities were offered – 'Coal, coke and firewood. Ales and Stouts in Casks and Bottles. Timber, slate, lime and cement merchant. Monumental Mason. Cabinet Maker and Upholsterer. Furniture and Bedding Warehouse. Agent for Bourne Valley Pottery, Anglo-Bavarian Brewery and Atlas Assurance Co.'

Messrs Shepherd, Neame & Co., the Ale Stores, Margate used the cheaper thin, buff card for their printed message in the 1870s. The card was addressed to themselves and the front read:

Please supply me with the following, viz:

|  | Per 36 gals | 18 gals | 9 gals |
|---|---|---|---|
| Stock Ale | 60s | 30s | 16s |
| Pale Ale No. 1 | 48s | 24s | 13s |
| Pale Ale No. 2 | 36s | 18s | 10s |
| Stout | 50s | 26s | 14s |
| Porter | 36s | 18s | 10s |

Those were the days!

The reply-paid, double postcard was highly convenient for business purposes. In the 1890s, Messrs J. & E. Wright of Birmingham had the top card printed on the back with their name and, 'Dear Sir, On the . . . we had the pleasure to quote you for . . . But as we have not been favoured with your commands, we should esteem it a favour if you would kindly state on the accompanying card if you have decided to give out the order. Yours respect-fully, John & Edwin Wright Ltd.' The accompanying card was printed on both sides. The front was addressed to the firm and on the back was a space for the date and 'To Messrs John & Edwin Wright Ltd: Gentlemen, In reply to your enquiry of the . . . Yours truly.'

Great ingenuity went into producing eye-catching advertisement cards. Size was one factor that brought a card special notice. Dewar's of 'White Label' whisky sent out cards in 1907 which measured $9\frac{1}{2}$ in. by 6 in. Also in 1907, J. A. Lawton, the coachbuilders, sent out a magnificent card. The front shows two elegant ladies alighting from a superb motor car, complete with chauffeur and brass carriage lamps and horn. In the background a cabby desperately hangs on to his horse which is about to bolt. The back advertises Lawton's stands at the Liverpool Motor Show, 25 January to 2 February 1907, and advises, 'If you want a tyre for your car or attire for your man Go to Lawton's.' It measures 9 in. by almost 6 in. For an earlier show at Olympia in 1906 Lawton's used a normal sized card, this time illustrated by a photograph of their latest model. It exhorted the reader, 'A Postal Card will bring you our new Illustrated Catalogue "D". Send for it now while Motor Thoughts are uppermost in your mind.'

These large cards were sent through the post for $\frac{1}{2}$d by book post.

There are also novelty advertising cards. In 1904 a jovial, pig-tailed China-man winks from a 7 in. by $4\frac{1}{4}$ in. card published by Livermore and Knight. 'What has Ah Sin got up his sleeve?' we are asked. 'Something of value as usual,' we see on opening up the folded paper from his sleeve. Johnson Brothers (Dyers) Ltd list their 150 branches and a sample of the host of articles they clean or dye, such as 'Nottingham lace curtains . . . for 9d per pair, equal to new and with even greater care than when done at home.' The advertisers were quick to dream up gimmicks to boost their sales. In 1904 and 1905 Crawfords, the Cream Cracker makers, sent out a detailed map showing the area of the eagerly followed Russo-Japanese War (Plate 28).

The Boer War was the background for the Thorneycroft Steam Wagon Co.'s advertising card which showed soldiers in the most extraordinary looking contraptions, rather like a cross between a steam roller and a milk float. 'Lord Kitchener says, "The Motor Lorries sent to South Africa did well; Thorneycroft's are the best!" (*Vide* War Commission Report)' is the printed message. On the back of this Tuck's card is a large red seal advertising 'The Automobile Show, Crystal Palace, February 12–February 24 1904.'

Kiwi, the shoe polish company, quickly took advantage of someone else's labours. Their card reads, 'Kiwi emblem cut out of chalk by the N.Z. Forces to commemorate their occupation of Sling Camp, Bulford during the Great War. The body covers an area of $1\frac{1}{4}$ acres, Height 420 feet, Length of bill 150 feet, Height of letters N.Z. 65 feet. Total area enclosed $4\frac{1}{2}$ acres. The emblem has been registered as a military encroachment by the Imperial authorities and on behalf of the N.Z. Forces, its maintenance has been undertaken by the Kiwi Polish Co.'

Messrs T. Kennedy, milliners of Moffat, had the chic idea of sending a card from Paris, showing the Eiffel Tower, which informed their clients that they 'have pleasure in intimating that their representatives are at present in Paris and will shortly return with a selection of the LATEST MILLINERY and OTHER NOVELTIES'.

In 1907 Grapevine Cigarettes borrowed the Southend Imperial Lifeboat and ran up a sail which read 'Smoke Grapevine Cigarettes'.

Royalty was indiscriminately exploited for advertising purposes. Gossage's produced a card headed with the name of their soap. Beneath is a picture of the fleet, with inset portraits of Edward and Alexandra and other members of the Royal Family. Underneath is the caption, 'The Right Sort'. A much later card by a firm of Kentish tailors shows a well-cut suit modelled by a figure with a blacked-out face. Despite the lack of features it is obviously Edward, Prince of Wales – the future Edward VIII.

Animal food products were widely advertised on the postcard. The beautiful series of champion dogs produced by Spratts and described in Chapter 7 would equally be classed as advertising. Walker, Harrison and Garthwaites show a picture of a gorgeous St Bernard on a card posted in 1910 and advertising 'Britain's Best. The City Meat Biscuit.' On the back, 'A Gentleman says, "Though Sceptical, yet tried 'Viscan' on young Foxhounds. Results most satisfactory." '

Some firms took popular series by well-known publishers and had their advertising message overprinted. Tuck's 'Early Days of Sport' series showing 'Polo in 600 BC' advertises Sainsbury's Crelos, 'The Wonder Margerine', and their famous Harry Payne painting 'Defenders of the Empire' of Navy, Army and other forces' figures is later used to advertise Claymore Scotch Whiskies.

Other cards (the Fry's series described later are a good example) were specifically designed for the product in question. It makes an interesting exercise to spot the borrowed cards from the custom made, and a fascinating search for both the plain and advertisement versions of such cards can be made.

The biggest publicity stunt by a firm of postcard publishers was undoubtedly Tuck's £1,000 postcard competition. If anything gave impetus to set the growing postcard snowball in motion, this was certainly it. In 1900 Tuck's launched this popular project to boost the many new lines they were producing since winning what Mr Adolph Tuck described as his 'uphill fight' with the Post Office to be allowed to publish Postal Union size full-out picture cards. They had already run successful competitions along the same lines with their Christmas cards. In the postcard competition the prizes were to be awarded to competitors with the largest collection of Tuck's postcards which had passed through the post, but the card need not have been addressed to the competitor. The same design could be entered more than once, provided each entry bore a postmark from a different locality. To make the competition more interesting, 'Consideration will be given in the adjudication of the prizes to the number of towns represented in the postmarks stamped upon the cards.' Imagine the frenzied travelling around the country and requests to friends in far-flung parts of the British Isles this stipulation must have caused. Mr Tuck described his motives for inaugurating the competition thus: 'To at once draw the attention of the great public to the pleasure to be derived from picture postcard collecting for its own sake,' and here we come to the crux, 'thereby enabling us to produce and publish more rapidly the large number of art designs that we have in hand for the purpose.'

At this time the Postmen's Federation was desperately short of funds. An advertisement in the *Postman's Gazette* suggested that postmen should combine together to win a £100 prize in Messrs Tuck's £1,000 competition. If they were successful the money should go to the Federation. The *Picture Postcard Magazine* also asked its readers to send any spare cards to the Treasurer of the Federation. After such an appeal, it is a credit to the honesty of the British postman that any of Tuck's postcards were actually delivered during the competition!

The competition was due to close in January 1902, but the deadline was extended to 25 February. In March a second £1,000 competition was launched and in May the prize money was doubled. In the same month the winners of the first competition were announced. The first prize was awarded to a collector of 20,364 cards!

Kodak instigated a competition for their DIY cards and in 1900 the proprietors of the *Sheffield Weekly Telegraph* started a competition for which the prizes were packets of picture postcards. Three thousand cards were given out as prizes, and they were all Tuck's.

In 1908 the *Daily Mirror* sponsored Britain's first beauty competition. There were 1,500 entries, and the lucky winner was an aspiring actress, Ivy Close. Ivy's face became news overnight and the term 'Beauty Queen' was launched. C. W. Faulkner quickly produced postcards of her and were also the publishers who brought out cards of the competitors for the *Daily Express* competition, known as 'The *Daily Express* and Seymour Hicks Beauty Quest', which soon followed. We have postcards of later *Daily Mirror* beauty competitions, including second and third prize winners, and these were published by Rotary.

Perhaps the most notorious or controversial advertising card was the famous 'Beer and Baccy' card issued in Victoria, Australia (see Plate 4). It was produced in 1895 by Victoria officials on a printed penny stamp card as a source of revenue, and on the address side advertised two firms selling the commodities that gave it its name, Havelock's 'Pure American Leaf' tobacco and Foster's lager beer. The outcry against it was so great, approaching in strength the reaction to the infamous Mulready envelope in Britain, that it was soon dropped.

Insurance companies were offering various degrees of cover to anyone who purchased one of their cards from as early as June 1900. In 1908 a card issued by 'Ocean Accident' guaranteed to pay the holder £50 on death! The offer expired in 1909, but in any case it was only open for seven days from the purchase of the card.

Britain, despite the enthusiasm of a few vociferous advocates like Adolph Tuck and Mr Henniker Heaton, was notoriously slow in the postcard pioneer days in introducing any innovations. New ventures, styles and uses for the postcard in the early days often came from the Continent, where the more tolerant postal authorities adopted a less restrictive attitude, making the whole atmosphere conducive to new ideas.

This state of affairs was deplored by contemporary postcard enthusiasts, and in October 1902 a certain H. R. Woestyn wrote an article in the *Picture Postcard Magazine* on railway and steam ship cards. He bewailed the fact that British railway companies and steam ship companies didn't use the same imagination that had gone into producing attractive pictorial posters to produce postcards. He pointed out that the Great Southern and Western Railway of Ireland had done so as early as 1898, but until this year of 1902 no British companies had thought to use this method of popularizing their routes.

These were useful comments, designed to jolly along the British companies, but Mr Woestyn's investigation could not have been exhaustive. One British company had, in fact, begun this innovation. It was the Great Northern Railway Co. and they had produced coloured cards as early as 1897. The original paintings of locomotives and wayside scenes are attibuted to F. Moore, and the well-printed cards show locomotives in three insets framed in gold, with plenty of room for a message below.

He had also missed the fact that in March 1901 the Locomotive Publishing Co. had produced a packet of twelve cards (which sold at 6d) of photos of railway engines and well-known express trains which freely advertised the railways they ran for. All were coloured, but one was outstanding for the period as it was printed by the three colour process. The set includes the famous Stephenson 'Loco No. 1' and a 'huge modern coupled express engine of the North-Eastern Railway'.

Of course the railways, like so many other businesses, had used the official pre-stamped postcard from its inception. It was, however, the sad dearth of picture postcards that Mr Woestyn was complaining of, and in his article he rejoiced that, at last, the Furness Railway had entered the field and had commissioned S. Grant Rowe, RBA to produce thirteen sketches of typical beauty spots covered by them in Lakeland. They were reproduced in eight colours by Messrs McCorquodale, and although the colours came in for some criticism, the innovation was welcomed. They sold at thirteen for 1s or six for 6d.

The Furness Railway opened the floodgates, and soon the North Eastern and North British Railway Companies produced cards for the East Coast Express route to Scotland – not very spectacular cards, however, for they merely show a train and the arms of the various companies. The cards were issued free to passengers in the dining-cars. They were well printed by Messrs Andrew Reid of Newcastle.

By 1903 the Cambrian Railway were issuing cards printed by the Picture Postcard Co., and in April 1904 the Publicity Department of the North Eastern Railway Co. advertised four 'Panoram' postcards of York, the four for 3d. The next year the Great Western Railway had cards with a printed message to acknowledge the receipt of a passenger's communication on the back, and on the front the Company's crest and a small picture and description of a town on their routes.

Later the Photochrom Co. published an attractive series for the Great Northern Railway, and by 1910 McCorquodale were printing cards for the London and North Western Railway Company, 'noted for Punctuality, Speed, Smooth Riding, Dustless tracks, Safety and Comfort and is the Oldest Established Firm in the Railway Passenger Business'. On an unposted card one can see, in the space for the stamp, the printed claim that over six million cards had been sold! At about the same time, Waterlow & Sons Ltd printed black and white view cards for the London, Brighton and South Coast Railway.

Naturally Tuck's made railway cards too. By 1904 they were issuing cards for the London and North Western Railway Company showing views along their routes, and later produced attractive 'Oilette'-type series for the Great Eastern Railway. The Furness Railway also had Tuck's cards. In glossy sepia, they show appropriate scenes, like Furness Abbey, with a description on the back and the name of the nearest station to book for.

Their most attractive railway cards are the 'Famous Expresses' series. The title also gives the line the express runs on, as 'Flying Dutchman. GWR'. This series was in use by 1904.

Mr Woestyn's article referred also to steam ship lines and he congratulates Mr David MacBrayne of the Glasgow and Highland Royal Mail Steamers, one of whose first cards is shown in Plate 29. In 1902 MacBrayne issued his passengers with this lithographed card free. The one we illustrate shows the paddle steamer RMS *Columba*, and on the back is an appropriate quotation from Wordsworth.

The larger shipping lines, notably the Pacific Line of Royal Mail steamers, produced most attractive cards. The Pacific Line's cards were printed by Andrew Reid of Newcastle and show their graceful ships. He also printed sepia pictures of the South America Pacific Line ships.

A line which combines rail and sea travel is shown on a McCorquodale card, posted in 1908. The front is illustrated by a steamer on choppy blue water with the caption, 'To Ireland via Holyhead'. The back shows us that it is a London and North Western Railway card and advertises the Royal Mail route from England to Killarney, Cork, Waterford, and South and West Ireland via Holyhead.

The P. & O., the New Palace steamers, B.S., and the White Star Line are a few of the many steamer postcards to look for in this very collectable category.

The hotels, of course, had their own printed pictorial stationery for guests' use long before the birth of the picture postcard and automatically continued the service with postcards when they became available.

The Prince of Wales Hotel, Southport proudly claimed in 1903 to have a passenger lift and electric light. It is difficult for us to realize that electricity only came into general use after 1906, when tungsten was first used in electric light bulbs by the General Electric Co. The Midland Hotel, Birmingham advertised another modern amenity on a card posted in 1906 – three telephone lines.

The hotel managements were always looking for a new angle to advertise on their postcards. The Hotel Metropole, Brighton issued an unusual card that had a picture of the hotel's façade over half the front. There is another picture on the back showing a carriage drawing up with a happy couple at the hotel entrance.

The Atlantic Hotel in Scilly showed the hotel 'bus' which met all the steamers – a cart drawn by a tiny donkey! The Grand Hotel, Scarborough is shown on a card produced by a local printer who shamelessly uses a drawing of Queen Alexandra as part of the trademark of his 'Queen Series'.

To judge from the vast quantity of Fry's advertising cards that were issued during our period, one may be tempted to imagine that the guests at these hotels spent most of their holiday supping cocoa, and that we were a nation of cocoa rather than tea drinkers. Fry's were prolific postcard advertisers and produced many different designs. The successful humorous postcard illustrator, Tom Browne, drew many cards for Fry's, one of which is shown in Plate 18. A particularly attractive series shows scenes inside and outside a chocolate shop.

In 1903 Chas Pearce drew a boy slithering in a most undignified fashion down an icy slope, black umbrella and silk hat flying. 'If you feel cold, fall back on Fry's Pure Concentrated Cocoa' is the advice offered him. Another Pearce card shows a sailor-suited boy pulling a train loaded with Fry's products, and a card by Maud Fabian shows a polar bear offering a steaming cup of cocoa to a frozen body emerging from a hole in the ice. 'No better food after a cold bath,' says the wise bear.

The famous five boys, showing 'Desperation, Pacification, Expectation, Acclamation' and finally 'Realization "It's Fry's"', appear on a later card, posted in 1917 during the reign of George V. Fry's were then 'Chocolate and Cocoa Manufacturers to HM the King'.

Cadbury's, their greatest rival, concentrated mostly on pictures of their village, Bournville. Discreetly written along the edge in what appears at first glance to be hand writing, is the message 'Don't forget to send the Bournville cocoa coupons, you will be delighted with the prize box of Chocolates.' The advertising potential was ruined by many a sender, however, who carefully snipped off the printed writing and sent a charming view card of Bournville.

The most attractive Cadbury's advertising postcard is one of Tuck's 'Collector's Postcard' series of 'Celebrated Posters. It is card no. 1,500 and shows a picture of a stage coach, with a smiling maidservant handing one of the passengers a cup of steaming cocoa from an inn door. This Tuck's series comprises many interesting adverts, including a Pear's soap picture by L. Cobrichon of a baby reaching for the soap. Pears also used that much-reproduced picture by Millais, 'Bubbles', with a small bar of Pear's soap added to the foreground. Underneath they state, 'After the original in the possession of Messrs Pears.'

Rowntrees, too, produced advertising postcards and were the most discreet of the chocolate manufacturers in their advertising. Typical is a black and white photograph by Col Stuart Wortley of 'Moonlight in the Bay', the only concession to advertising being the words 'Rowntrees Postcard Series'. Another chocolate manufacturer, Bensdorp, shows a pretty Dutch girl with the message 'Absolute Purity. Use Half Quantity – Half Cost.' The back is printed with Messrs Bensdorp's address, with an invitation to send for a free sample of cocoa.

Many firms advertised in this subtle way, producing cards that were aesthetically pleasing, with only a tiny mention of the company's name. Unfortunately they were obvious targets for advertising saboteurs, who had only to neatly cross out the offending words.

Now that foreign travel was becoming quicker, more reliable and more comfortable, travel agents began to come into their own. In 1904 Thos Cook & Son issued the beautiful coloured card of Naples shown in Plate 10. We have two copies of this card, addressed respectively by a mother and daughter to themselves at their English address. Why? So that they would both have a postcard with the rare postmark 'Vesuvius'! Cook's, of course, could have their cards printed in any of the many countries in which they arranged tours. In Hungary, for example, they produced a fascinating set of Hungarian gypsies in traditional costume.

Wilkie & Son, Tourist Agents of Cook, relied on more homely humour on their postcard. 'Morrow Paddy. Where are you going wid de Pigs?' 'Whist! Ye Divil! They'll hear ye. It's to Cork I'm going, but it's Kinsale they think I'm takin' thim to!!' By one of those happy slices of luck that makes postcard collecting such a rewarding hobby, our copy of this amusing card also bears an interesting postmark – a TPO (see Chapter 9).

Small local firms found the postcard a most convenient medium for advertising. Haydock Coals, Liverpool and Bootle coal merchants, produced at least three series: one of reproductions of paintings such as 'Industry' by H. King, and another of 'Stately Homes', such as 'Balmoral Castle, the King's Highland Home', and a third of London views. Haydock's advertise their Household Coal at 14s a ton!

Browns of Birmingham catch the eye with the heavily printed words, 'GIVEN AWAY!!', on the back of a card showing Paradise St, Birmingham. They continue, 'Lovely Leather Purses for Ladies and Fine Leather Pocket Books for Gents, during Xmas and New Year, at BROWN & CO's with the Best Value ever offered in FINE FOOTWEAR by these well-known Price Cutters.'

Theatre managements, noting the quantity of postcards showing their actors and actresses eagerly bought by the public, did some advertising on their own account on cards which were often distributed in the theatre foyer. One of the most colourful sets, printed by David Allen & Sons, was issued by the Opera House, Southport to publicize *The Earl and the Girl*, a musical comedy by Seymour Hicks and Ivan Caryll, 'as played at the Lyric Theatre, London'. They show bright drawings of scenes from the play in a distinctly humorous vein (see Plate 18).

In 1908 the Lyceum Theatre, Sheffield issued a portrait of Sir John Hare reproduced from a painting by Millais, to advertise his *Farewell*, which extended over six nights and a matinée. A most dramatic series were printed by Foulsham & Bamfield for the Assembly Rooms Theatre, Malvern for the momentous visit of H. B. Irving and his wife Miss Dorothea Baird in *The Lyons Mail*, *The Bells* (of course), *Charles the First* and *Hamlet*. Irving and Dorothea were shown in action stills from each of these plays, he with eyes rolling in terror as Mathias; she sad and dignified as Queen Henrietta Maria. Perhaps the most exciting entertainment advertised on postcards was Buffalo Bill's Wild West show touring Britain in 1904.

Exhibitors issued cards with a flavour of the exhibition at which they were showing: M'Clinton, who built the Irish Village of Ballymaclinton at the Franco-British Exhibition at Earls Court in 1908, for instance, and Virol for the Ideal Home Exhibition in 1910. They produced a series of black and white cards showing 'Virol Children of all Nations'. Other cards of the same vintage show sketches of houses and bungalows priced at about £150.

Reward cards were issued by local county councils and other public bodies to commend children for good attendance at schools and other institutions, or for ability in particular subjects, such as 'French Sentences', 'Memory Maps', 'Botany' or even 'General Work'. The London County Council and Hampshire County Council were among the authorities to issue such rewards. Cadbury's published many series of them, including coloured butterflies and moths, birds and maps. Tuck's also printed as reward cards series they had already issued. A typical card shows one of their 'Oilette' series, 'Inns of Court', painted by Charles E. Flower. The back is printed, 'London County Council – Reward Card' and it gives a simple description of Mitre Court, which is pictured on the front. It was used in March 1907. They also printed sepia reproductions of classic paintings, such as Millet's ubiquitous 'Gleaners', with a short biography of the artist on the back. This series was issued for the School Board for London. Hildesheimer & Co. printed cards such as their 'Zoo Series' as reward cards. A typical one shows 'Jingo (Indian Elephant)', and the back simply states, 'London County Council – Reward Card'. We have one issued in 1908. Many reward cards are marked with the rubber stamp of the school or other institution awarding them, such as 'Finsbury Division. Hugh Myddleton School' or 'Clerkenwell Schools, Amwell Street, E.C.'.

Cards were also given away free with a variety of products. Godfrey Phillips, the tobacco company, gave away thousands of cards 'with the larger packets of the brands manufactured by Godfrey Phillips Ltd and Associated Companies'. Their series include 'Beauty Spots of the Homeland', 'Famous Paintings', 'Our Glorious Empire', 'Garden Studies' and 'Dogs'.

The gift cards that you will come across most frequently were inserted in novels and magazines, which gives them the generic name of 'inserts', which extends to apply to all cards given away in a product of any kind.

Some publishers seemed boundless in their largesse – series after series was printed to give away. Familiar names to insert collectors are Shurey's and Brett's. Shurey's coloured view cards were published by Delittle, Fenwick & Co. and are 'British throughout'. They advertise Shurey's series of 'Smart Novels', 'Yes or No', 'Dainty Novels' and 'The Finest 1d Magazine – Weekly Tale-Teller'.

Shurey and Brett are the big names in inserts, but they were by no means alone in the field. A card showing a black and white picture of 'The Ancient Church, Shoreham' has on the back, '4 Picture Postcards presented weekly with *Idle Moments*. All Newsagents, 1d.' *Tit-Bits* magazine produced a card showing a boy thoroughly enjoying reading the publication. Underneath they claim, '*Tit-Bits* insures your life for £1,000.' *T.A.T., the New Penny Magazine Journal* produced a series for every month. We have a 'November' card, posted in 1903, showing a Regency couple, the dashing gentleman holding an umbrella to protect his dainty lady.

The idea of giving away cards was not new. In November 1900 the magazine *Girl's Own Paper* issued with its 'weekly and monthly parts' two sets of four picture postcards printed on one sheet. When cut out they gave the reader four cards illustrating various aspects of the paper. One bore eighty-seven tiny portraits of some of their readers and another was a reproduction of a tablecloth with signatures of contributors. In April 1902 Cassell's gave away with their fortnightly magazine *Living London* ten postcards illustrating pictures from the journal. In comparison with the reproductions in the magazine itself, the postcard colours are poor. They include titles like 'London's Toilet', 'Oriental Types in London', 'Printing Banknotes at the Bank of England' and 'Polo Playing'.

In March 1904 the *Postcard Connoisseur* magazine, in its first issue, said in the editorial that they hoped to explain the new processes and issues of cards and to 'disparage carelessness and vulgarity in art and to praise the best cards as they appear'. One special feature would 'constitute a new departure, for each number will contain at least six actual postcards, in themselves of equal or greater value than the published price of the magazine' (which was

6d). Some would be original cards published 'expressly for the *Postcard Connoisseur*' and would 'present types and designs not usually taken up from the commercial standpoint'.

Some magazine publishers had far more enterprising schemes to publicize their magazines. In June 1904 'The People on Earth' received a postcard from Mars! The card, printed by J. M. Bacon, was dropped from a passing balloon and was postmarked 'Posted in Mid-Air'. The picture side shows a balloon ascending into the clouds, with the legend, 'All newsagents keep *Smith's Weekly*. Get a copy yourself and see how very interesting it is. 32 pages. One Penny. Every Tuesday.' and 'A Message from Mars (per balloon post) to the People on Earth – "We like your new Penny Paper *Smith's Weekly* very much!" ' It also advises the recipient, 'You should preserve this card as a curiosity. It is the only one ever posted from the clouds.' Smith's obviously had a publicity agent who would be the envy of many a modern one.

In tune with the current craze for round-the-world trips, the *Candid Friend Magazine* (weekly, 6d) sponsored an automobile expedition round the world in 1902 – itself no mean feat in those pioneer motor days. The public was invited to subscribe to the tour and would receive cards posted en route by the intrepid travellers, led by Dr E. E. Lehess, from the principal stops. The cards, costing 5s for five, 10s for twenty, and £1 for fifty, would be stamped with the authentic expedition stamp.

Accessories for deltiologists were also advertised in the magazines. In October 1900 the *Picture Postcard Magazine* described the predicament of a guest wanting to write a postcard in a hotel. If a pen could be located, then there was often difficulty in finding ink. The answer to this problem was a pocket pen, self-supplied with ink – to wit, the Swan Fountain Pen. The magazine had made arrangements for this, the best self-feeding pen in the world, made by Messrs Mabie, Toad and Bard, price 10s 6d, to be made available to all their readers. No reduction could be made for them, but 'on mentioning the fact that they are readers of the *Picture Postcard*, the firm will take especial pains to supply the best and most suitable pen to applicants whose requirements they guarantee to satisfy'.

Shops, famous and obscure alike, used cards for advertisements, from Swan & Edgar's, 'The Most Popular Shop in the Best-Known Spot in the Largest City of the World', in 1905, to Barker & Moody's of Leeds, with their 'Reliable Unshrinkable Flannels', which helped the customer 'to escape irritation of mind and body', in the same year.

Many charitable concerns advertised on postcards with a view to obtaining money for some good cause. St Paul's Hospital had an enterprising method of raising money. They issued booklets of sepia views of London taken by 'Aero Films Ltd' on the back of which was written 'St Paul's Hospital Competition. £1,000 for 1d (penny). 64 prizes. Any Penny Postcard of this series you buy may win £1,000.'

The hospital's best friend was Jack, a black spaniel sort of dog with a collecting box strapped to his back. Jack, with the help of his gallant fireman owner of the fine moustache, collected nearly £150.

Many charitable drives were organized to help the armed forces. A set of sepia cards was produced for the Welsh Troops Picture Postcard Day in aid of the National Fund for Welsh Troops. Coloured cards for the same cause include a photograph of the youthful King Edward, Prince of Wales, in Army uniform – 'Our Soldier Prince' – and Owen Glendower from the painting by Michael.

There are black and white and coloured versions of a C. W. Faulkner card of a British ambulance shattered by shellfire at the Verdun front. The card promotes the 'British Ambulances for French Wounded' fund. The Ambulance Committee staffed and maintained 120 ambulances at the French front.

A sepia photograph of Nurse Edith Cavell illustrates a card for the Belgian Soldiers' Fund, 1916, and there was a scheme to nourish our very own boys at the front. The latter cards are described in Chapter 5, and one is shown in Plate 12. On the back of the Duke of Wellington card is the message, 'The profits derived from the sale of these postcards and the Lord Roberts and Lord Nelson postcards (six for 7d post free) are devoted to Miss Gladys Storey's Bovril Fund for our soldiers in the trenches. By arrangement with the Military Authorities the Bovril is despatched and delivered direct to our men in the firing line who have now, by the kindness of the public, received sufficient Bovril to provide 200,000 cups.'

Six years earlier, another nourishing food drink had sustained other brave men. A card shows Lieutenant Shackleton's ship *Nimrod* leaving New Zealand for the Antarctic. In the sky is the legend 'OXO for stamina' (Plate 28) and on the back, ' "Found Oxo excellent in sledge journeys and throughout winter. Christchurch, N.Z., 26/3/09. Shackleton." ' Lieutenant Shackleton sent the cable to Oxo, London when he reached New Zealand on his return from the Antarctic. 'It is the most striking tribute ever paid by a great man to a great food.'

Another way of advertising a famous product in conjunction with postcards was used by Nestlé's in October 1901. By sending in six labels from their 1lb. tins of milk one could obtain free four coloured postcards depicting 'Types of the British Army'. Several sets of these gift cards were available.

From this cross-section of these early advertisement cards we get a small but vivid glimpse of what the late Victorians and Edwardians were being wooed to buy and, what is even more fascinating, in many cases we learn how much they were asked to pay for the products. Perhaps 'Drunk for 1d, dead drunk for 2d' would then only apply to those with the weakest heads, but mild euphoria for such a price was still a distinct possibility.

PLATE 17

*Left*—Japanese Official
Postcard: General
Kuroki, 1904

*Right*—Jarrold's: 'The
Great War' Series I,
September 1914

The Celebrated "Famous Advertisement" Series, by permission of Messrs. J. S. Fry & Sons, Ltd.

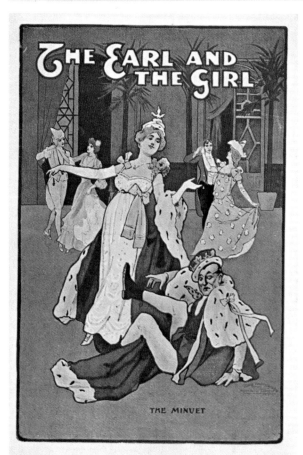

THE MINUET

PLATE 18

*Above*—Advertisement for Fry's Cocoa in 'The Celebrated "Famous Advertisement" Series', c. 1904

*Left*—Advertisement for a musical comedy at the Lyric Theatre, London, c. 1904

A Happy Christmas.

PLATE 19

*Left*—'Popular Series':
Christmas card, c. 1910

*Below*—Philco Series No.
5205, 1918

Welcome Home

MY BOY

WELCOME HOME.
GLAD NEWS OF OUR VICTORY, GREAT AND GRAND,
THRILLS EVERY HEART IN THE MOTHERLAND,
AND WITH LOVING PRIDE AND WELCOME TRUE
WE AWAIT THE HOME-COMING DEAR BOY, OF YOU.

COPYRIGHT.

THE BIG FIGHT OPENS.

THE AIR RAIDER

'it er "'Arry'

PLATE 20

*Above*—Davidson Bros:
Imperial Preference versus
Free Trade—A. Ludovici,
c. 1903

*Left*—Tuck: Oilette—'The
Zeppelin Raider', c. 1916

PLATE 21

*Left*—'Art and Humour' Publishing Co.: 'Leap Year' Series, 1916

*Below*—Millar & Lang: 'National' Series—'When Father Says "Turn" . . .', c. 1903

On the postcard, handwritten:
*Ungreave House.*
*With love. Emily.*

PLATE 22

*Left*—Tuck: 'Modern Art'
card by Eva Daniell, c. 1901

*Below*—Misch: 'World's
Galleries' Series—'The Four
Parts of the World' by Rubens c. 1

The Four Parts
of the World
P. P. Rubens
Vienna

PLATE 23  *Above*—Tuck: 'Real Japanese' card, Connoisseur Series, c. 1905. *Below*—WWI embroidered card, c. 1916

Metz S. M Reichsluftschiff Zeppelin I wird in die Halle geführt
Garage du dirigeable Zeppelin I

Herzliche Weihnachts=
und Neujahrsgrüsse
1915
aus der
Kriegsgefangenschaft
im
Alexandra Palace.
London.

PLATE 24

*Above*—Klingenstein:
Zeppelin I, c. 1909

*Left*—POW card issued at
Alexandra Palace, London,
December 1915

# 9

# Curious

Of all your categories of cards, this is likely to be the most fascinating. The 'curious' cards fall naturally into two main sub-divisions: the Novelty and the Special. To start with the Novelty, we would define it as a card which (a) does something, (b) has something stuck on it, (c) is made of some unusual material.

*Novelty cards – type (a)*

These cards have a variety of intriguing instructions printed upon them. For example:

> *Pray hold this card up to the light*
> *And you shall see a charming sight.*

Follow these instructions and all sorts of exciting things happen. You will be looking at one of two types of cards, a Hold-to-the-Light (commonly known as an HTL) or a Transparency. There are two main types of HTLs. One type has a blue tinted picture side with little creamy yellow patches and a creamy yellow back. On holding the card to the light one discovers that the yellow patches are usually windows, moons, lanterns, etc. that have been cut out of the blue layer and give a most realistic impression of being lit up. The other kind are coloured, very pretty pictures, with white backs. They work on exactly the same principle and are often greetings cards, with the message, such as 'A Merry Christmas', lit up as well. Most HTLs seem to have been made in Berlin especially for export to this country as they show typical British views, such as the Memorial Theatre at Stratford-on-Avon or the Exchange, Liverpool. They were made by a firm with the initials W.H. and both varieties were being sent through the post in 1903.

Transparencies are more sophisticated. A transparency probably looks like a perfectly normal card – perhaps a black and white photograph with a colour wash over it. Holding the card to the light reveals a variety of surprises. Charming colours may appear on what seemed a dull card; a whole new picture may be exposed or additional figures seen. In 1900 a series of Wagner's operas and also the fairy story 'Puss-in-Boots' were produced, on which parts of the picture disappear while other parts miraculously appear, when held to the light. In other versions daylight pictures turn into moonlit views, or buildings go up in flames!

'Rub this card with the edge of a silver coin and witness a startling result' commands an otherwise blank card (actually produced by Hornimans, the tea firm). And a picture does magically appear. This type of card is called a Frictograph, and rubbing with any metal object such as a coin or a watch will bring up the picture. Hartmann pioneered them and produced three series in November 1902, the first 'Portraits of Royalty', the second of the King receiving Boer generals, and the third 'Patriotic Devices'. They sold at twelve cards for 6d.

'Heaters' produce the same result by a different method – 'Hold to heat and picture appears'. Phosphor cards glow in the dark after being held under a strong light for a few minutes.

Some cards appear to be written in gibberish until we follow the instruction to hold them to a mirror. They are written in looking-glass language. Other novelties request us to tilt the card. They may be tilt messages, with curious elongated letters that can only be deciphered when the card is held at a certain angle, or tilt pictures which at first glance look quite unremarkable but which, when held at an angle, reveal a completely different picture.

Another sort of card which reveals a surprise when viewed in a certain way is like the one which asks us to 'Find Sir Edward Gray'. His face is skilfully hidden in the clouds. A Boots 'Patriotic' series card shows a picture of a lion – 'A tribute to our Colonies' by William Armitage. The lion's mane is formed by the words Canada, Australia, New Zealand and African Colonies.

Folded cards often open to show a surprise – a bird which pops out at the viewer or a Christmas paper chain. The contents of these folded cards are skilfully cut and creased to open up as the card is opened, and to fold flat again when the card is closed. A card entitled 'The Mystery Hinge Card' has two flaps, with a different picture under each.

Jigsaw cards were popular, although not so easy to come across now complete with all their pieces. You may be lucky enough to find a Tuck's set in its original packet, with one 'Oilette' card to use as a guide, the other cut up in jigsaw shapes to assemble. Valentine's also made jigsaw puzzle cards. In some cases a whole card is merely a piece of a jigsaw puzzle, although it probably appears to be a complete picture in itself. The whole set forms a large picture, like the set of twelve cards which show pictures of Napoleon. Placed in the right position they make a 20 in. high portrait of him. Another such set depicts a seventeenth-century Japanese tapestry when placed side by side, and in 1905 Wrench produced a set of five cards which together form a cat.

Also in the Novelty category come the mechanical cards. These are worked by pulling levers, tabs or rotating discs, by activating pivots or disc wheels. Girls dance, fans wave, heads nod, anglers cast for fish, good children go up and down on seesaws and naughty children put their tongues out. One of the more spectacular types bears the instruction 'Blow' near a small hole at the top edge of the card. A tube runs from this hole between layers of card leading to certain portions of the illustrated subject's anatomy. These portions are cut out of the face of the card and filled in with thin rubber. They inflate with dramatic results when the instruction is complied with and Rubensesque bosoms and rears billow out from the flat card.

Pullouts are perhaps the most common type of novelty. Seaside resorts went in for fishy ones: 'Cromer is the "Plaice" for a holiday', 'From a Giddy Shrimp at Newport', with the fish forming a flap which holds a pull-out strip of miniature views of the town. Pullouts are happy hunting ground for punners. 'R.U. Cumming to Worcester?' asks the message on a gay traveller's suitcase which contains the view strip. Valentine's called them 'Mailing Novelties', but managed to get the shape passed by the Post Office for ½d postage. They warned, however, as did Woolstone Bros. on their 'Pocket Novelty Cards', 'If any Message is written, 1d Postage Inland.' The sender was allowed to write his name at the foot for ½d, and later could add 'Five Words of a Complimentary Character'. Warren Williams, who painted views for E. T. W. Dennis's facsimile cards, also painted for pullouts and the Photochrom Co. produced pullouts in their famous 'Celesque' series.

The idea of flaps cut in the main picture which lifted to show a series of smaller views was an obvious choice for the resorts. As with many other types of cards, the manufacturers printed the words 'Greetings from . . .' or 'Happy Holidays at . . .', the name being added for the particular town which ordered them. So we see the same scenes of happy holidaymakers and sunlit sandy beaches representing a host of different holiday centres.

Other cards using the principle of a hinged flap fall into more romantic and sentimental categories. Sometimes the flap took the form of a velvet rose which pulled down to reveal a cutout doll which popped up from her garden.

Another type of card requiring some sort of action by the purchaser or the recipient is the painting card. These sold in booklet form, like the G. W. Faulkner & Co.'s *Floral Studies Post Card Painting Book*, in which the postcards are perforated for tearing out. The booklet contains eight coloured postcards of flower studies with eight uncoloured duplicate cards for painting. The cover and back of the booklet are illustrated with coloured flowers.

Yet another 'action' novelty, Tuck's 'Butterflies on the Wing' Series, is described by the manufacturers thus: 'A novel and highly interesting pastime for young and old. Six Postcards of Groups of English and Foreign Butterflies and Moths . . . with the outlines perforated so that the wings may be easily bent upwards giving the Butterfly its natural flying appearance. Cut away from the postcard in this position, and placed on a dark background with a pin inserted through the body, a realistic collection of thirty different butterflies and moths can be formed with this single Packet of Six Postcards.' They were drawn by R. J. Wealthy.

In 1914, The Office Appliance Co. Ltd of Birmingham patented a most ingenious postcard. Double normal postcard size, and thinner, the card, known as a 'Duplex Postcard', could be typed on, taking a carbon copy at the same time. The card could then be folded in half, and the three already gummed edges sealed. It then looked like a normal postcard, with the usual 'Postcard' heading printed on the back.

It was not, however, as original an idea as the company imagined. The very same principle had been used by the Italian postal authorities for some of their official issues well before 1900. At that time the main advantage was thought to be the privacy this type of card afforded to the message.

Our own postal authorities were not so keen on the idea, and in 1920 they issued a regulation stating that duplex cards could only be sent at the current Letter Rate.

Perfumed cards unfortunately have long ago ceased to smell. We have to trust the inscriptions upon them to know that fir trees on cards once were fragrant with the tang of pine, that velvet roses once were perfumed like real ones and that the picture of a scent bottle really contained cologne.

Sandpaper has various uses when applied to cards. One card depicts a cat whose fur is made of sandpaper and the recipient is invited to strike his match on the animal.

There seemed no end to the invention and ingenuity of the postcard manufacturers in those early days. The idea of a three-dimensional picture strikes us as such a contemporary idea, and yet a set of 3D cards was published in 1910 – perhaps earlier, as the card we have seen was posted in that year. The special two-coloured spectacles for viewing were attached to the bottom of the card with the instruction to tear them off for use.

The manufacturers seemed determined to appeal to each of the senses of their customers. We have described cards that smell, cards that excite the eye, cards that we have to use our sense of touch to operate, and there also exist cards that we have to listen to. A card posted in 1904 shows a bird which proclaims 'Squeeze me and I sing to thee'. This type of card, of course, is known as a 'Squeaker'. So far we have not come across a card with an edible portion, but we are sure it was not beyond the inventiveness of the manu-facturers. It is one of the fringe fascinations of collecting that one comes across completely new types of cards every week.

*Novelty cards – type (b)*

This group consists of cards which have something stuck on them – a form of decoration normally described as appliqué, but hardly appropriate for describing some of the extraordinary substances which were used to embellish postcards. The usual materials are velvet or silk. These are used to form the dresses of the ladies depicted on the cards, or their enormous hats. 'The Pet of the Boys', a Valentine's 'Hattire' series card posted in 1911, is coyly hiding under her huge velvet hat. She got herself into trouble with the Post Office, however. Her large hat made her qualify for Letter Rate and a 1d stamp, which her card did not bear. Result: 1d postage due.

Lush flowers too are made of these same materials – velvety roses or irises in brilliant colours. These appliqué cards are amongst the prettiest, in their sentimental late-Victorian/Edwardian fashion, that one can find. Others are edged with lace and some are decorated with crochet – real works of art in their parochial way.

The lily is sometimes gilded with jewelling or tinselling, which often trims the dresses of the Edwardian beauties who were the subjects of so many cards. Davidson Bros., Beagles, Armstrong and Rotary were among firms to brighten up their stars in this way.

This form of decoration was also much used on greetings cards. 'The Popular Series' included many such sets as Christmas cards. Embossed, gilded and tinselled, decorated with angels and cupids, bells and flowers as well, they appear to our more sophisticated eyes as the epitome of Edwardian sentiment, exuberant and sugary. An advert by the Philco Publishing Co. in 1904 described their forthcoming novelty – the jewelled Christmas and New Year postcards – 'The effect of which is very striking and the cards will doubtless find many admirers as the style, so rich, is appropriate to the Festive Season.'

Tinselling proved popular with the public but not with the postal authorities. On the Continent there was much concern about the harm that the mica or powdered glass used to give the tinsel effect might do to postal workers' skin and lungs. The Continental countries refused to allow the cards, and from February 1905 they could not be sent out of Britain. The manufacturers seemed to have hit upon a solution when they made transparent envelopes that had a hole over the stamp space, through which the cancellation could be made. The Post Office didn't like the idea, and in a Circular dated 16 May 1905 Postmasters were instructed not to deliver cards in transparent envelopes.

It was not until June 1907 that tinsel cards were forbidden to be posted uncovered in Britain. They had attracted Letter Rate almost from the beginning, but from 4 June they had to be either enclosed in sealed envelopes at Letter Rate or in unsealed envelopes at Postcard Rate. The public were not very good at obeying this regulation and at frequent intervals up to the First World War official reminders were issued that tinselled cards could not be posted uncovered – but they were. In much the same way people often forgot to put the 1d stamp on the cards in the early years when they were accepted uncovered.

We have one card which shows a bird looking so realistic and lifelike as it perches on a mountain crag that one almost expects it to fly off the card. It is made entirely of real feathers, skilfully graded and mounted. Feathers also decorate hats to great effect.

Pressed flowers stuck on a card and decorated with a small coloured bow make charming cards, and must have had great appeal to the many young ladies whose hobby was pressing flowers.

To add realism to animal subjects fur fabric was used, and human hair on human figures for the same effect, the subjects often having long, flowing locks. Buttons are to be found sewn on cards and pins were sometimes stuck into padded pincushions. The bosoms of rotund ladies were favourite places for the pincushion. Glass eyes and wire tails that wag were other devices.

Among the more unusual objects attached to cards were packets of clover seeds from Ould Ireland, sprigs of heather from Bonnie Scotland and mother of pearl.

Of all the manufacturers of the types of novelty cards so far described, the undoubted leaders were Ettlinger & Co. Mr Ettlinger started production in London in 1902 after some years in the trade in Germany. By November of that year his lines were selling well, especially his musical cards. There were cards of children, animals and birds with a squeaking mechanism. The wily Mr Ettlinger used them as a passport to the various retailers he visited. On being greeted with a 'Not today, thank you,' he would produce one of his squeakers and inevitably would be asked to step inside so that this ingenious novelty card could be examined. Once inside, Mr Ettlinger would produce his more serious lines and a sale usually resulted.

In December 1903 Ettlinger dreamed up a really striking novelty – the Smoking Postcard. The card showed a coloured comical head with a miniature cigar in its mouth. When lit, the cigar smouldered, emitting a 'pleasing perfume'. The card itself wasn't at all damaged by this pyrotechnic display and it carried three extra cigars for repeat performances. It sold at the astronomical price of 3d.

March 1903 saw two other Ettlinger Novelties: a 'Bird Postcard' of the type described above, with real feathers, and what was described in a contemporary advertisement as 'an absurdity' – jumping postcards. Unfortunately, it didn't describe exactly how this mechanical wonder worked.

The postman's lot in those pioneer days of the novelty postcard must have been an exciting one. The pile of mail he picked up to deliver was liable to jump out of his hands, squeak as he touched it or emit a variety of odours.

*Novelty cards – type (c)*

In this group we examine the cards made of unusual materials. Amongst the most attractive of them are the celluloid cards. There are two main types of celluloids. One had a paper backing (Tuck's made this kind) for writing the address and message. The other kind have no paper on the back and the sender was expected to write his message on the shiny celluloid itself. Both types were frequently heavily embellished with downy velvet flowers, glitter, gold and silver paint, the decoration being on the matt side of the celluloid. They are frequently found in the form of greetings cards for Christmas, New Year and Birthdays, and are often hand painted.

Unfortunately for the second time round collector, celluloid is extremely brittle, and it is rare to find a card uncracked or with all four corners intact. In fact many novelty cards, especially mechanical specimens, probably have been much played with and handled and are therefore likely to be in poor condition.

The opposite of the celluloid card decorated with velvet is the plush or velvet card decorated with celluloid. These are incredibly elaborate cards, with lace-decorated celluloid fans, celluloid flaps that open to form objects such as boats, or celluloid flowers.

Aluminium is a surprising medium for cards, and indeed cards made of this metal were not popular with the Post Office. They were thought to cause damage to the other mail and soon aluminium cards bore the instructions 'This card *must* be sent under cover only.' At first they were allowed to be sent bare through the post so long as they bore a penny stamp, and we have one which was posted in 1905. Many bear views of Liverpool, which tempts one to deduce that they were manufactured locally. The only reference we can find to their place of origin, however, is that some were exported from Rome. Occasionally one comes across hand-painted metal cards.

Having to put one's card into an envelope destroyed most of the point of sending an aluminium card, and the manufacturers were quick to produce 'mock aluminium cards' in cardboard which gave the effect of a metal card without the inconvenience. Tuck's made a 'Silverette' series of views and actresses; the 'Palatine' series made an 'Alumino' card; Misch & Co. made them as Easter cards with cuddly coloured chicks; Birn Bros. made them as name cards with, for example, 'Florrie' and 'Emily' written in glitter on the silver background. Wildt & Kray made a series of them with appealing kittens and children.

Also imitated were leather cards. Usually of American origin, one occasionally finds in an old British album two buff coloured cards side by side. On closer examination one will be found to be made of leather, the message burnt on by poker work, and the other one merely a leather-coloured card.

Even more curious, and harder to come by, are papier mâché cards – a true rarity these. Wooden cards, such as those made of $\frac{1}{8}$ in. cypress wood, are hardly more common and we have yet to see a card made out of dried moss, but they do exist. Perhaps the most charming cards in this category are the Japanese veneered cards, with delicate compositions of mountain views, flowers or insects on branches made of razor-thin marquetry of different coloured woods. Peat cards are an unusual Irish novelty. One in our possession states, 'This card is made from Paper manufactured by the Callender Paper Mills, Celbridge, from Peat taken from the bog of Allen.' It is a very coarse, dark brown card, was posted in 1904, and depicts a colleen and an appropriate Irish verse.

In the Japanese style, so greatly in vogue around 1905, are Tuck's 'Real Japanese' postcards in their 'Connoisseur' Series. These are exquisite cards with a rough linen texture finish, in vivid reds, purples, blues, greens, and yellows, showing typical Japanese interior scenes. In the right-hand corner is a paper 'stamp' of a most peculiar shape (Plate 23).

There is one card which to our knowledge is unique – in the true sense of the word. This is the famous Khaki Card. For Christmas 1901 a sergeant of the Grenadier Guards serving in South Africa sent to his family a large square piece of khaki, worn by him through several engagements. On the top was written 'S. Africa, 1899, 1900, 1901', showing the time he had been on active service in that country. The 'card' showed his regimental colours, with the words 'A Soldier's Compliments'.

Our present category includes what are the most expensive cards in any collection. Expensive, that is, for the card itself, rather than the postmark or stamp it bears. These are the woven silk cards and they are so valuable because they took such skill on the part of the machine operator to manufacture. Craftsmen naturally commanding a comparatively high wage were required to programme the weaving machines to produce their complex pattern of different coloured silks. The three main manufacturers of this type of card were Stevens, Grant and Alpha, foremost of whom was T. Stevens of Coventry, who made the sought-after Stevengraphs. You will probably have to part with several pounds to become the proud owner of a Stevens postcard.

Stevens started manufacturing silk postcards in 1903 in Coventry, and continued production into the 1920s. The range of subjects was enormous; probably well over one hundred different designs were produced. A favourite Stevens subject was ocean liners like the RMS *Lucania*, *Etruria*, *Capanania*, *Invernia* and *Caronia*. 'Hands across the Sea' was another favourite, like the card showing clasped hands, the American and British flags and the name of the RMS *Dominion*.

The silk cards are mounted with embossed paper borders and bear the words 'Woven in Silk'. The colours are bright and realistic and the pictures incredibly lifelike and detailed. At first glance they might appear to be photographs, so accurate are they.

Grant started production shortly before Stevens, in 1902, but also had his works in Coventry. By July 1905 he had already produced forty different subjects on postcards and finally produced over one hundred titles on a wide range of subjects. There are Grant silk cards of Royalty, of printed song sheets, views, exhibitions (such as the Scottish Exhibition in Glasgow, 1911), homely subjects entitled 'Home Sweet Home', 'The Old Armchair' and even 'The Foxhunt Meet'.

You will have to pay about half as much (but we are still talking in pounds, not shillings) to buy a Grant woven silk card. There seems no readily apparent reason for this; Grant cards are equally detailed and beautifully produced. As with Tuck's 'Oilette' series, which are eagerly sought while the equally attractive Salmon, Faulkner and Hildesheimer facsims tend to be neglected, collectors seem to have seized on the name 'Stevens' and underrated Grant.

Grant cards usually have a printed credit on the paper surround, often with the words 'Woven in Silk' or 'Real Silk Woven Postcard'. To help distinguish the two, it should be known that Grant cards have a printed border on a smooth surround which is not embossed like the Stevens surround. In 1903 Morgan & Co. of Sydenham were selling silk woven cards manufactured by Stevens. Their stall was near the Crystal Palace, which was shown on their first silk postcard.

'Alpha' is the name on the third brand of silk postcard. Alphas are worth about a third the price of Stevens cards, although it seems that Stevens actually made these cards, which were then retailed in London by Messrs Stiebel whose trademark was 'Alpha'. Stiebel introduced silk cards in June 1912, but most Alphas are to be found later, continuing into the twenties. Many of them are greetings cards – 'Birthday Wishes', 'May Thy Life Be Full of Joy', 'Wishing you Much Happiness', etc.

W. N. Sharpe of Bradford produced a series known as 'Fab Patchwork Cards'. These are cardboard cards with a silk or satin-like square stuck on the picture side. At each side of the patch are pictures of industrious ladies sewing their Fab squares into cushion covers. We have one of series A, showing the Leeds town crest, and the message on the back reads, 'I have sent you this card. You can make a cushion of them when you get tired of your book.'

This series A, which is unnumbered, comprises many town arms and clans. Other series, and the later ones are numbered, include flowers, portraits of Royalty and stage stars; and there are several series of views.

Again, because there was something stuck on them, the Fab cards required a 1d stamp. All cards with full-out silk pictures were also subject to the 1d Letter Rate.

Readers wishing to know more about the fascinating subject of silk postcards are advised to read *Stevengraphs and Other Victorian Silk Pictures* by Geoffrey A. Godden, published by Barrie & Jenkins.

Perhaps the greatest success story in the whole of our period was the silk embroidered card. They were produced almost exclusively during the years of the First World War – few had been made before 1914 and few were made after 1919 when the army of occupation dispersed.

Their immense popularity was due to a variety of factors. Perhaps the most significant was that they were visually perfect vehicles to express the strong feelings of patriotism, courage, hope, faith, pride and strength that the war, the greatest and most terrible so far in the history of man, had produced in soldiers and civilians alike. Their bright, sometimes even crude and garish, colours exactly reproduced the strength and violence of these feelings. Patriotism is considered a very tame virtue these days and tends to be played down. But during the First World War pride in one's nation and fighting heroes was almost frenzied. These colourful little cards with their messages of hope and confidence exactly summarized what everyone wanted to shout. 'Onward to Victory', 'We Shall Win', 'Right is Might', 'Victory and Liberty', 'Rule Britannia', 'For Right and Humanity', 'To the End', were the slogans they expressed so aptly.

Pride in the individual regiments engaged in the fighting was echoed in the cards showing regimental badges, crests and battle honours, like those of the Hampshires, the RIR, the ASC, the AOC and the RE. Even the novelty heroes of the war, the aviators, were celebrated on these postcards, such as the one which shows an aeroplane with its wings made of Allied flags and the message 'Honour to the aviators'. Faith in the invincibility of the Allies was depicted by flags of the various nations involved and the slogans 'Allies Forever', 'Glory to the Allies', and 'United we Stand'. The Stars and Stripes were added when the first American contingent of troops arrived in the autumn of 1917.

The cards perfectly expressed the other emotions so deeply felt during those fearful years; the fear experienced by 'our brave lads' at the front, their love for the girls left behind. The sometimes inarticulate soldier in France with no time or opportunity to write long letters found exactly what he wanted to say, yet far more prettily that he often knew how, on the sentimental examples of the silk embroidered card.

'Remember Me Dear While I'm Away', 'Far From You, but Thinking of You', 'May Your Thoughts Be Mine', 'God Be With You Till We Meet Again', 'I Miss You More Than Words Can Tell', expressed to perfection what Tommy wanted to say. No-one was forgotten; there were cards addressed to 'My Dear Mother', 'With Love to My Dear Wife' or 'To My Dear Sister' and general purpose salutations such as 'With Loving Wishes', 'All Kind Thoughts'. Others like 'Greetings From France' and 'Greetings From the Trenches' brought home the grim reality of where they were and why.

The mood of cards bearing these messages of love and hope is quite different from the formal, stylized design of the regimental types. Flowers abound in all hues and shapes and sizes, with forget-me-nots being far and away the most popular, often with the embroidered words 'Forget Me Not' forming the focal point. They were sometimes made like envelopes, the flaps raising to show a small card bearing a more personal message, a small photograph of the sender or a tiny silk handkerchief, itself lavishly embroidered. Good luck symbols such as black cats and horseshoes are also frequently found.

Far more of the cards bearing these tender messages were sold than those bearing patriotic sentiments, with those showing regimental badges coming third in popularity. The home-loving British Tommy wrote regularly to his wife or sweetheart and chose his cards accordingly. It therefore follows that cards with regimental badges are scarcer and therefore command a higher price than the sentimental variety, with patriotic cards falling between the two in price. Of the sentimental cards, those in the form of envelopes which still contain their original inserted cards are worth more than the conventional variety. A few regimental cards are of the envelope variety, and these, of course, are the most expensive category.

Appropriate cards were available for every special occasion: there are

Christmas and birthday cards and cards for the New Year with the year embroidered in large figures.

Why did the market in this type of card boom overnight from almost nothing in 1914 to the estimated eight to ten million produced during the war years? A large proportion of the British and Allied soldiers engaged in the war were keen deltiologists. The postcard collecting craze was still in its heyday. Therefore the soldier writing home to his family and friends was conditioned to do so on a card, not a letter. No effort was spared to ensure that forces' mail got through as quickly and regularly as conditions allowed. Many Forces' Post Offices were set up, dealing with a tremendous volume of mail daily.

Back at home the manufacturers of cards left in business because they were too old or unfit for active service were experienced in their commerce. They were quick to realize the potential market and swiftly and efficiently catered for it. They sensed the rightness of the embroidered silk as a vehicle for the sentiments their customers wished to express at this particular time, and the cards themselves with their brash tones and lavish decoration appealed immensely to current popular artistic taste. Never can an article have been so right for the times and the market for which it was produced.

The cards retailed at the equivalent of between 12 np and 25 np each in today's money – a large chunk out of any private soldier's pay. It put them beyond the reach of most of the continental Allied troops, and it is a measure of the devotion of the British husbands and sweethearts that so many of these expensive items crossed the Channel every day to become treasured exhibits in family albums all over the country.

Conditions for manufacturing these cards were very favourable in France. For nearly 200 years France had enjoyed a high reputation for the manufacture of silk. It was a country slow to adopt many of the new concepts and gadgets of this fast moving era. Conservative in many ways, her attitude to female emancipation was not as enlightened as that prevalent just over the Channel. The young French girl of every class was still being taught the skills of the needlewoman and other domestic arts. She was an adept embroideress, whereas at that time in England Valentine's were making a series of cards of 'Girls We Miss'. One, called 'The Domesticated Girl', shows an industrious newly-wed darner, watched by a smug-looking husband.

The French soldier was poorly paid in comparison with the British private and the women left at home were often glad of some form of employment to supplement their meagre allowance. The work of embroidering was congenial and convenient; often it could be done in the house after a normal day's work. It was popular work, as the end product was something that would give pleasure to the lads at the Front. In some cases war orphans were employed in embroidering cards and the comparatively few British manufacturers utilized the skill of French and Belgian refugees. Tuck's were among the few British manufacturers and called their embroidered cards 'Broderie d'art' series. They were also published in England by the Inter-Art Co. A few embroidered cards were made in Switzerland, but the bulk were produced in France.

The embroiderers were issued with long strips of silk or organdie. On this strip, roughly 75 in. long and 4½ in. wide, they would embroider with brightly coloured silk thread the same design 25 times, holding the section they were working on in a wooden frame to keep it taut. Even when made by the same worker, each card would have slight variations. We have three versions of the same Christmas design featuring mistletoe. On each of three cards the leaves are almost imperceptibly different in size. The obviously handmade, personal quality of the design is one of the silk embroidered card's greatest charms. The standard of embroidery does vary. We have two cards produced by the same French firm in identical embossed cardboard frames. The pattern on one is exquisitely embroidered in a neat and meticulous style. The embroidery on the other is far more slapdash and altogether more crude.

The strips were collected from the needlewomen and sent to the factory where they were highly starched to hold the tightly-worked stitches taut and then cut into rectangles about 2½ in. by 4½ in. and glued onto a cardboard backing. The cardboard frame, often embossed, was then glued into place, completing the card. These final processes were usually executed by machine and the finished product was a well-made, aesthetically pleasing card.

The cards were placed in brown, translucent envelopes. Cards are occasionally found still in their original envelopes, which were to protect the fragile embroidery and afford a small measure of privacy to the message. The cards were posted in these envelopes.

A few woven silk cards were produced in France and the United Kingdom during the war years, also aimed at the vast soldier market. They had nothing like the success of their flashier rivals as they were more subdued in effect and subtler, and somehow didn't capture the intensity of feeling and sentiment then prevalent.

They were also far more difficult to produce under wartime conditions of deprivation and requisition. Mills and skilled machine operators were needed for the war effort, to weave cloth for uniforms and blankets, tents and even occasional parachutes for the new aviators. Examine a woven silk picture carefully and you will see how fantastically detailed it is. Great skill and experience was required to set up the looms to make their complex patterns. It made sense to turn to the cheap, technically unskilled labour force that was available to make the embroidered cards, and the plain silk or organdie used for the background of these cards was relatively cheap and simple to weave.

Those woven silks that were made during this period are fine examples. Portrait pictures of the allied leaders King George V, President Poincaré and General Joffre are strikingly accurate and lifelike representations. Flags were used as subjects in an attempt to capture the patriotic market, but the woven silks never had the mass appeal of their humbler relations the embroideds (see Plate 23).

*Specials*

These cards characteristically have an added value because of some factor unrelated to the card itself. The special feature is often a postmark. Postmarks are a whole subject in themselves and we will only deal with some of the main and easily recognizable types that increase the interest, and the value, of one's cards.

Any postmark which deviates from the normal double ring cancellation can add value, so long as it is a clear, legible mark – a 'good strike'. Naturally the commoner deviations will only add pence or a few shillings, but the really rare, unusual postmarks can be worth pounds.

In the slightly more unusual category are 'skeleton' date stamps: large, roughly produced single rings; squared circles, with barred edging to the normal sized circle that squares it up; duplex marks, which are barred spoon cancellations with the number of the issuing Post Office in the centre; and some of the rarer branch office small, single ring cancellations. The more obscure the name of the Post Office stamping such marks the more valuable the post-mark will be, with Post Offices no longer in existence being the most desirable.

Postmarks from small islands, such as Lundy, Anglesey, the tiny Scottish islands and even, to a lesser degree, the Channel Islands and the Isles of Wight and Man, are also collectable items.

Any cards depicting a scene at an exhibition are enhanced if they bear a clear postmark of the exhibition itself. Cards of the Franco-British Exhibition of 1908, the first exhibition to be held at the White City, are to be found by the score and are therefore of little value. Concentrate on the cards posted at the White City and stamped 'Franco-British Exhibition London', or in the Irish Village of Ballymaclinton erected in the Exhibition by the makers of M'Clinton's soap. The same applies to any exhibition, fair or congress.

Postmarks from railway sorting tenders and carriages or Travelling Post Offices (TPO) or even those from more obscure stations add interest to your card, especially if the picture side shows a view of the station.

Military postmarks of various kinds are collected: Field Post Offices from Bulford, Westdown Camp, Perham Down, Tidworth or Sling Camp, to name but a few. Rarer are Boer War postmarks from 1899 to 1902, but one has a good chance of finding Field Post Office marks from the First World War or even prisoner of war camps, and the various military expeditions.

Postmarks on mail carried by ships are the most financially interesting of all. Ship letter marks from British ports, India ship letter marks from privately owned ships carrying letters, and the especially prized packet letter marks are eagerly sought. A packet boat is a ship under Post Office control and rarer packet or 'paquebot' marks can be worth several pounds. After the Postal Union Congress in Vienna in 1891 most nations adopted this word 'paquebot' for stamping letters posted on board mail boats.

The other great prize of the postmark collecting deltiologist is the stamp of the first airmail delivery. The first letters officially carried by air in Britain were those flown from London to Windsor, and in the reverse direction, in September 1911 to celebrate the coronation of King George V, as described in Chapter 4. Other airmail was soon carried, if not officially, at various flying meetings and from the *Daily Mail* propaganda flights up to the First World War.

Any 'Royal' postmarks or cancellations for the coronations of Edward VII in 1902 or George V in 1911, Royal deaths, marriages and other events are also worth looking for, as are any events in the Post Office calendar celebrated by special date stamps – the Penny Postal Jubilee in 1890, for instance.

Any failure to comply with postal regulations which is stamped on a card makes the card collectable: postage due marks for any infringement such as 'Posted without late fee', 'Exceeds limit of size', 'Stamp not visible', etc. Various slogans, like the First World War 'Feed the Guns With War Bonds' and later, 'You are wanted on the telephone' always add interest. So do the marks due to war, like 'Service Suspended' on cards addressed to Germany during the First World War or 'Part of a Mail Captured by Germans and Delayed', or the sad messages on cards sent to relatives of missing servicemen, 'Reported Missing' or 'It is regretted that this item could not be delivered because the addressee is reported Prisoner of War.'

Another special feature is the subject's autograph on a card. The commonest autographed cards are those signed by the popular stars of the stage or silent screen, such as Gladys Cooper, George Robey, Vesta Tilley or Chaplin. The deltiological autograph hunter is usually on the lookout for cards which belonged to the vast autographed collection of Reginald Bray, who was known as the 'Autograph King'. He had thousands of cards printed for him reading as follows:

From the Autograph King. Owner of the largest collection of modern autographs in the World. Awarded Diploma at the International Sports Exhibition, Crystal Palace, 1904.

My I ask you to kindly add your Autograph on the other side and return this to me for my collection. Thanking you in anticipation and apologising for addressing you by postcard.

I remain,
Yours faithfully,

PS . . .

The PS was a personal message from Mr Bray to the person he was addressing. For instance, he requested the Hon. Frances Wolseley, President of the School for Gardening, to 'add the date you first presided over the School' and he asked a 'Lady Councillor at Wycombe Abbey School' to 'Kindly also add the date you were elected.'

His collection includes politicians, judges and professional men as well as actors and actresses. A man of many parts, Mr Bray was also known as 'The Human Letter'. He posted a curious variety of objects over the years, from himself to a turnip on which the destination was carved, an addressed shirt front, a cigarette and a bowler hat.

The main hope of striking gold in the philatelic field is the unlikely one of finding a first day issue – and, to be strictly accurate, it is the postmark which counts, not the stamp itself. The dates to look for are King Edward VII $\frac{1}{2}$d and 1d, 1 January 1902; King George V $\frac{1}{2}$d and 1d, 22 June 1911; and on 3 June 1918 the postcard rate was raised from $\frac{1}{2}$d to 1d, so a postcard posted inland on that day which did not qualify in some odd way for the Letter Rate would count as a first day issue. The only other hope is to scrutinize every ordinary stamp for a misprint!

The subject matter of many otherwise perfectly ordinary card-sized, card-shaped, cardboard cards puts them in the 'curious' category. Often these cards are best filed under different headings: for instance natural disasters and accidents may come under 'Commemorative'; freaks of nature, such as dwarfs or giants, under 'Portraits', and we have dealt with such cards in their appropriate chapters.

Cards which show the gruesome, the macabre and the mysterious, however, can only be classified under sub-headings of the curious. There are many collectors who specialize in cards showing various forms of torture. Cannibalism is illustrated in a set of cards showing tribesmen cutting up human bodies, and there are plenty of cards to be found showing skulls and other relics. Cemeteries, including the Dogs' Cemetery in Hyde Park, jails and prisons (Dartmoor seems to be the most frequently illustrated – see Plate 6), stocks, like the ones at Brading, Isle of Wight, ducking stools – all are to be found on postcards for those interested in crime and punishment and the life hereafter.

Occasionally one comes across pictures of opium dens which remind us that drug taking is not such a modern evil, and for students of spiritualism there are cards depicting ghosts, haunted houses and a variety of spooky legends. An anecdote in a lighter vein on a Valentine's card tells the story of the 'Wiltshire Moonrakers' – smugglers who fooled the 'Zizeman' (Excise man) by pretending to rake for the moon in a river, believing it to be a cheese. They had in fact dropped their cask of smuggled brandy in the water! There is a circular inset in the middle of the picture with a legend that sounds like the title of Number One in the Hit Parade – 'Rake, Daddy, Rake'. This popular legend was also depicted by other publishers.

Sometimes one happens upon really odd cards. One, posted in 1908, shows Mr Geo. M. Schilling who, believe it or not, 'Walked round the World in his Airship'. Equally eccentric was H. W. G. Belbin who, at about the same time as Mr Schilling was struggling round the world in his airship, was pictured riding his bicycle on the Thames. He called it his 'Land and Water Cycle' and claimed to have ridden over 700 miles on river and sea. He specialized in demonstrations at seaside resorts like Westcliff and Southend, where he rode along the pier and straight into the sea.

Since the turn of the century there had been a marked preoccupation with circumnavigating, circumflying, or circum-motoring the globe in ever-decreasing time. In December of 1900 the editorial of the *Picture Postcard Magazine* describes such a feat. 'When Jules Verne, some quarter of a century ago, wrote one of his most exciting stories, based on the then extravagant idea that a man might go round the world in 80 days, nobody dreamed that before the century was out any postcard would have actually performed this peripatetic feat. A least a postcard has recently travelled round the world in 81 days, 19 hours – an average rate per day of 306 miles, 5 furlongs' – a feat surely equalled by the mathematical tour de force of working out the daily mileage.

In 1902 – a great year for postcard innovations and novelties – a completely new venture was started. This was the private Do-it-Yourself card. Kodak, Mallandain's and Velox ('the well-known makers of gaslight papers') all sold sensitized cards at about 2s a dozen, 420 for 3 gns, 1,080 for £7. The method was the same for all. Mallandain's 'Vandyke' brown cards instructed one to take the cards out of the packet one at a time, stick on one's own negative, expose the card to the light for a few minutes, pull off the negative, dip the card into cold water, then in a weak hypo solution and dry, and hey presto! one's own picture on a postcard ready to send to admiring friends.

The following year Rotary added their name to the list of DIY card publishers. Mallandain's were now charging 6d for ten and Velox 1s per dozen. Trade was obviously going well to enable such a reduction in price after only one year's production.

About this time an enterprising German lady deltiologist thought of a novel way to increase her collection. On the border of a 100 mark note she wrote her name and address and invited any gentleman into whose possession the note might come to send her a picture postcard. Many did, until she received a letter from an even more enterprising gentleman who agreed to do so, provided she reciprocated by sending him 100 marks – as his craze was to collect notes!

Even before 1900 machines were installed on railway stations to dispense cards by the penny in the slot method. The Automatic Postcard Machine was advertised at 4 gns, but although the initial outlay was small, profit was obviously not very great, for selling at 1d cards already franked with ½d stamp proved 'unremunerative', and in May 1902 they changed to selling two unstamped cards for 1d.

There were several makes of vending machines. We have a card from an Elite Pictorial Postcard Machine, with a view of the Royal Victoria Pavilion at Ramsgate.

Other postcard inventions included Charles Voisey's stereoscope called 'Le Merveilleux'. He produced it in January 1903 and it cost 4s 6d or 7s 6d, depending upon quality. Voisey also produced special stereoscopic cards for viewing through his mahogany box, price 1s per dozen.

The Reflectoscope was another gadget for viewing postcards. Made by

Thomas H. Nichol, it helped one to see otherwise hidden detail in one's cards by viewing them reflected and greatly magnified in a convex mirror.

The private postcard box was another accessory of the boom period. Beautifully made and covered in simulated leather, they were the exact size of a postcard. The writer of a postcard thus knew that if his card would not fit exactly into the box, it would be liable to Letter Rate for being of excess size.

Picture postcard clubs were being formed all over the country and magazines for collectors were mushrooming. They carried lists of all the new publishers and the various new sets they were producing. For the collector's benefit they also ran exchange clubs and printed the names and addresses of collectors who wished to swop cards. Among the more successful were the *Picture Postcard Magazine*, started in January 1900, price 1d; *Postal Cards and Covers*, 1901; the *Poster and Postcard Collector*, 1903; the *Postcard*, which claimed to be 'The World's Smallest Journal', and the *Postcard Connoisseur* which started in March 1904.

Another aid to the collector was Tuck's *Postcard Exchange Register*, published annually. It contained 'the names of upwards of 2,000 ladies and gentlemen, collectors of TUCK'S POSTCARDS in every part of the World, who will exchange TUCK'S POSTCARDS with you.' It is interesting to see that in 1902 a Mrs Pritchard of Essex was already advertising used Tuck's postcards for sale at 2s per dozen.

A really curious feat was performed in 1900 by an eighty-five-year-old Norwegian. After four years' hard work he succeeded in writing a 46,000 word novel on one postcard.

'Philocartophical' clubs existed for collectors who were interested in stamps as well as postcards. They flourished in the United States, on the Continent, in Japan, Egypt and Asia. Members of the British club each had a number, preceded by the letters BEV. We have one much-travelled card, a view of Bedruthan Steps, which was sent to BEV371 in Brussels, where it was postmarked and stamped with a Belgian stamp; on to BEV126 in Moscow, where it was postmarked and stamped with a Russian stamp; on to BEV578 in Boras where it was postmarked and stamped with a Swedish stamp, and finally back to BEV637 in London, from whom it had started with a British postmark and stamp. The international journey took place in 1913, and as was always requested by such 'philocartophiliacs', all the stamps were stuck on the picture side of the card to make a handsome item for display in an album.

One novel method of delivering mail was by pigeon post. Pigeons had first been officially used to carry mail during the siege of Paris in the Franco-Prussian War in 1870. There had also been a military pigeon post during the Boer War in South Africa. The only regular civilian pigeon postal service was the Great Barrier Reef post. In January 1902 the inhabitants of the Great Barrier Reef sent a loyal address to the Duke of York, then visiting New

Zealand. The postcard bearing the address travelled the sixty miles to the mainland by the pigeon post. Later in the year the *Picture Postcard Magazine* published postcards called 'Pigeongrams', showing pictures of the carrier pigeons and of the pigeon post stamp.

Some cards are curious because of their size or shape. The world's largest postcard deserves a mention, even though it is outside our period. It measured 7 ft. by 4 ft. and was made of plasterboard. It had to be delivered by truck and was a Saint Patrick's Day Greeting.

In terms of cards that could actually be posted in the normal way, Valentine's made a 'Giant Postcard' as part of their official series of views of the Franco-British Exhibition in 1908. It measured $7\frac{1}{2}$ in by $5\frac{1}{2}$ in and could be posted with a $\frac{1}{2}$d stamp. It pales into insignificance, however, beside the Graphotone Co's 'Giant Card', which measured $8\frac{1}{2}$ in. by 12 in. This could also be posted for $\frac{1}{2}$d, but 'No writing other than Address and Signature' was to be on the card.

The Photochrom Co.'s 'Reform View Card' is only slightly smaller at $9\frac{1}{2}$ in. by 8 in. This went 'Per Book Post' for $\frac{1}{2}$d, with address and signature only. This company also made a 'Panoramic Card', $9\frac{3}{4}$ in. by 4 in. and the same postal conditions applied.

The 'Trent' postcard of the Trent Bridge Publishing Co. is 12 in. by $5\frac{1}{2}$ in. It required a 1d stamp, 'being above Regulation Size', but one was allowed to write a normal message on it.

At the other extreme are the Rotary 'Photo Series' of bookmark cards, measuring $1\frac{3}{4}$ in. by $5\frac{1}{2}$ in. They went by Book Post for $\frac{1}{2}$d, provided the sender's name and address only were written on the address side. The sender was invited to write his signature on the picture side. These were very popular series and seem mostly to have been posted in 1903 and 1904.

At about the same time, Rotary made a series of 'Midget' postcards, $2\frac{3}{4}$ in. by $3\frac{1}{2}$ in, which had a small space for communication and went for $\frac{1}{2}$d. The ingenious Mr Ettlinger also made 'Midget Postcards', $3\frac{1}{4}$ in. square or diamond shaped with 3 in. sides. He called them 'The Royal Series' and they had the added refinement of being hand tinted (see Plate 32).

Cards come in all sorts of peculiar shapes. Anything of extraordinary shape could first be submitted by the manufacturer to the General Post Office for approval. If passed, the card bore the words 'Shape passed by General Post Office for transmission by Post.'

Tilley & Son, a small local firm at Ledbury, Hereford, have this message stamped on a card shaped like a donkey. It is a Malvern card, as in Edwardian times donkeys used to carry sightseers up the beautiful Malvern Hills – in fact they did so right into the twenties. On the front is written, 'On the Hills. Waiting for You.' This particular card does all sorts of things! Open it up and a boy on another donkey pops up. It also contains a pull-out strip of miniature views of the town and the hills.

There were many series of cards illustrating strange languages. Valentine's made one around 1906 showing the 'Language of Vegetables'. Tomatoes, for example, meant 'An Acquired Taste. Wait! Love will Come.' Fruit also has its own language and, of course, the language of flowers had been in use for many years between suitor and courted.

The First World War produced another idiom: the language of stamps. The Inter-Art 'Comique' series illustrated this strange form of communication. The angle of the stamp on a card or letter expressed different phrases, from upside down, 'Do you Remember Me?'; horizontal with the Monarch's head tilted to the right, 'Thinking of You', or head tilted to the left, 'Answer At Once'; to the normal position for the stamp which signified 'Write Soon'.

There is even a series of cards which illustrated the deaf and dumb language and another, published by P.P. & P., has a different card for each letter and is called 'The Alphabet Series'.

Amusing things to look for on your cards are mistakes – deliberate or unintentional. Publishers were quite unscrupulous at providing the same view to umpteen resorts for them to write in the name of their town. A card posted in 1904 purports to show 'The Harbour, Southwold'. The annoyed sender has scored out 'Southwold' and substituted 'Walberswick'. Wrench published a card showing a London Technical College. It is labelled 'People's Palace, London', and is in a way prophetic, for he could not have known at this time that the People's Palace would indeed become part of a college, Queen Mary College.

A card showing the Waterloo Monument to Fallen Prussian Soldiers translates the German inscription thus: 'The King and Country, with Gratefulness the Fallen Heroes. May They Rust in Peace.'

The fact that many cards were printed in Germany led to many mistakes in titles. We have a Hartmann card, posted in 1903, which is entitled 'Howth Head and Irland's Eye'. The writer explains to the recipient, 'This card was printed in Germany, hence mistake in name, Howth Harbour and Ireland's Eye.'

Sometimes pictures were printed the wrong way round. Regent Publishers produced two versions of a card entitled 'Haymaking'. The hay wagon is facing a different way on each card.

Objects were often superimposed by the printer. A photograph of the Toll Bar, Gretna Green bears a patently drawn in ornate coach and horses. It is entitled 'A runaway marriage at Gretna Green'. Nicholson & Carter published a coloured version of it, posted in 1904 and a black and white version posted in 1905. Versions without the coach also exist.

Popular selling cards were altered by some printers to bring them up to date, and substituting motor vehicles for horse-drawn ones was one way. One such card must qualify in the long life stakes: first issued in 1912, it was still being sold in 1958, but the two Household Cavalrymen it pictured were bereft of their luxurious moustaches and a poster in the background dated 1910 was almost obliterated.

Finally, the world's most expensive cards were made for an Indian Prince. Sixty elephants were killed to get the right sort of ivory for the thin cards and his state artists were kept busy for six months producing the designs!

Here, then, we have described just a few of the cards you can file under 'Curious'. It is literally 'a few' when one realizes that cards were sold at the rate of millions per year during the boom period. As early as October 1903 it was predicted in the *Glasgow Evening News* that 'In ten years Europe will be buried beneath picture postcards.' Had the craze not died a natural death in 1918, it might well have come to pass.

# 10

# Miscellany

After acquiring a certain number of postcards the collector will find several types that will not fit readily into any of the categories discussed. Many of them are beautiful or interesting cards, and we cannot complete our book without devoting a special chapter to them.

There are many famous postcard illustrators who did not paint views, advertisements, military or humorous subjects, portraits of specific people or scenes of topical interest. Some just drew pretty children or women, not from life, but from their own imagination. A whole new category suggests itself for the connoisseur, but it would denude other sections of a collection. Classification by artist, to be filed or displayed in alphabetical order, would have several distinct advantages. It always seems a shame to split the works of a versatile artist like Harry Payne, whose work belongs to several different categories. Before the boom period of the picture postcard Harry Payne specialized in illustrating books of military history. He worked for the publishers W. & A. K. Johnston of Edinburgh, Glasgow and London, who published Lt Colonel Percy Grove's *History of the 91st Princess Louise's Argyll Highlanders* in 1894. An album of Harry Payne, or Mortimer Menpes (another versatile artist of children and views) cards would make a most attractive and interesting exhibit in any collection. Menpes had been a war correspondent during the Boer War for the magazine *Black and White*, but his postcard work, as far as we can ascertain, did not start until well after 1902.

The alternative for those particularly interested in signed or identified artists' work, is to have a sub-section in every main category devoted to artists who excel in that particular field.

Ethel Parkinson was such an artist. Her postcard work is typified by a charming series of cards for Faulkner in 1904: happy scenes of adults and children against a wintry background, with predominant shades of brown, framed in what can only be described as a pale shade of khaki. The pictures all bear titles such as 'A Winter's Tale' or 'A Frosty Morning'. Another series, also for Faulkner, has no border, and again shows children. 'Who Likes Ices?' is the caption to a picture showing a well-dressed boy and girl eating strawberry ice-cream. The Parkinson series are clearly numbered and further classified by the letters A–F, there being six to a set.

Florence Hardy is another artist who drew for Faulkner. Her favourite themes are Dutch, and many of her pictures show delightful children in adult situations, often with a romantic connotation. 'Thus you wind yourself round my heart', the little Dutch boy is saying to the little Dutch girl as he holds the

149

skein of wool for her to wind. Other Hardy pictures are more sophisticated. One series shows fine eighteenth-century ladies and their suitors in romantic situations. 'Love's Questioning' is the caption to a picture which shows a pensive beauty seated at a harpsichord while her lover presents her with a bouquet of flowers.

Two famous artists who designed postcards of children are Kate Greenaway and Mabel Lucie Atwell. The Greenaway cards were issued at the beginning of our period and are most elusive today. Kate Greenaway died in 1901 in Hampstead, aged fifty-five. Besides illustrating books like Browning's *Pied Piper of Hamelin* and several of her friend Ruskin's works, she also composed verses for many of her own books, for example *Under the Window*. Her work was exhibited at the Royal Academy in 1877 and in 1899, and there were four exhibitions of her works at the Fine Arts Society: in 1880, 1891, 1898 and after her death, in 1902.

Kate Greenaway's popular fame resulted from her charming studies of children, dressed in the costume of the beginning of the nineteenth century. So widely were her pictures appreciated that she was said to have 'dressed the children of two continents.' Her children made perfect designs for cards, and she produced Christmas and Valentine cards for Marcus Ward. Greenaway postcards are widely catalogued and advertised for in American publications. In view of her early death in 1902, however, doubts as to the existence of genuine Kate Greenaway cards are felt by some British postcard experts. It is thought that those cards that do exist may well have been produced some time after her death, reproducing pictures drawn by her for Christmas or Valentine cards or book illustrations. Mabel Lucie Atwell, born in 1879, started drawing her chubby children on postcards in the teens of the century. But be careful in dating unposted cards, as she continued long after 1918.

The signature 'Ellen M. Clapsaddle' on a postcard is highly prized in America at the moment. Although several British publishers like Misch & Co. issued her cards, they are not as yet sought after in this country. No doubt they will be, for she drew charming pictures. Often Dutch in flavour and printed in Delft tones, children are her usual subjects, with several delightful series of Valentine cards.

Tuck's produced a very pretty series of Jennie Harbour paintings, pretty girls like 'A Fayre Lady' in a special 'Oilette de Luxe' series. In their 'Art' and also their 'Modern Art' postcard series they printed some gorgeous art nouveau pictures. One by Eva Daniell is reproduced at Plate 22.

One of the most interesting artists to draw postcard designs was famous for his paintings in a completely different medium. His name was Charles Baldwyn, always known as Charlie, and he was one of the Royal Worcester Porcelain factory's most accomplished painters. Charlie specialized in painting birds; exquisite studies that he made from life, often 'borrowing' birds for a few days from friends to sketch.

Success came when some of his paintings were exhibited at the Royal

Academy. But porcelain painters were abysmally paid, and when Charlie married he had to augment his meagre income. One of the ways he did so was by selling postcard designs to a firm of Clifton dealers, Richard & Mackay, and in 1891 he received the sum of 19s for bird pictures for postcards. They were obviously a success, as on 12 April 1893 Charlie received £6 15s for forty-eight cards. Unfortunately we have yet to find any of the postcards Charlie painted.

Towards the end of our period L. Barribal drew some sophisticated sirens for the Inter-Art Co's 'Artistique' series. The heavily made up, sultry redheads are very reminiscent of the women in Toulouse-Lautrec's paintings, especially 'La Goulue'. In direct contrast, A. A. Nash painted some innocent little girls in Regency dress for the same series.

Some sirens of the sea, in untypically revealing bathing costumes, were drawn in 1898 by Jack Abeille. They appeared on cards posted soon after the turn of the century, and at about the same time some lovely ladies in revealing stages of déshabillé were painted by B. Wennerbery. 'Now is this Art?' comments the sender of one. Under the protective, respectable title of 'Art' many extremely provocative cards were sold and ogled in this rather hypo-critical age. Photographs of live models who, in many cases, revealed far less were outrageously denounced as obscene or pornographic and banned or destroyed. But under the cloak of 'Art' anything was allowed. Just as static nudes were allowed at the Windmill, but 'if it moves it's rude', so anything drawn, painted or sculpted, or a photograph of any work in these media, was not only permitted, but praised for its artistic qualities; whereas anything photographed from life was vulgar and degrading. A supreme example of this was demonstrated by the act of a group of performers called 'The Seldoms'. With the absolute minimum of clothing they posed in tableaux representing classical sculptures, plastered in makeup to look like marble. They appeared at the London Pavilion and Rotary produced a set of postcards showing their act. Their realistically marble-like makeup elevated the performers from nudes to 'Art'.

## Art Gallery Reproductions

The range of subject matter here is, naturally, limitless, but even more interesting is the wide range of methods of reproduction and the varying degrees of success with the processes used. These processes are described in Appendix 4.

In July 1900 Tuck's were advertising such coloured series as 'Landseer's Masterpieces', and they went on to attain a high standard of reproduction in their 'Bartolozzi' series, paintings from the British Museum engraved by J. Bartolozzi. More beautiful still is the fine series of 'Gallery Pictures', mostly Turner reproductions, with gold edges on the cards. Then followed the 'Olde Print' series of English Old Masters such as Reynolds and Romney, by

different engravers. 'Seaside Gems' include sweet pictures of little girls by
E. Van Goethen, and there are many, many more Tuck's art reproduction
series.

Other publishers early to reproduce old masters and contemporary artists'
work were Wrench, Eyre & Spottiswoode, Valentine's, Hildesheimer, Jesse
Boot and Faulkner. All are printed in either black and white or sepia on very
matt card, and at a quick glance are practically indistinguishable. Wrench,
Eyre & Spottiswoode and Valentine's favoured oval pictures with plenty of
space around them for a message; while from the beginning Hildesheimer,
Faulkner and Boot almost filled the card with a rectangular picture.

Reproductions of pictures from the Tate and National Galleries, the
Wallace Collection and provincial British art galleries form the bulk of the
output of the first group, while Hildesheimer, Boot and Faulkner often
reproduced jolly pictures by Maude Goodman, Fred Morgan, A. Verey,
John A. Lomax, L. Emile Adan, C. A. Weatherstone, G. Sheridan Knowles
(better known for his familiar painting of 'Good King Wenceslas'), Lucien
Davis, Florence Fitzgerald, P. Tarrant *et al*. Pretty ladies and children in
Regency dress in pastoral settings predominate, and typical titles are 'Fond
Mothers', 'Crossing the Brook', 'Happy Days', 'Dressed for the Wedding',
'The Reconciliation' and 'Little Trespassers'.

The British Museum and the National Gallery also had their own official
reproductions in similar style, printed by the Medici Society and the Oxford
University Press. But the youthful Wrench was the first to think of, and obtain
permission for, selling Picture Postcards from public buildings like the Tower
of London and the national art galleries.

Photochrom's early reproductions are glossy sepia photographs which,
unfortunately, fade rather badly. They tended to concentrate on the full
frontal, or even rear views, of nudes allowable only in the name of 'Art' at
this time.

It is when the reproductions launch into full colour that they truly become
miniature works of art in their own right. Photochrom's style changed completely, and they produced some fine copies of such paintings as Millais'
'The Boyhood of Raleigh' or Yeams' 'When Did You Last See Your Father?'
Cassell's now produced 'Art Postcards', but they are in rather wishy-washy
tones, as are those of the 'Knight Series'. It was an unpleasant fact to contemporary postcard connoisseurs, but patently obvious, that most of the best
quality reproductions were printed abroad in Saxony, Bavaria, Austria or
Switzerland. Tuck's, Photochrom, Wrench and Faulkner all used Continental
printers for many of their early series.

Perhaps the finest colour reproductions of all were published by Misch &
Co. in their 'World's Galleries' Series, and as Misch & Stock in such series as
'Millet's Masterpieces'. Their range is wide: British, Dutch, Italian and French
masterpieces in jewel-like, glowing colour. We have in our collection a
'Portrait of a Young Girl' by Greuze – one of the most reproduced pictures

on postcards. On the back of this card, as on most Misch & Co.'s 'World's Galleries' cards, there are two series numbers, in this case 'Series no. 1086 (29744)'. The first number is Misch's own series number, the second is Stengel's. Stengel printed cards numbered from 2900 for sale in England by Misch & Co., while selling the identical cards, even to the number, on the German home market. Stengel's were the supreme printers in this field and continued to produce their fine cards at their works in Dresden until they were destroyed by bombing in the Second World War.

It is incredible how poorly the truly contemporary style of art was represented on art gallery reproduction postcards. The Impressionists are almost totally ignored; one of the very few publishers to include this style in their series being Huardel & Co. in 1904. Examples of Art Nouveau were confined almost exclusively to 'girlie' pictures. The publishers obviously catered for demand, and the lack of innovation denotes a most conservative, even reactionary, taste in the collectors of 'Art' postcards.

Another interesting point, which is hardly surprising in view of their real beauty, is that very few of the cards by Misch & Co., and the other fine examples available, have been posted. They were bought to put straight into the purchaser's own album – luckily for the present-day collector, as so many of these gorgeous cards are thus available in absolutely mint condition.

Many beautiful series of flower pictures and artistic still life compositions of fruit, berries and vegetables were published, mostly drawn specially for the postcard, while some were photographic studies. A large proportion were printed by the skilled Continental firms who exported in vast quantities to this country, but the British firms are well represented too.

M. Billing painted a delectable series of still life pictures of fruit and vegetables for Ettlinger. They include asparagus, artichokes, cherries, mushrooms, apples, grapes and melons and often have a bottle of wine for good measure.

Some beautiful display albums can be compiled using these fruit and flower cards, and they are an interesting source of material for comparing the different techniques used in reproducing paintings and photographs.

### 'Classical' and Historical Scenes and Characters

As well as reproductions of classical paintings and sculpture, reproductions of scenes and characters of classic authors, especially Shakespeare and Dickens, were widely collected.

In February 1901 Tuck's produced a series of Shakespearian cards drawn by Harold Copping. Copping was the artist of the painting often reproduced in Edwardian children's books, 'The Hope of the World', which shows Jesus surrounded by children of different nations. Faulkner, at about this time, also produced a series of scenes and characters from Shakespeare – cards with that delicate air so typical of the early coloured pictures. Unfortunately the artist was not identified. In 1905 Clarion Postcards issued a set of illustrated 'Songs from Shakespeare', drawn by Frank Chesworth. And of course there are cards with portraits and busts of Shakespeare, and cards showing every aspect of Stratford that has any tenuous connection with the Bard.

Some early Tuck's issues of 'Dickens Cards' show black and white pictures of characters from Dickens, such as Mr Jingle of *The Pickwick Papers*, which occupy only about half of the picture side. Later sets in the series are coloured reproductions of drawings by Kyd which have tremendous character. In the later 'Oilette' series 'In Dickens Land' are sets showing coloured reproductions of drawings by Phiz and other original Dickens illustrators. Delightful cards, they show scenes from *The Pickwick Papers*, *Nicholas Nickleby*, *Martin Chuzzlewit* and other favourites.

Hildesheimer produced amusing sketches in black and white of scenes from Dickens, such as 'David Copperfield', and in 1901 J. M. Goldwyn of Rochester, taking advantage of the author's connection with this town, issued a series of Dickens cards. About 1905 J. Welch & Sons produced 'Trichromatic Studies from Life by Charles Dickens', also drawn by Kyd, and Faulkner produced a coloured 'Charles Dickens Series'.

As with Shakespeare, portraits of Dickens and scenes of places where he was born, lived or had written about feature on scores of cards.

Almost as popular an occupation as compiling an 'art gallery' album was the making up of an 'historical' album. Some of these albums are historical labours of love, with immense pains being taken to follow up portraits of famous characters with reproductions of scenes from their lives and views of locations connected with them. Let us take Charles I for example. A collection would have portraits by Van Dyke and other painters, sculptures by Chapman and others, portraits of his family and his opponent, Cromwell. Then there would be photographs of various battlefields, like Edge Mills and Naseby, and the famous oak tree in which he hid. Worcester would be well represented, with pictures of 'Ye Ancient Commandery', 'King Charles' Hole' and 'Ye Olde King Charles' House'. Chester view cards would show the spot on the city walls 'where King Charles stood on 24 September 1645 and saw his Army defeated at Rowton Moor'. Finally there would be scenes of his trial and then the execution on 30 January 1649.

Napoleon, Joan of Arc, John Knox, Nelson and many other famous characters have been given this exhaustive treatment in any Edwardian 'Historical' album worthy of the name. The charming pictures of R. P. Phillimore, especially his historical series, will be well-represented in any good collection.

Another subject frequently collected has a far stronger flavour of our period. It is the collection of sets representing Faith, Hope and Charity. Countless series were produced, reflecting the current desirability of these three virtues, which were also popular Christian names in Victorian times. Among the most beautiful sets is that drawn by Mailick for the G.B. Co. (his 'Hope' is shown in Plate 27). They are artistically embossed with touches of gold, and this particular set also includes representations of those other qualities, 'Purity', 'Patience' and 'Innocence'. The 'E.L. Theochrom Series' of F.H.C. (as they are commonly known) are glossy pictures in white frames. Wildt & Kray produced several sets on this theme, one drawn by Ortel, and there are many anonymous sets, some jewelled, and many by foreign publishers. Several publishers produced cards showing three virtues on one card. Philco is one of them, and by each picture is an appropriate caption

> *Faith. Our Trust in thee we place.*
> *Hope. Thy sweet influence we trace.*
> *Charity. We're hallowed by thy grace.*

Rotary represent the three by photographs of pretty children on the one card.

Sets representing the seasons were also collected, such as the Cynicus series of 'Spring, Summer, Autumn and Winter' drawn by J. Douglas and one of the few designs published by this company not drawn by Cynicus himself.

*Illustrated Songs*

In the years preceding the First World War music-making was one of the principal forms of amusement for all classes. The cinema was in its infancy, and the theatres and music halls were the most popular entertainment. To most families a visit to the theatre had to be a rare treat, not a regular outing, but for those who could afford it, the sheet music of songs from the shows and the music halls could be eagerly bought and played at home. For those who couldn't afford the luxury of a piano these same songs would be sung with gusto at the local public house. So new songs that caught the public's fancy soon enjoyed nation-wide popularity; nor were the old, traditional songs neglected. This enjoyment of singing and music-making was reflected in the postcard by the numerous series which featured popular songs, old and new.

Tuck's produced in their 'Oilette' range several series of 'Illustrated Songs', featuring such favourites as 'Comin' through the Rye', 'My heart's in the Highlands', 'Swanee River', 'Darby and Joan' and 'The Lost Chord'. The same idea was used by Bamforth's, who produced an even greater number of titles, aimed more specifically at working-class tastes in many cases. Their songs are illustrated by action photographs posed for by members of the Bamforth family and employees, and were sold in sets, usually of four, with a different card for each verse of the song. The verses were acted out with great gusto and dramatic effect by the amateur models, and the picture was often completed with inset 'thinks' vignettes, as the main character remembers happier times or a loved one far away.

> *I'm sometimes afraid to think, Daddy,*
> *When I am big like you,*
> *And you are old and grey, Daddy,*
> *What you and I would do,*

*If when we got up to Heaven,*
*And Mother was waiting there,*
*She shouldn't remember the two she left,*
*So sad and lonely here.*

Happier notes are struck with 'Apple Blossom Time', 'If you were the Only Girl in the World', 'Not Because Your Hair is Curly' and 'When Love Creeps in Your Heart', and Daddy is always a faithful standby in cases of neglect and jilting. Some songs were photographed both in black and white and in colour series, with different casts.

Hymns are also treated by Bamforth's in this way, with devout-looking models, lots of running water, visions of Jesus and angelic choirs in profusion. It's hard to realize that the sophisticated, brittle attitude of the twenties was just round the corner when these scenes wallowing in bathos were taken.

## L.L.

A French photographer who issued many of his large number of series in Britain merits a place in this chapter. Known merely as 'L.L.', he produced many photographs of old master pictures from British & French galleries.

But L.L.'s greatest talent was as a photographer of views. The earliest of his cards that we can trace was posted in 1903. When we consider how basic the camera he used would seem to any modern photographer with a host of sophisticated gadgets at his disposal, his photographs must be regarded as superb works of technical and artistic achievement. Every millimetre of his tremendously detailed pictures is in perfect focus. It is his photograph of Broadstairs that we chose as a typical crowded beach scene (Plate 7). Many of his cards were issued in booklet form showing scenes of towns both in peacetime and during the First World War.

His best and most representative photographs show busy scenes at race tracks or markets; full of atmosphere, life and character. Each L.L. card is clearly numbered, starting with no. 1, a panoramic view of Le Havre, and he was still issuing cards when our period ends in 1918. The name 'Lévy fils' appears on the back of some of his postcards, indicating, perhaps, that one 'L' stands for Lévy.

## Fantasy

A curious feature of the Edwardian era was the latent but strong streak of almost surreal fantasy that sometimes erupted to the surface to find expression in a postcard design. Some of these fantasy compositions are described in Chapter 7, but far more way-out designs were often used. The Alphalsa Publishing Co. produced some fantastic, ingenious compositions, one of which is shown in Plate 30. Another in the same series shows a profile of Napoleon I, his nose and eye formed by a horse and rider, his chin by a prone soldier, his lips by the soldier's hat and his ear by a cannon!

Another type of fantasy card featured babies, bare and chubby, or clad only in their shifts. One shows part of a tree in whose branches are sixteen nests – each one occupied not by a bird, but by a baby! Another is filled with toad-stools upon which a score of babies sit or lean.

Animals, too, came in for this strange treatment. A photograph by Perkins & Sons of Lewisham shows a small promontory of land peopled by twenty-four rabbits of all shades. It is obviously a deliberately posed picture as they are not wild rabbits; it is as if we are given a glimpse into part of a rabbit wonder-land.

Far-seeing Wellsian and Jules Verne visions of what the world would soon be like, produced imaginative scenes of towns crammed with the most un-likely looking vehicles. The sky is often filled with flying machines that would never have a hope of getting off the ground in reality. Speed was a great pre-occupation in this era of accelerated development of all types of transport and communication, and the joys of living in this machine age inspired exuberant fantasies.

## *Tuck's First Editions*

Tuck's, who seemed to possess a genius for concocting novel schemes to promote the sales of their cards (cf. their £1,000 competitions), came up with another bright idea in May 1903. The publishers sensed, or imagined, that finality was one of the prime requisites in any collecting field. They feared that the public might be put off collecting postcards with any great enthusiasm as, owing to the vast quantities of cards produced in any one week, no col-lector, even in his wildest dreams, could ever hope to collect every card that had ever been produced – in other words, he could never *complete* his col-lection. This was one of the reasons why so many publishers produced cards in sets: at least the collector could complete a particular set of cards, and it was hoped that if he bought one, he would be anxious to go on and buy the other five so that he could complete the set.

Now Tuck's went one better by announcing that they intended to produce special limited sets which the collector could easily complete, and with the knowledge that very few other collectors would have the opportunity to do likewise. Moreover, there would only be a specific number of such special sets. They were to be limited first editions of 1,000 copies, and were proposed as an investment, the value of which, Tuck's maintained, was bound to increase phenomenally. Each special set of four or six cards bore an individual proof number, was marked with the word 'Proof' in gold, and protected by a trans-parent wrapper in which it could even be posted. These first edition sets were printed on specially thick board with gold edges and sold at 8s each, Tuck's reserving the right to raise the price of the final sets of each issue to 10s. They were issued one month in advance of the normal edition of each set as it was produced, and were distributed to lucky collectors all over the world.

A registration certificate was sent with each set to be filled in by the purchaser and returned to Tuck's to keep in a special registry. Intending purchasers could then be put in touch with collectors who might at some time in the future wish to sell their special, limited, first edition proof set at a handsome profit. Tuck's emphasized as the main attraction of the scheme its 'finality, the desideratum of collecting'.

*Engineering*

All manner of modern man-made marvels have occurred in all the categories we have so far proposed, but the mechanically, technically or engineering minded may wish to make a totally separate classification to encompass them all, with sub-headings like 'Bridges', 'Dams', 'Towers', 'Motorised Vehicles', or simply 'Motors', 'Ships', and so on.

The most aesthetically pleasing of these groups is ships. It is a vast subject in itself, which can easily be broken down further into photographs and paintings, sail, paddle, steam, civil, naval, pleasure craft, functional boats and so on. It can also include ferries, docks, harbours, ports and shipyards and any other constructions remotely connected with shipping. Cards aplenty exist which show all of these and more. Models of ships, wrecks and stranded ships can also be moved into this group.

Perhaps the most fascinating ship featured on postcards is the White Star Liner *Titanic*, which struck an iceberg on her maiden voyage and sank with the loss of 1,513 lives on 15 April 1912. The subject of many books, plays and films, the *Titanic* was also the subject of a deltiological investigation conducted by Mr John Smith, Editor of the *International Postcard Market*, through his magazine. Readers sent in details of a staggering variety and number of postcards illustrating the ship and the disaster.

Bamforth's produced a set of six, numbered 21 to 26, with drawings of a ship not named but obviously the *Titanic* going down. They bear, naturally, the words of the hymn 'Nearer my God to Thee'.

Another set of six shows the *Titanic* at Belfast in 1911, her launching, captain and officers. Among famous publishers, Tuck's (in their 'Celebrated Liners' series), Salmon, Rotary, Valentine's and Beagles all produced *Titanic* cards.

Millar & Lang ('National Series') produced mourning cards with a black edge, bearing the words of the ever-appropriate hymn and photographs of the ship and Captain Smith. E. A. Bragg of Falmouth was perhaps the first off the mark with mourning cards. One of his has been found postmarked 7 May 1912, 22 days after the disaster. It bears the caption, 'In Memoriam – Heroes All.'

Among the novelty cards reported on the subject are a large-sized card and a woven silk card.

Mr Smith came to the conclusion that well over fifty different known cards had been issued on the subject, and details of more are still coming in. But beware – one *International Postcard Market* reader pointed out that some *Titanic* cards are superimposed prints, while others reported that several cards purporting to be of the *Titanic* are in fact of her sister ship, the *Olympic*. The two ships were the largest in the world at the time of the disaster. Similarly, cards purporting to be of the *Lusitania* are sometimes of her sister ship, the *Mauretania*.

Ships also confuse postcard collectors by changing their names occasionally; the *Alsatian*, for instance, after doing her stint of war service in the First World War, was renamed *Empress of France*. However, it makes an interesting exercise to find cards of the same ship under different names.

The wealth of cards available depicting other candidates for this classification – transport of all kinds – have been described elsewhere; but here could be mentioned canals, rivers, aqueducts and viaducts. Canal scenes can be quite charming, for of course they were still being employed for commerce and pleasure before a doldrum period from which they are only now beginning to emerge, thanks to the dedicated efforts of a few enthusiastic experts. Activity at locks is often featured, but pretty, restful stretches of canal are just as often shown on canal postcards. Commercial scenes, too, showing laden barges negotiating locks and docks, can often be found.

It is a sad fact that many of the mills illustrated on Edwardian postcards have long since been demolished or fallen into ruins. More reason to collect these cards, which are often so charming and romantic, as they are valuable historical records, sometimes the only type which exist. There is a surprising variety, too, in this relatively small sub-classification. Cards with Dutch content enjoyed a great vogue, and there are many Dutch landscapes, either drawn (like those of Florence Hardy) or photographed (like the sepia series of Dutch cards for which Salmon was the British agent), which feature windmills. And there are far too many British windmills to enumerate – not to mention water mills. The most illustrated of all is the great water wheel at Laxey in the Isle of Man. Known by local inhabitants as 'Lady Isabella', it pumped water from the lead mines. The huge wheel, 72 ft. in diameter, has been photographed in black and white, sepia and colour by many publishers, but perhaps the most attractive version, a Tuck's 'Oilette', is shown at Plate 11.

Factories and works, large and small, from Cammell Laird's steel works in Sheffield to the Milk Factory in Middlewich, and mines of every description are illustrated on cards, and would find a natural home in this classification. Dams are well-represented; weirs and floodgates and, one of the most interesting groups, bridges. Suspension bridges and railway bridges, ferry bridges, town bridges and tiny country bridges all have postcards of their own. The Tay Bridge, described on a Valentine's card as the 'longest bridge in the World. Cost £650,000. Length of viaduct 10,780 feet', and of course the

Great Forth Bridge, are the subject of cards by many publishers. Valentine's describe the Forth Bridge thus: 'the labour of 5,000 men (day and night) for seven years. Engineers – Sir John Fowler and Sir Benjamin Baker. Contractor – Sir William Arrol. Cost over £3,500,000.' They also tell us that the steel used weighed 51,000 tons and that 5,000,000 rivets were used, but neglect to say that the bridge was completed in 1890 and that of those 5,000 men who worked day and night for seven years, an average of nine per year were killed on the job.

For the really dedicated machine enthusiast, a series of cards printed for the National Science Museum and others must be very appealing. They show such delights as 'the low pressure rotative steam engine' and 'Joule's Calorimeter'. The sets, however, also include some models of more general interest, such as Langley's 'Aerodrome of 1903 – the experimental man-carrying aeroplane evolved by Prof S. P. Langley in the USA from his earlier successful models. It was tested in October and December 1903 but it failed to fly on each occasion.' We're not surprised after having seen its picture!

*Panel Cards*

An interesting type of card, but one which had a limited appeal and was never produced in great numbers by the majority of publishers, is the extremely thick card. Faulkner were the main producers and called them 'Panel Cards'. Many of them are greetings cards and are called, appropriately enough, 'Panel Greeting Cards', with suitable inscriptions for birthdays and Christmas. Faulkner reproduced some of their attractive facsim series of views on them. Unfortunately the view is often unnamed and the artist uncredited. Wildt & Kray also printed thick cards remarkably similar to Faulkner's; they even called them 'Panel Cards'. In addition to facsim views they also reproduced Old Master paintings in sepia. Nearly all the panel cards have gilt edges.

Their main disadvantage was that, because of their weight, they had to bear this cautionary message: 'The postage is One Halfpenny provided there are not more than five written words (formulas of courtesy, or of a conventional character) – Vide *Post Office Guide*.' They were also expensive to buy.

*Embossed Currency and Stamps*

One of the most sought after and expensive types of cards today are those embossed with realistic coins and stamps. A card showing the embossed stamps of Mexico is reproduced in Plate 29. The price of these cards is continuing to rocket as they are most difficult to find. This may well be due to the reactionary attitude of our Edwardian Post Office and Bank officials. As we have seen, the Post Office was extremely pernickety about what it would and would not allow to pass through the post. Before launching the large-scale production of novelty postcards, many publishers were wise enough to submit their

OUR LOCAL EXPRESS   TAUNTON TO BARNSTAPLE

BEFORE I ENGAGE YOU, I SHOULD LIKE TO
SEE YOUR CREDENTIALS.
WELL YOU WONT! I'M A RESPECTABLE
GIRL AN' I'D SOONER LOSE THE JOB FIRST!

PLATE 25

*Above*—Cynicus: 'Our Local
Express', c. 1906

*Right*—Card by Donald
McGill, c. 1913 (publisher
anon.)

PLATE 26

*Left*—L-E, Paris: 'L'Avarice' from Series 'Les Péchés Capitaux' by Raphael Kirchner (notice 'pin-up' holes)

*Above*—Gibson Girl, shown on card of c. 1906 (James Henderson & Sons)

*Below*—Rotary: Camille Clifford, c. 1906

2902 A    MISS C. MILLE CLIFFORD.    ROTARY PHOTO. E.C.

PLATE 27

*Left*—Tuck: 'Gladys' by A. Asti, Connoisseur Series, c. 1905

*Right*—GB Co.: 'Hope' (one of a set of three—'Faith, Hope and Charity') by Mailick, c. 1905

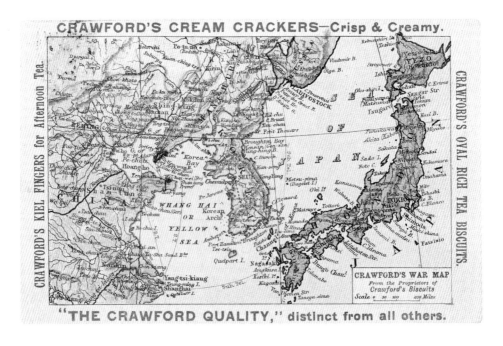

PLATE 28   *Above*—Crawford's War Map, 1904. *Below*—Shackleton's Oxo card (publisher anon.), 1909

Lieutenant Shackleton's ship "NIMROD" leaving New Zealand for the Antarctic.
Note.—The "NIMROD" is open to the public at Temple Pier, Embankment, London, until about end October, 1909,
and will probably subsequently be visiting other ports in the country.

PLATE 29  *Above*— McCorquodale & Co.: advertisement for Glasgow and Highland Royal Mail Steamers, 1902. *Below*—Embossed card with stamps of Mexico (publisher anon.), c. 1904

FLYING SCENES AT BLACKPOOL.

Un faune

PLATE 30

*Above*—The Times: 'Flying Scenes at Blackpool', 1909

*Left*—Alpha Publishing Co.: 'Un Faune', fantasy composition, c. 1912

WOVEN IN SILK

*R.M.S. LUCANIA.*

PLATE 31  *Above*—Card woven in silk by T. Stevens, 1905. *Below*—W. N. Sharpe: 'Fab' Patchwork card, 1910

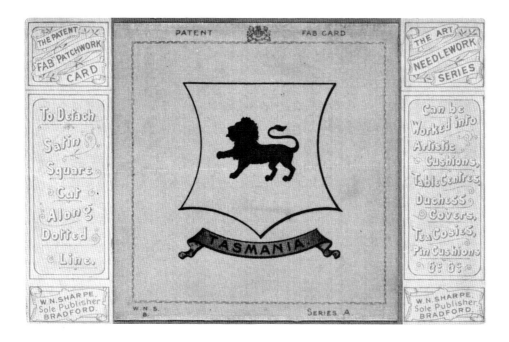

229 X          MISS MARIE STUDHOLME.          ROTARY PHOTO, E.C.

PLATE 32

*Above left*—Ettlinger: midget card, 1904

*Above right*—Rotary Book card, jewelled: Edna May, c. 1902

*Left*—Rotary: Marie Studholme, c. 1905

designs to the Postmaster General for his approval, thereby avoiding the financial loss that they would incur if large quantities of postcards were pronounced offensive by the sensitive Post Office. For even if the design was approved, if the card had to be posted at the current Letter Rate of 1d a loss was still likely. The public was used to being able to send its postcards for a halfpenny and disliked having to pay more.

In May 1900 Swiss-made postcards started appearing in this country decorated with stamps that were so cleverly printed that they looked absolutely real. They were published by Menker & Huber of Zurich and were widely admired.

In November 1902 an English publisher, C. J. Engle & Co. of Boscombe, decided to produce these 'philatelic curiosities' in Britain. Luckily he took the precaution of sounding out Post Office reaction, for Mr Engle received a letter from the Postmaster General saying that he was unable to sanction the issue of postcards bearing illustrations of postage stamps.

At about this time an admiring stir was also caused by postcards bearing reproductions of the bank notes of various countries and their coinage in gilt relief. Nothing had ever been seen like them in England, nor, if the Bank of England had its way – which it did for a long time – would any such postcards ever be manufactured in this country.

The Post Office even went to the extraordinary lengths of asking local Postmasters in March 1905 to report to them the names and addresses of any shopkeepers in their district who stocked these cards. Should any of the troublesome cards still manage to slip through and be observed in the post, they were to be stopped and sent to the Returned Letter Branch.

Luckily for the second time round collector, Continental Post Office and banking authorities had no such qualms about permitting the manufacture and sale of this particularly effective type of card. The most accomplished publisher in this field was Otmar Zieher. They produced embossed cards showing the stamps, currency, flags and even exchange rates. Sometimes they incorporated different combinations of these four motifs on cards representing countries as far apart as Russia and Monaco, Japan and Mexico. Their cards are all clearly numbered.

Other publishers were Muir and Moodie, who numbered their cards, and sometimes included crests in their designs.

### Doll Postcards

A charming category of cards collected by an enthusiastic minority comprises any cards showing dolls, puppets, golliwogs and doll houses. Greetings cards for birthdays, Christmas and Easter often feature toys, as do the cards especially made for children. As mentioned in Chapter 4, Tuck's produced some delightful cards featuring golliwogs and wooden 'Dutch' dolls. Unfortunately the best cards in this group are later than our period. They are the series produced by Tuck's in 1924 of 'The Queen's Doll's House', forty-eight cards in all. Sets of 'Titania's Palace' are also eagerly sought by doll-card collectors.

*Bill Doolin*

We end this pot-pourri chapter with one of the most hard-to-resist-looking-for foreign cards in the history of the postcard. Postcards have been used for conveying every conceivable form of message or information, from proposals of marriage to coded messages between spies. But here is one of the most curious uses of all.

The outlaw, Bill Doolin, has been the hero or villain of many books and films. In the course of his turbulent career in Oklahoma Territory he and his gang got away with a daring and profitable bank robbery. Immediately the bank offered a reward for information leading to the recovery of the money, and showing great initiative, the sheriff (who sounds like a keen deltiologist) hit upon a novel way to spread the news. He had printed on postcards, which he mailed all over the area, the following message:

BANK ROBBED $450 REWARD

Ford County Bank, Spearville, Kansas was robbed today by three men. One small, dark-complexioned man 23 years old, small, very dark moustache and dark clothes (Ol' Yantis). One medium-height man, sandy-complexioned, short beard, light hat and clothes (Bill Doolin). One dark man, 25 years old, medium weight, dark moustache (Bitter Creek New-combe). Three horses, bay, sorrel and dun, latter with lined back, all medium size. Robbers have large number new $5 bills issued by First National Bank, Dodge City, Kansas.

A reward of $450 is offered.

C. M. Beeson,
Sheriff, Dodge City, Kansas
November 1st 1892

N.B. Keep watch for the new $5 bills.

Happy Hunting!

# Appendices

# I

# British Official Postcard Issues, 1870-1899

*Notes*

1. *Sizes*. These are given to the nearest millimetre. However, there is likely to be up to 1 mm. variation in card sizes, even between cards of the same batch.

2. *Specimen cards*. Official cards can be found with 'Specimen' printed over the stamp. These may or may not be cards of a type that were finally issued for sale, and may have been produced for circulation and approval within the Post Office, within the publishing house or even for submission to the UPU headquarters in Berne.

3. *New issues*. New Inland issues, i.e. halfpenny cards, usually superseded previous similar issues in that these were allowed to waste out, and this can be assumed in the table unless otherwise stated. Cards for foreign use usually became invalid on the first day of sale of a new issue.

4. *Green printing*. Blue-green printing began for Inland cards in February 1901 and changed to yellow-green in December 1904.

5. *The Address This Side*. Instructions were removed from the address side of Inland cards after March 1908.

6. *'T' stamp*. If a postcard for transmission to Britain contravened the postal regulations in its country of origin, it was there marked with a letter T as incurring an additional tax which was raised in this country. A reciprocal arrangement existed for cards posted from Britain.

7. *Adhesive stamps*. Although these were only acceptable as full payment for Inland Postage from 1 September 1894, they had been used on postcards for foreign use from about 1875 to 'make up' postage rates that were not exactly prepaid by the cards available.

8. *The official cardboard*. The buff cardboard used varied in colour from dark to very light, and also in thickness; but it is always 'thin' in comparison to the 'stout' white card.

| Serial | Date first issued | Face value | Size (mm.) | Card | Colour of printing | Plate no. | Notes |
|---|---|---|---|---|---|---|---|
| 1 | *1870*<br>1 October | ½d | 122×88 | Buff | Violet | 1 | In coat of arms, end of lion's tail touches, or is very close to, his mane. |
| 2 | late November | ½d | 121×74 | Buff | Violet | | The 'oblong card' same design as serial 1. |
| 3 | *1872*<br>17 June | ½d | — | Light buff | Various: e.g. black, brown | | Privately printed cards. Size to be 'as nearly as possible the same size as the official postcard'. Oval pink/orange stamp impressed by Post Office. Royal Arms should not appear, but sometimes does. |
| 4 | *1875*<br>1 January | ½d | 121×74 | Buff | Violet | | Same design as serial 1 except 'To' omitted. |
| 5 | 1 February | ½d | 121×74 | Thick white | Brown | | Mr Gladstone's 'stout' card. Same design as serial 4. |
| 6 | 1 July | 1¼d | 122×87 | Buff | Brown | 1 | 'Foreign Postcard'. The first British postcard which could be sent abroad for countries within the GPU. Discontinued 31 March 1879. |
| 7 | *1878*<br>1 January | ½d | 122×75 | Buff | Brown | 2 | New design. No border; tip of lion's tail now about ½ mm. from his mane. Arms 14 mm. wide. |
| 8 | 1 January | ½d | 122×75 | Thick white | Brown | | Same design as serial 7. |

| | | | | | | | Notes |
|---|---|---|---|---|---|---|---|
| | *1879* | | | | | | |
| 9 | 1 April | 1d | 122×88 | Buff | Brown | 2 | 'Grande Bretagne'. The card that upset Ireland. Sale of serial 6 stopped. |
| 10 | 1 April | $1\frac{1}{2}$d | 122×88 | Buff | Brown | | 'Grande Bretagne' same design as serial 9 but oval stamp. |
| 11 | October | 1d | 122×87 | Buff | Brown | 2 | 'and Ireland'. Note: from 1 July 1879 adhesive stamps could be added to the printed stamps on the Foreign postcards to make up the overseas rate, e.g. to Australia (2d) via Brindisi. |
| | *1882* | | | | | | |
| 12 | 1 October | $\frac{1}{2}$d+$\frac{1}{2}$d | 122×75 | Buff | Brown | | Same design as serial 7 plus instructions for use. The first 'Reply Paid Card'; perforated. |
| 13 | 1 October | $\frac{1}{2}$d+$\frac{1}{2}$d | 122×75 | Thick white | Brown | | Same design as serial 12; perforated. |
| | *1883* | | | | | | |
| 14 | 1 January | $\frac{1}{2}$d+$\frac{1}{2}$d | 122×75 | Thick white | Brown | 2 | Same design as serial 12; white linen hinge. |
| 15 | 1 January | 1d | 140×88 | Buff | Dark brown | | Inscription changed. |
| 16 | 1 January | 1d+1d | 140×88 | Buff | Dark brown | | Same design as serial 15 plus instructions for use. Perforated. |
| 17 | 1 January | $1\frac{1}{2}$d | 140×88 | Buff | Brown | | Same design as serial 15 but oval stamp. Discontinued October 1891. |
| 18 | 1 January | $1\frac{1}{2}$d+$1\frac{1}{2}$d | 140×88 | Buff | Brown | | Same design as serial 17 plus instructions for use. Perforated. Discontinued October 1891. |

| Serial | Date first issued | Face value | Size (mm.) | Card | Colour of printing | Plate no. | Notes |
|---|---|---|---|---|---|---|---|
| 19 | 1 January | 2d | 140×88 | Buff | Brown | | Same design as serial 17, but new stamp. For use via Brindisi to British Pacific possessions. Discontinued October 1891. |
| 20 | 1 January | 2d+2d | 140×88 | Buff | Brown | | Same design as serial 19. Perforated. Discontinued October 1891. |
| | *1888* | | | | | | |
| 21 | January | ½d | 122×75 | Buff | Light to dark brown | | Same design as serial 7, but inscription differs in detail. Overall dimensions of inscription and also Arms increased by 1 mm. Allowed to waste out from 1 November 1899. |
| 22 | — | ½d | 122×75 | Thick white | Light to dark brown | | Same design as serial 21. Several issues up to July 1889, when a slightly thinner version issued. Allowed to waste out from 1 November 1899. |
| | *1889* | | | | | | |
| 23 | — | ½d+½d | 122×75 | Buff | Brown | | Same design as serial 21 plus instructions for use. Perforated. |
| 24 | — | ½d+½d | 122×75 | Thick white | Brown | | Same design as serial 23; white linen hinge. |
| 25 | September | 3d | 140×88 | Buff | Carmine | 2 | 'British Empire' card for use to Australian colonies. Full length portrait stamp. Discontinued January 1891. |
| | *1890* | | | | | | |
| 26 | 16 May to 19 May | 1d | 141×89 | Buff | Carmine | 2 | Jubilee Card. Only 10,000 printed. Sold at the Guildhall Postal Exhibition but many forgeries exist. |

| Serial | Date | Value | Size | Card | Stamp | | Notes |
|---|---|---|---|---|---|---|---|
| 27 | *1891* June | ½d | 122×75 | White | Brown | | Same design as serial 22, on thinner July 1889 version. Reverse side carries blue printing 'Royal Naval Exhibition' and 'Top of Eddystone Lighthouse'. A blue sketch of the lighthouse is to the left. |
| 28 | *1892* 1 April | 1d | 130×83 | Buff | Vary from orange to vermilion | 2 | Full length portrait stamp. Allowed to waste out from 1 November 1899. |
| 29 | 1 April | 1d+1d | 130×83 | Buff | As serial 28 | | Same design as serial 28 plus instructions for use. Perforated. Allowed to waste out from 1 November 1899. |
| | *1894* 1 September | | | | | | Privately printed cards allowed to be used with adhesive stamps |
| 30 | *1895* 21 January | ½d | 115×89 | Stiff white | Brown | | Same design as serial 21. The first official court size card. |
| 31 | *1899* 1 November | ½d | 115×89 | Stiff white | Brown | | Same design as serial 30, except 'ONLY' omitted. |
| 32 | 1 November | ½d+½d | 115×89 | Stiff white | Brown | | Same design as serial 31 plus instructions. White linen hinge. |
| 33 | 1 November | ½d | 141×89 | Buff | Brown | | Same design as serial 31. |
| 34 | 1 November | ½d+½d | 141×89 | Buff | Brown | | Same design as serial 31 some perforated, some folded. |
| 35 | 1 November | 1d | 140×89 | Buff | Carmine | 2 | Full length portrait, heading re-set to include Coat of Arms. |
| 36 | 1 November | 1d+1d | 140×89 | Buff | Carmine | | Same design as serial 35 plus instructions. Some perforated; some folded. |

Private cards could now (1 November 1899) be produced to a maximum size of 140 mm. × 89 mm. (5½ in. × 3½ in.) to correspond with the size of the new official card.

# 2

# A Chronological List of Postcard and Related Events

*1 October 1869*. Austria issued the world's first postcard (Plate 1).

*1 October 1870*. Britain issued her first postcard, for Inland use only (Plate 1; Appendix 1, serial 1).

*1870*. Besnardeau's illustrated cards were used at Conlie.

*1871*. The decorated Belgian card issued (Plate 3).

*March 1872*. Grant's Doré card issued.

*1 April 1872*. Privately printed cards were allowed in Britain (Appendix 1, serial 3).

*1873*. The first official German postcard issued.

*9 October 1874*. The first meeting of what was to become the Universal Postal Union (UPU) ended in Berne, having established a 'Convention' for dealing with mail between member countries.

*1 February 1875*. Mr Gladstone's 'stout' card put on sale (Appendix 1, serial 5).

*1 July 1875*. As a result of the UPU Convention in 1874 Britain issued her 1¼d Postcard, her first for Foreign use (Plate 1; Appendix 1, serial 6).

*1878*. UPU Congress in Paris. The first official French Postcard issued.

*1 April 1879*. As a result of the UPU Congress in 1878 Britain issued two new Foreign Postcards. One upset Ireland. (Plate 2; Appendix 1, serial 9).

*1 May 1882*. Zrenner produced for the Nuremberg Exhibition what was probably the first commemorative picture postcard.

*1 October 1882*. Britain's first reply paid postcards put on sale (Appendix 1, serial 12).

*June 1889*. The Eiffel Tower was opened to the public.

*5 August 1889*. The Heligoland postcard was posted.

*16 May 1890*. The Guildhall Postal Jubilee postcard was put on sale (Plate 2; Appendix 1, serial 26).

*June 1891*. The Royal Naval Exhibition Eddystone Lighthouse card was put on sale (Appendix 1, serial 27).

*1892* (approximately). Rotary presses developed in Germany for photo-lithographic printing.

*1 September 1894*. Privately printed postcards for use with adhesive stamps allowed in Britain.

*11 December 1894*. The Post Office reminded manufacturers that their names and trademarks should not be on the address side of a postcard.

*1894*. Messrs Geo. Stewart of Edinburgh and F. T. Corkett of Leicester produced what were probably Britain's first picture postcards.

*21 January 1895*. The first official court size card issued in Britain (Appendix 1, serial 30).

*1895*. The firm of Blum & Degen was established to produce Picture Postcards.

*1896*. Pictorial Stationery Co. founded.

*16 June 1897*. Writing a message on the address side of a card no longer formally forbidden.

*1897*. Valentine's produced their first postcards.

*11 October 1899*. The start of the Boer War.

*1 November 1899*. Full UPU size private cards allowed in Britain. Tuck's issued their first postcards.

*28 February 1900*. Ladysmith relieved.

*17 May 1900*. Mafeking relieved.

*July 1900*. *Picture Postcard Magazine*, Editor E. W. Richardson, was published by the Collectors' Publishing Co. Tuck's announced their £1,000 competition.

*December 1900*. John Evelyn Wrench issued his first postcards.

*1900*. By the middle of the year the following firms were among those manufacturing picture postcards: the London Stereoscopic Co., Ellis & Wallery, C. W. Faulkner & Co., Beeching Ltd (of the Strand), the Collectors' Publishing Co., the Picture Postcard Co., and Frith's.

*22 January 1901*. Death of Queen Victoria.

*23 January 1901*. C. W. Faulkner & Co. issued Queen Victoria commemorative cards.

*January 1902*. The Postmaster General sanctioned the use of divided back cards. Henry Stead issued his first 'Current Event' postcard.

*30 January 1902*. The Anglo-Japanese Alliance was formed.

*31 May 1902*. The end of the Boer War.

*26 June 1902*. The day set for the Coronation of Edward VII, which had to be postponed due to the King's illness.

*9 August 1902*. The Coronation of Edward VII.

*1902*. Bamforth & Co. of Holmfirth began to produce picture postcards. F. Hartmann introduced the divided back card.

*23 May 1903*. Death of Angelo Asti.

*May 1903*. D. F. & Co. published their first picture postcard.

*5 August 1903*. Death of Phil May.

*1 January 1904*. Book Post changed its name to Halfpenny Packet Post.

*8 February 1904*. The start of the Russo-Japanese War.

*21 June 1904*. Metal cards had to be put into covers.

*21 October 1904*. The Russian Navy fired on Hull trawlers fishing on the Dogger Bank.

*1904*. The Collectors' Publishing Co. published only three issues of the *Postcard Connoisseur* from March. A facsimile of Grant's Doré card was among six others given away with the first issue. Philco introduced 'jewelling' for the Christmas season. Donald McGill drew his first cards. France accepted the divided back card.

*16 May 1905.* The Russo-Japanese War ended.

*5 September 1905.* Postmasters were instructed not to deliver cards posted in transparent envelopes.

*1905.* Germany accepted the divided back card.

*June 1906.* UPU Congress in Rome accepted the divided back card.

*November 1906.* The 'T' stamp introduced on postcards (Appendix 1, Note 6).

*1906.* Wrench & Co. ceased publication.

*April 1907.* The minimum size of postcards was raised from 3¼ in. by 2¼ in. to 4 in. by 2¾ in. (82 mm. by 57 mm. to 101 mm. by 70 mm.).

*4 June 1907.* Tinsel cards had to be put in a cover, but if the cover was unsealed they could pass for ½d.

*1907.* America accepted the divided back card.

*16 March 1910.* Death of Tom Browne.

*6 May 1910.* Death of Edward VII.

*22 June 1911.* Coronation of George V.

*9 September 1911.* First United Kingdom Official Aerial Post (Plate 4).

*1911.* McCorquodale & Co. took over the printing of Official cards from Thomas De la Rue and Co.

*4 August 1914.* Britain entered First World War.

*1 November 1915.* Book Post reintroduced.

*14 December 1915.* Cards to neutral countries subject to censorship.

*2 May 1916.* HM Ships not to be shown on postcards.

*11 August 1916.* Death of Lance Thackeray.

*6 September 1916.* The first *Daily Mail* War Cards issued.

*6 April 1917.* America entered First World War.

*August 1917.* Death of Raphaël Kirchner.

*3 June 1918.* Postcard Rate raised to 1d.

*October 1918.* The Pig Control postcard issued.

*11 November 1918.* First World War ended.

*December 1918.* Censorship relaxed. The end of the Golden Age.

# 3

# Publishers of Picture Postcards with some Information on Trademarks and Series

The information below has been assembled from a study of postcards in our own and other collections and from searches at the Public Records Office, Companies House and the Patent Office.

It is not easy to establish when any particular organization first produced picture postcards. The majority of the publishers already in business as companies before they began to print cards have not retained their records; others which came into card publishing around 1900 often did so as trading associations and not as limited companies.

It was not until 22 December 1916 that 'business names' of trading associations had to be registered, and by that time many of the postcard entrepreneurs had gone out of business. In any case business names only had to be registered if they were different from those of the proprietors, so some associations continued on into 1917 without being registered. Such a case was J. W. Ruddock and Sons. Their name was not registered until 1928 although they started in 1904, and it was probably registered only for commercial reasons. Some, however, like Cynicus, started off as limited companies, and records exist for these from the 1890s; others, such as Birn Bros. Ltd, changed from trading associations with business names to limited companies. Sometimes, as was the case with Birn Bros., the same name was used for the limited company and the trading association, but often not. It is surprising that trading associations could register business names ending in 'Co.', thus giving the impression of being a limited company, e.g. Nister & Co.

Unfortunately, many of the records concerning the limited companies once held by the Board of Trade have been destroyed because of their age. Thus there is no easy way of assembling details of publishers. Indeed, for a large proportion of them their only legacy is the cards they printed, and by collecting and exchanging information the deltiologist should be able to work slowly back to find the earliest days of any publisher.

*Alphalsa Publishing Co.*, London
The limited company was dissolved before 1950 and its records were destroyed in July 1963. Alphalsa cards are mostly found with postmarks in the 'teens' of our period. Many skilfully composed fantasy cards. 'Smile Messengers' and other humorous series.

173

*Aristophot Co.*, London

The limited company was wound up before 1950. Aristophot cards are mostly found from the latter years of our period. Photographic studies of beauties; greetings cards.

*Bamforth & Co.*, Holmfirth, Yorks

James Bamforth founded the firm in 1870 and became known as 'King of the Lantern Slides'. The firm made lantern slides and films, using members of the family and employees as models. In 1902 they began producing postcards. They carried over the life modelling techniques they had developed with lantern slides, and created a unique and successful format which many others tried to copy.

The firm became a limited company in June 1910 and celebrated its centenary in 1970 with the publication of Frederick Alderson's book *The Comic Postcard in English Life*.

Specialists in sentiment, they produced many series in sets of three and four cards of illustrated songs and hymns, many humorous series, and patriotic and sentimental cards during the First World War. Their early cards were in black and white, but most of the later series were coloured.

*J. Beagles & Co.*, London

The firm was in production by 1903. They were specialists in photographic portraits of royalty, other personalities and commemorative cards; usually direct photographic prints or 'bromides'.

*Birn Bros.*, London    Trademark 'B.B.' on London series

Joseph and Sigmund Birn traded for many years as Birn Bros., and on 3 March 1915 formed the limited company of the same name. This company is still extant.

These versatile publishers were in production by 1905. They produced series of greetings cards, crested views, animals and pretty girls in the Asti style.

*Blum & Degen*, London    Trademark 'B & D'

The firm started production in 1895. Many examples of their early views are still available. Later they produced many series of coloured portraits of actresses. They were reported as having habitually 'in stock over 1 million cards' and 'between 2,000 and 3,000 distinct designs' in July 1900.

*Boot, Jesse*, Nottingham

Some of the firm's cards bear the words 'Boots Cash Chemist'. The firm was producing cards by 1901 and their early series were art gallery reproductions in black and white in the style of Faulkner and Hildesheimer. Later they produced series of facsims, ships, etc. in the 'Pelham' series.

*Cynicus Publishing Co.*, Tayport and Leeds
The firm was incorporated on 3 March 1902 by Messrs Yorston & Hogarth of Glasgow. There is no record of earlier trading as a business association, nor is there any record of when the company moved from Tayport to Leeds. The company was dissolved on 9 June 1916.
As far as we can ascertain, the company mainly published the designs of 'Cynicus' himself – Martin Anderson. Anderson had published books of his cartoons from 1890 and his cards all bear his own brand of distinctive cynical, satirical humour. The cards are always clearly signed. Notable series were 'Our Local Express', 'Scottish Character Sketches', 'Characters from Shakespeare'.

*Daily Mail*, London
'Battle Postcards' of official war photographs of action scenes of the First World War. The cards printed by the three-colour process were on sale at the end of September 1916. Series I to III were titled:

*Series I*
  1. Wounded 'Tommy' to the photographer: 'I'm not a German.'
  2. Highlanders pipe themselves back from the trenches
  3. Church service before battle
  4. A British heavy gun in action
  5. Helping an ambulance through the mud
  6. Sir D. Haig introducing Sir Pertab Singh to General Joffre
  7. Army chaplain tending British graves
  8. Thirsty German prisoners in their barbed-wire cage

*Series II*
  9. Ypres after two years of war
 10. RAMC picking up wounded in a captured village
 11. A 'fag' after a fight
 12. 'Tommy's' lookout in a captured trench at Ovillers
 13. British mine exploding at Beaumont Hamel

14. Crawling to the German trenches under fire
15. British machinegunners wearing gas helmets
16. A gallant rescue under fire: this man saved twenty lives like this

*Series III*
17. 'Tommy' finds shell holes comfortable to sleep in
18. After the first cavalry charge, July 1916
19. Firing a heavy howitzer in France
20. 'Tommy' at home in German dugouts
21. Black Watch pipers playing to the captors of Longueval
22. Bringing in prisoners
23. Burial of two British soldiers on battlefield
24. Saving a wounded comrade under fire


Series IV, V and VI in photogravure were available from 6 September 1916, as were Series VII, VIII, IX and X in Silver Print style (photographic facsimile). The coloured sets were not on sale until about a fortnight after the black and white sets as they took longer to produce. Issues continued at least until Series XX in April 1917.


*Davidson Bros.*
The limited company was dissolved in 1950. The company was in production in the era of the undivided back, i.e. before 1902. Davidson Bros. were the great humour specialists and produced many series of original cartoons by the best humorous artists of the day, including Tom Browne, John Hassall, Louis Wain and Ludovici. They are represented in many other categories as well, notably facsims, like the 'Arcadia' series by Prof. Van Mier.


*Delittle Fenwick & Co.*, York

This title was registered as a business name on 26 February 1917 and the partners were named as William Drinnan Delittle, Feargus Delittle and John Fenwick. The business was carried on from Railway Street, York, and on 31 March 1923 became a limited company. This company was liquidated in July 1968.

The firm started production in May 1903. As well as the usual trade name 'D.F. & Co.', they occasionally used the name 'Defco'. Notable for their 'fake' moonlight views, they also produced humorous cards and some attractive series of art reproductions, especially those of paintings by A. Greenbank.

*E. T. W. Dennis & Sons*

The firm was publishing views by 1901, when the only clue to their identity was their tiny initials on the picture. Later cards always bear the 'Dainty' series trademark. They produced many series of views, humour and pullouts. They are current members of the Postcard Publishers Association and are based in Scarborough.

*Ettlinger & Co.*, London

Max Ettlinger's limited company was dissolved before 1950. Ettlinger started production in Britain in 1901. Originally he specialized in novelty cards (Chapter 9). He also produced art gallery reproductions, portraits, greetings cards and many other types in the 'Royal' series.

*Eyre & Spottiswoode*    Trademark 'Woodbury Series'

The firm was producing black and white art gallery reproductions soon after the turn of the century. Their later cards were of many types especially view cards.

*C. W. Faulkner & Co.*, London

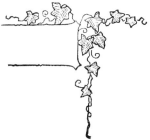

This trademark is also found on some Rotary cards.

Charles William Faulkner incorporated the limited company on 13 September 1905. It was wound up on 16 April 1959.

Faulkner was producing cards by May 1900 and advertisements in the April and December 1901 issues of the *Picture Postcard Magazine* listed forty series. If the lists are chronological, which is likely, the earliest series was the 'British Statesmen Series'. This was followed by a 'Comic Series' in the 'Write Away' style, with sets numbered from 3 to 6, with six cards in each; then 'Society Sketches', 'Shakespeare' and 'British Generals'.

Faulkner was a versatile and prolific publisher, with many fine series in a variety of categories. Besides the early series mentioned above, we would single out: 1. early black and white art gallery reproductions. 2. superb, early crested or heraldic cards. 3. fine 'Opera Series'. 4. reproductions of contemporary artists' work, notably Florence Hardy, Ethel Parkinson and Shepheard. 5. panel greetings cards. 6. commemorative cards. 7. facsim views.

### *F. Frith & Co.*, Reigate
The company was in production before 1902 and produced countless series of good quality view cards.

### *Gale & Polden Ltd*, Aldershot

This firm produced cards in the era of the undivided back. They always specialized to a large extent in cards with a military flavour, and used the trade name 'Wellington' for most of their series. Their most famous series shows the uniforms, colours and history of all the British regiments (Chapter 5). The cards were issued in 1908 and 1909.

Gale & Polden were the official publishers for the I.R. Austrian Exhibition, 1906 and the Balkan States Exhibition, 1908.

### *W. H. Goss*
This trading name was registered by William Eliot Thomas on 26 July 1920, that date being given as the first day of trading. The place of business was the Albion Printing Works, Torquay. On 29 September 1920 the business became a limited company.

The earliest Goss card that we have seen was posted in 1906. The company produced distinctive reproductions of their own armorial and ancient pottery and porcelain designs.

*F. Hartmann*

Hartmann started production in 1902 and was the innovator of the divided back card. He produced many series of views and pastoral scenes, including several hop-picking series and 'Rural Series'. Composite views and fine embossed cards were also issued.

*James Henderson & Sons Ltd*

The firm was in production by 1904 with its 'Pictorial Comedy' series, notably by C. Dana Gibson. Henderson published Gibson cartoons as well as 'Gibson Girls', and other artists' work in their 'Head Studies' series.

*S. Hildesheimer & Co.*, London and Manchester

The firm was in production by 1902. Their early cards were black and white art gallery reproductions. Later they produced many series of coloured facsim views and greetings cards.

*Inter-Art Co.*

The information on this publisher was provided by Mr R. E. Collier of Derby, who has a collection of over 2,000 different Inter-Art cards. The cards are all numbered and were published from 1909 to 1935, and from 1951 to 1952. Artists who contributed designs include Donald McGill, Frederick Spurgin, Lawson Wood and Agnes Richardson.

Their cards were printed six to a plate, generally with adjacent numbers and a related theme. Overall classification may be into six types, which are, chronologically:

1. *Photogravure series*. Not coloured, numbered on the front, from Southampton House. First published 1909, numbered 501 to 524.

2. *Writing on back in red*. First published from Southampton House, 1909 to 1912, numbered 1 to 100 and 600 to 1,000. Also reprinted in black lettering from Red Lion Square or Florence House.

3. *Writing on back in black*. First published from Southampton House 1912 to 1914, numbered from 100 to 1,000. Also in black lettering as type 2.

4. *Holborn series*. First published from Red Lion Square 1914, numbered H102 to H118 and drawn by Phil Martin.

5. *Early numbers*. 100 to 8,000, published from Florence House or Red Lion Square, 1915 to 1935.

6. *No address given*. Numbered 400 to 700, published 1951 to 1952.

During the Florence House period (early numbers) artists such as A. A. Nash (pretty children) and L. Barribal (glamorous sirens) drew designs for the 'Artistique' series.

*Ja-Ja*

There is some confusion as to the name of the publishers of this famous series. We have seen it attributed to Jackson of Grimsby, but we have in our

possession a Ja-Ja card published by Stoddart & Co. Ltd. Unfortunately this
limited company was dissolved before 1950 and all its records have been
destroyed.

*Ja-Ja* produced vast series of heraldic crested and clan tartan cards.

### *Jackson & Son*, Grimsby

John Middleton Jackson incorporated his limited company on 23 June 1914.
It was liquidated on 5 February 1953.

Jackson's postcards appeared towards the end of Edward VII's reign. The
company is notable for publishing series of composite views, the cards divided
into geometric shapes each with its own small view.

### *Jarrolds Ltd*, Norwich

The firm started producing postcards in 1898/9 and is still thriving and
now a member of the Postcard Publishers Association. They produced series
of facsims, including some by Walter Hayward Young. Their most famous
cards were produced for the 'Great War' series during the First World War.

### *Knight Bros.*

The firm was in production by 1904. They issued some attractive art
productions, notably still lifes; views and humorous cards.

### *McCorquodale & Co.*

The limited company was dissolved before 1950. They were producing
cards in 1900 and published some early cards for railway and steamship lines.
In 1911 McCorquodale took over the government contract from De la Rue
to print postal stationery.

### *Millar & Lang*

George Grandison Millar started producing postcards in 1903 and in 1905
formed the limited company which is today a member of the Postcard Publishers Association. Millar & Lang were prolific publishers and are represented
in most categories of postcards. The firm produced many humorous series, the
most famous of which is the 'Father says "Turn" ' series. They also produced
some splendid 'Hands Across the Sea' cards; exhibition cards, notably for
the Scottish Exhibition, 1911; and a delightful series to illustrate nursery
rhymes. Frequently their cards were printed and distributed by smaller firms
and bear these firms' names, e.g. 'Varsity Oxford City', on cards showing the
various college crests.

*Misch & Co.*

The limited company was dissolved by 1950. Some cards bear the name 'Misch & Stock', with the same trademark.

Their cards were being sold in Britain by 1904 and their most famous series are the 'World's Galleries' reproductions printed by Stengel. These cards always bear two numbers, one being Stengel's series number and the other Misch's. They also produced greetings cards and humorous cards, notably the 'Motorist's Series'.

*Ernest Nister*, London

On 31 January 1927 Karl Ernst Nister and Leopold Benda, both of Nuremberg, registered the business name 'Nister & Co.' for the purpose of fine art publishing and printing. The name appears to have been used since January 1920, but the association ceased to trade on 18 June 1927. The place of business was given as London, and Karl Ernst is certainly the printer who called himself Ernest Nister.

Nister was producing cards in Britain in the period of the undivided back. He printed art gallery reproductions and greetings cards.

*The Philco Publishing Co.*, London

This business name was registered on 15 March 1917. The registration form stated the general nature of the business as 'fine art publishing' and it was signed by the proprietor, Philip Lawrence Cohen. The place of business was given as Holborn Place, W.C. The firm ceased to trade on 1 January 1934 and was incorporated with Millar & Lang Ltd.

The earliest Philco card we have seen was posted in 1904. The firm's main output was in photographic portraits. They also produced greetings cards and some facsims.

*R. P. Phillimore & Co.*, Berwick

The company was formed in Berwick to publish Phillimore's own work – mostly delicately drawn views, historical houses and other subjects with historical interest. An added bonus is often found on the back: another small Phillimore drawing connected with the picture on the front. Some postcards are in Phillimore's named 'Historical Series'.

*Photochrom Co.*, London and Tonbridge Wells

The limited company was dissolved in the 1960s. The company was publishing cards by 1902. Some of their early series were photographed reproductions of classical paintings and sculptures. Later they produced views and novelty cards. Their most distinctive series are the attractive 'Celesque' and blue 'Wedgwood' range of views.

### Pictorial Stationery Co., London

The company was founded in 1896 and in 1900 was reported as having brought out 350 new designs in 1899. They were prolific publishers of views in the 'Peacock' series in a variety of styles. They also produced an 'Autochrom' series.

### Rapid Photo Printing Co., London

The limited company was dissolved before 1950. They were publishing cards by 1903 and specialized in photographic portraits.

### Regal Art Publishing Co., London

The company was publishing cards by 1903. They issued fine facsim views very similar in style and quality to Tuck's 'Oilettes'.

### Rotary Photo Co., London

There is no record of this firm in Companies House. It is possible that the title was a trading name and that the firm was not a limited company. An identical business name was registered in 1952, so the original organization no longer exists.

The company was producing cards soon after the turn of the century and was credited in 1902 by the Editor of the *Picture Postcard Magazine* with being the first publisher to produce New Year cards (for January 1902), and with introducing the rotary photographic reproduction process to British postcard production.

Rotary produced thousands of sets of stage stars and 'Hand Coloured British Beauties'. Rotary sometimes used a trademark similar to that of C. W. Faulkner.

### Rotophot

This company, which specialized in photographic portraits, was in production before 1902.

### J. W. Ruddock & Sons, Lincoln

The trading association began in 1904 and was based in the High Street, Lincoln. It was not registered until 30 November 1928. At that time the partners were given as John William Ruddock, John Davis Ruddock and James Herbert Ruddock.

The firm specialized in facsim views, especially of the Lincoln area, many reproduced from watercolours painted by a local artist.

*J. Salmon Limited*, Sevenoaks

Joseph Salmon acquired his business in 1880, and his eldest son, also Joseph, produced the company's first postcards some time between 1900 and 1904. These were collotype views, monochrome and colour, reproduced from his own photographs of Sevenoaks and district.

In 1904 a local water colour artist, C. Essenhigh Corke, was commissioned to paint pictures of the district, and pictures of Knole in collaboration with the then Lady Sackville. These were published that year as postcards. About 1911, A. R. Quinton, a well-known artist, was commissioned to paint a set of water colours for reproduction and publication as postcards. These were quickly followed by other sets of different places by the same artist.

The company was incorporated on 24 October 1930 and the present Managing Director is the great-grandson of the first Mr Joseph Salmon. Today J. Salmon Ltd is a member of the Postcard Publishers Association.

*E. A. S. Schwerdtfeger & Co.*, London

Most of their cards are postmarked in the 'teens' of our period. They produced countless series of photographic portraits of beauties and children, and greetings cards.

*Stengel & Co.*, Dresden and Berlin

The company exported thousands of cards to Britain and they were being sold here by May 1901. Their main works were in Dresden. Their early photographic views, both black and white and coloured, are distinctive for their sharp detail, but they are famous for their superb art gallery reproductions in glowing colour. (See also Misch & Co.)

*Geo. Stewart*, Edinburgh

The firm started postcard production in 1894. They claimed to be the first British picture postcard publishers with their views of Edinburgh in September 1894. The cards showed vignetted scenes. They also produced early commemorative picture postcards of the Nile Expedition in 1897.

*Stewart & Woolf*, London

The limited company was dissolved before 1950 and its records have been destroyed.

Cards were being sold by April 1904. Stewart & Woolf cards always reached a high standard of printing and finish. They include views with a pastoral flavour, greetings cards, humorous cards and some fine embossed cards.

*Alfred Stiebel & Son*, London

Their cards are mostly seen later in our period. They produced humorous cards, greetings cards and woven silk cards under the trade name Alpha.

*A. & G. Taylor*, London

This business name was registered on 20 March 1917 by Mrs Christine Lawrence of Cardiff. The limited company has now been dissolved and its records were destroyed in July 1963.

Their cards claim 'By Appointment to Her Late Majesty': therefore they must have been producing postcards before 1901. Later issues include a 'Reality' series, an 'Orthochrome' series and many glossy greetings cards.

*Raphael Tuck & Sons.*

Raphael Tuck & Sons were well-established art publishers to Queen Victoria when the Picture Postcard developed. They published their first postcards on 1 November 1899. In July 1900 they advertised their first numbered series, and Series 1 was given as '12 London Views'. Their first Harry Payne series was no. 18, 'The British Navy', comprising six cards. The 'Souvenir of Ladysmith and Mafeking Relief' set of six cards was Series 27. Other notable first series, each of six cards, were 'The Amewsing Write Away! Series', no. 42, and the 'Empire Series', no. 49. The majority of Tuck's cards are coloured, including all those mentioned above.

Tuck's went on to produce so many thousands of fine quality postcards that it is almost impossible to single out any for special mention. However, here are a few outstanding series: Limited Edition Proof Sets (Chapter 10); Educational Series; Rough Seas series, printed in black and white on green and blue tinted cards from August 1901, and later as 'Oilettes'; Empire, Royal, Political, Military and other early series with undivided backs; Harry Payne series of military uniforms; series of Louis Wain, Asti, Prof. van Hier, Lance Thackeray, Phil May and other contemporary artists' work; Jotter and others' 'Oilette' views.

*Valentine & Sons*, Dundee

Like Tuck's, Valentine's also produced Christmas and other greetings cards in mid-Victorian times. They first produced postcards in 1897.

Although examples of their vast output will be found in practically every category we have dealt with, Valentine's were the view card manufacturers supreme (Chapter 4). Their greatest achievement is in their comprehensive range of photographed view cards, covering the whole of the British Isles. They also produced many series of cards showing regional occupations, costumes and pastimes, and novelty cards, such as pullouts and jewelled cards.

They were official publishers to the Franco-British and other exhibitions, for which they produced fine cards.

*J. Welch & Sons*, Portsmouth

This name was registered on 19 March 1917 and the place of business was given as Portsmouth. The principal partner was Joseph Welch, and other signatures, presumably his sons, were Joseph Horace Welch, Ernest James Welch and Claude Cullum Welch.

The first Welch card we have seen was posted in 1904. They produced many series of finely detailed photographic view cards and humorous cards, including a fine set of Dickens sketches by Kyd.

*Wildt & Kray*, London

Adolph Ernst Wildt and Henry Joseph Kray formed their limited company on 3 November 1934. It was wound up in December 1954. The first of their cards we have seen was posted in 1905.

Their great speciality was greetings cards, especially for birthdays, and many have a high gloss finish. They also produced views and novelty cards. When initials alone appear on a card there is sometimes confusion between their cards and those of another firm of publishers with the same initials, Watkins & Kracke.

*Woolstone Bros.*, London

This business name was registered by Gustave Woolstone on 7 January 1925. The place of business was given as Aldersgate St, EC1. They were producing cards before 1902 and later published many glossy greetings cards and views in the 'Arlette Glazette', 'Glossette' and other series.

*W. R. & S.*

Unfortunately the full name of this company has not been revealed by research. The first card that we have seen was posted in January 1903. The trademark 'Reliable Series' usually appears on their cards, which are represented in many categories, notably views and topical cards. They also produced some 'Hold to Light' cards.

*Wrench*, London

John Evelyn published his first postcards on or soon after 29 November 1900. His early cards were all printed in Germany by collotype, with the inscriptions in red. In 1902 the inscriptions changed to brown and then varied in colour. Wrench ran his own trading association until late in 1902, when he formed a limited company, but his expansion had been too rapid and, short of capital, he handed over control of the business to Amalgamated Press in 1904. They were unable to revive the business, which closed in 1906.

Always enterprising, Wrench was an innovator in many fields. He was the first publisher to obtain permission to reproduce paintings and sculptures from national institutions and to sell his cards on the spot. His black and white art reproductions were soon imitated by other publishers. He pioneered the subscription card with Henry Stead and introduced the insurance card to Britain – the sender was insured for £250 for twenty-four hours against death by accident and while travelling in any public conveyance.

Wrench's views covered most of the principal resorts and places of interest in the British Isles, and his series of animal studies included many fine photographic studies by Landor. Among his humorous series, Wrench issued some political cards reproduced from *Punch* cartoons. Perhaps his most famous postcards are in the 'Links of the Empire' series (Chapter 4).

# 4
# Printing Processes

The techniques used in different printing processes often overlap, and plates may be produced by a combination of methods in order to achieve some particular effect. Also, the image which is to be reproduced may be specially drawn or printed by one method and the printing onto the cards done by another. To complicate things still further, different terms are frequently used to describe the same processes and today it is almost impossible to describe any printing process as being of one particular type. Our aim in what follows is to look into the art of printing just enough for the collector to be able to identify, or at least appreciate, the printing techniques that created his cards. Should the reader require a more technical understanding of the subject we recommend a study of the books listed in the bibliography.

Printing processes may be classified by the position of the image to be printed in relation to the surface of the block or plate on which the image is marked.

*Intaglio* processes are those in which the image to be printed is sunk below the level of the block surface.

*Lithography* is a process in which the image lies at the same level as the block surface, and is distinguished from it by the use of greases.

*Letterpress* printing uses an image which stands above the block surface.

## *Intaglio*

A simple print or *line drawing* uses only lines. Shade is obtained by cross-hatching or by varying the spacing between lines. Plate 26 shows a line drawing. The earliest ones were scratched directly on the printing plates to produce intaglio images. The ultimate refinement of this process is *engraving* and when it is aided by chemical erosion it is known as *etching*. The resulting printing block may be called a *line block*.

*Gravure* is sometimes used as a collective description of intaglio processes which may be engravings or etchings.

*Photogravure* uses a direct photographic image which might be touched up, added to or subtracted from by engraving. *Dry point* is an engraving process done on a plate through an image marked on a thin layer of wax. *Aquatint* is an etching process that uses a particularly porous acid-resisting film to cover the plate surface and, like dry point, its particular benefits lie probably more in the area of the printer's work than the eye of the beholder.

*Mezzotint* is an interesting engraving process. The printing plate is pricked all over with small holes – not through-holes – and the image then engraved on the plate. Tonal values are obtained by scraping out the holes partly or wholly according to the amount of ink they need to hold. There is a characteristic ridged surface to intaglio prints and a tendency for the ink to squash over its correct boundaries. Nevertheless it will be necessary to study the cards very carefully in order to detect these characteristics. Bank of England notes are printed by intaglio methods and exhibit the ridged effect.

In general, intaglio or gravure processes may be said to have been those first used for picture postcards, but their limitations were the time and expense involved in producing the block. Photogravure, also known as *heliogravure*, speeded things up, and with the rotary press beginning to displace the slower flat bed press around the turn of the century, the quicker *rotogravure* process became available, but was not widely used. It was not used to print stamps until 1914, and during the intervening years the more convenient lithographic processes became popular.

*Lithography*

Photography provides a perfect tonal image of a subject, but the image cannot be put directly on a photo-sensitive printing plate because there would be no way for the printing ink to reproduce shading. The printing image on the plate either exists or it does not; there is no in-between state. A direct photograph would print as a silhouette. Shading is achieved by converting the photographic image into very small dots, and the size, shape and number of dots determines the intensity and shading of the picture. The conversion to dots is achieved by taking the photograph through a fine mesh known as a *half-tone screen*.

The majority of postcards produced up to about 1904 used the half-tone block that was produced by the screen in combination with any of the three printing processes, and if these cards are examined with a magnifying glass the dots can be clearly seen. The better quality half-tone prints use very small dots, but the regular pattern can still be seen on close examination. Some cards were made by using a half-tone screen which produced a grain-like image structure in an attempt to avoid the regularity of the dot pattern. These were known as *mezzographs*.

Photography was by far the most commonly used method of producing images on printing plates for postcards, and it could be employed for use with any of the printing processes. One of the most popular of such methods, which produced results approaching the standard of the direct photographic print, was *collotype*, and all of Wrench's early cards used the process. Collotype is a lithographic process and does not use the half-tone screen. Light is passed through a photographic negative and then made to fall on a smooth, gelatin-surfaced printing plate. By chemical treatment the gelatin wrinkles (reticulates) in proportion to the intensity of the light that falls upon it; thus the full tonal range of the photograph can be represented by the wrinkles on the plate, and the printing is done directly from the gelatin surface.

The process relies upon the fact that grease and water repel each other, and a water-absorbent block is used. The non-printing areas of gelatin are made to hold water, which rejects the greasy ink, while the dry printing areas hold the ink.

Examination of a collotype card using a glass will reveal not a regular pattern but a smooth, grainy change of tone. The process was used on the cheapest cards as well as the most expensive, and the high standard of repro- duction possible is well illustrated by Misch & Co's 'World Galleries' series, actually printed by Stengel (see Plate 22).

There are many variants of the collotype process, which was also known as *Albertype*, *phototype*, *heliotype* and *photocollotype*. One particular variant, *aquatone*, is sometimes claimed on more expensive cards. Collotype is par- ticularly suitable for pictures with a wide tonal range, but although relative intensities within each print are determined by the wrinkling of the gelatin, print to print differences are possible due to varying wetness of the gelatin. The aquatone process controlled the wetness so that consistent results could be obtained.

*Autolithography* describes the process in which the artist draws his picture directly on the printing surface using special chalks and crayons; but in general lithography is associated with photography and is sometimes known collectively as *photolithography*. However, we must point out that lithographic printing was developed long before the camera, and was widely used in Europe in the mid-nineteenth century; the artist usually drew his picture on a specially coated paper, and by virtue of the coating the image was transferred to the printing block by direct contact. The word 'lithograph' originates from the limestone blocks, which were smoothed and polished to act as water holding printing blocks when the process was invented by the German Alois Senefelder in 1796.

*Chromolithographs*, *oleographs* and *chromos* are all names for coloured lithographs. All three basic processes can be used with colour, and the im- portant development in colour printing was the discovery that an adequate colour range could be given to a picture by printing in three colours only. The first practical process was probably that devised by Joseph Albert in Germany around 1874, and from 1900 the *three-colour process* was rapidly introduced into Britain. The colours used are yellow, red and blue in that order, followed by the picture outline in black. One printing block is used for each colour and used successively. If the blocks are not identical and superimposed exactly the colours do not overprint or register properly, and blurred images result. This effect can be seen in many cheap German and British cards published by local stationers.

Colour printing, therefore, became a practicable proposition for quantity production at the turn of the century, and coloured cards replaced the earlier monochromes and black and whites. Some manufacturers stuck to the earlier slower and more expensive methods of applying fourteen or more colours, each with a different block.

*Letterpress*

This is the reverse of intaglio, and as the earliest form of printing was, as its name implies, used for reproducing print. How much it was used for postcards it is hard to establish, but cards bearing writing only, and the early De la Rue official cards, were probably produced by it, since the firm used it for their stamps well into the early 1900s. There is no list of variants as with the other two processes, and its major disadvantage in comparison with intaglio would seem to be that associated with finishing or modifying the printing plate. A line, say, drawn on an intaglio plate will produce a line in the printed picture, but to obtain such a required line in letterpress, it would have to be built up on the plate – a much more difficult and expensive procedure. Nevertheless, a simple design was cheaply reproduced by letterpress.

*Photography*

In addition to printed cards, the mass-produced photographic card was introduced into Britain by the Rotary Photographic Co. It had different names: *real photograph*, *bromide portraiture*, etc. As the company's name implies, they used rotary presses to print their cards. The commercially available photographically coloured print did not appear until the *autochrome* system in 1907, and until then almost all colouring was done by hand. This can be seen by tilting a coloured card to reflect the light, when the wash effect of hand colouring becomes apparent by its lower reflectivity in comparison to uncoloured areas of the card. The detection of hand colouring in this way is even easier with cards such as half-tone prints where the wash of colour contrasts strongly with the dot pattern of the picture.

# 5

# How to Date Postcards

It is possible to date most cards to within a few years of their issue. Some cards can be dated exactly, such as the early German officials, which carry the month, year and day in the bottom right-hand corner, e.g. 191k represents January 1891, 11th day. However, these cards are exceptional, and as far as we know there are no similar date marks on British Officials.

British Officials up to 1899 are listed in Appendix 1, and using this list, a ruler and Plates 1 and 2, any official card published up to that time can be readily identified. Picture cards are more difficult to date. If the card has been used the postmark can give an idea of when the card was produced, but it cannot be relied on. Manufacturers often unloaded old stock at cheap prices some years after it had been originally printed, and cards sold at museums and galleries could have waited a long time for a buyer. Early Wrench cards from the National Gallery quite frequently turn up dated well after 1906, when the firm stopped production. The postmark at least tells you the date before which the card was printed.

The picture on the card can help, and in Chapter 3 we have looked at the way in which dress evolved and discussed the introduction of the tram with respect to dating subjects. Researching the subject matter in the picture by use of our index or by library research will narrow the possibilities down. Pictures that commemorate some significant event are readily dated, and Appendix 7 lists the major British Exhibition dates, and Appendix 2 those dates that have significance in the postcard world.

The size of the card, its shape, the material and the printing all help. The index to this book will locate much information for you.

The address side of the card can be very helpful, and there are four places to look as shown in the sketch overleaf:

1. The stamp space is often marked with a postage rate. If it is not specified whether the rate applies to Inland or Foreign postage, it is safe to assume that it is for Inland use.

The Inland rate for postcards remained at ½d from the first use of the adhesive stamp on private cards in September 1894 until June 1918, when it was raised to 1d. But do not immediately dismiss a card specifying 1d Inland postage as being outside our period, because certain cards were liable to Letter Rate, e.g. appliqué designs and some mechanical cards which contravened the Treasury Warrant of 1894 because they had attachments.

The stamp itself can be a great help, but the same remarks that we made about postmarks apply to both card and stamp. The significantly different halfpenny issues in our period were:

September 1894.      Queen Victoria.   Orange (vermilion).
17 April 1900.       Queen Victoria.   Blue-green.
1 January 1902.      Edward VII.       Blue-green.
26 November 1904.    Edward VII.       Yellow-green.
22 June 1911.        George V.         Green.

Penny stamps differ widely in shades of red throughout the period, but two useful dates are 1 January 1902, when the Edward VII scarlet was introduced, and 22 June 1911, when the red George V issue was made.

A final point about the stamp, should any collector feel the need to remove it for examination, is that if it has a multiple watermark it will be a 1912 or later issue.

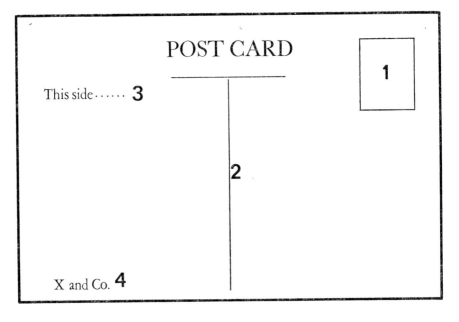

2. The divided back was introduced in 1902, and a card with a line down the middle is almost certainly of that date or later; some thrifty local publishers added lines to their old stock, and this can often be detected because the line is not the same colour as the other printing on the card. Also the added line is sometimes not parallel with the sides of the card because of the difficulty of registration, or because it was added by hand stamping.

3. When the divided back was introduced different manufacturers put a variety of guiding instructions here. At first only Britain would accept the

divided back and this was made clear on the cards. As other countries accepted it they were sometimes indicated. Thus if France were named the card was made in 1904, and if Germany, 1905. Once the UPU accepted the idea in 1906, manufacturers were quick to advertise the wider use to which these cards could be put by printing suitable instructions on them. But after a year or so the novelty wore off, and the fact that postcards could be sent abroad with writing on the address side did not need to be mentioned on them. We have listed a few typical instructions below with their likely dates, but these must be used with discretion for dating purposes because publishers often printed from the original plates for some years in order to avoid the trouble and expense of making new ones.

1902–4.          For Inland Postage this space, as well as the back, may now be used for communication.

1902–6           For Inland Postage only, this space may be used for communication.

1904 onward.     This space may be used for communication.

1904–7.          This space may be used for communication in the British Isles or to France at Postcard Rate.

1906 onward.     This space as well as the back, may be used for Inland Communication Postcard Rate, and for Foreign at Letter Rate.

1907 onward.     This space for communication.

Cards sometimes have 'per Book Post' written on them, or some reference to that post is made. Such cards are usually the larger ones such as Frith's 'Pictorial' series or Photochrom's 'Reform' cards. Book Post Rate was generally required because the cards contravened the postcard regulations in some way, usually in size. Book Post was available as follows:

| | |
|---|---|
| 1894–1 Jan. 1904. | Book Post. |
| 1 Jan. 1904–1 Nov. 1915. | Halfpenny Packet Post. |
| 1 Nov. 1915–1918. | Book Post. |

During the whole of the period 1894–1918 the charge was $\frac{1}{2}$d for up to 2 oz. of a maximum size of 2 ft by 1 ft. No message could be written on the card. If it was, the card incurred a surcharge to the Letter Rate. Habits die hard, however, as can be seen by the number of cards with messages written on the picture side after 1902, and 'Book Post' continued to be printed on some cards for a few years after 1904. Nevertheless a reasonable guess at a date for a card marked 'Book Post' would place it between 1900 and, say, 1910, or after 1915.

4. The manufacturer's name and series offer a clue to the age of a card. The index provides some information on series and some of the major publishers are listed in Appendix 3. The location of the publisher's name is mildly helpful. In December 1894 the Post Office warned that the publisher's trademark must not be put on the address side of the card, and from early 1895 to June

1897 cards should have had 'X and Co.' on the picture side. Treasury Warrant No. 429 of 16 June relaxed this rule, and most manufacturers had moved their names and trademarks to the address side by 1902, although early Wrench, Hildesheimer, Boots and Faulkner cards can be found with their names on the picture sides after this date.

Note. The reader should now be able to date the card shown at page 38 to within two years of its printing.

# 6

## How to Value Postcards

It would be an impossible task to compile an infallible and comprehensive catalogue of postcard prices. Value can vary enormously depending on such factors as age, condition, rarity and source of supply. What we will attempt is to provide a limited guide to the approximate prices you may expect to pay from a reputable postcard dealer or fellow collector.

We will take as our norm a card with no outstanding features – say a view – in good condition. We call the price of that card 'X'. At the present time this may range in value from 1 to 5 new pence, and the reader must establish its average value from his normal source of supply. We feel this to be the most practical method of assessing the comparative values of the particular types of card listed below at any given time, whether now or in the future. Although prices of cards continue to rise as deltiology grows in popularity, the relative values, always excepting any fashionable 'discoveries' that suddenly boost the price of a particular artist or type of card, remain fairly constant. The reader will be easily able to establish the current value for X and base his assessment thereon.

Undoubtedly the fastest rate of growth at the time of going to press is in the official cards. Very little information up to now has been researched or published in this field; yet interest is accelerating as collectors realize the fascination of the difficult but possible feat of trying to obtain every different issue of many different countries, as well as those of Great Britain. They are not easily available, and when discovered can fluctuate wildly in price.

The reader may expect to pay slightly less for a card in only fair condition, more for a card in mint condition, or for each card in a complete set; and more for coloured than sepia or black and white cards.

|  | Relative value |
|---|---|
| Views with middle distance illustrations of subjects such as canals, transport, mills | 2X |
| Views with clear foreground detail of any sought-after subject | 4X |
| Humorous cards | 2X |
| Humorous cards by signed artists, depending upon calibre and availability | 4X–6X |
| Photographic portraits of stage stars | X |
| Photographic portraits of more elusive stars | 2X |

| | | |
|---|---:|---|
| Photographic portraits of politicians, royalty, clergy and other personalities, depending upon rarity | | 2X–10X |
| Signed cards painted or drawn by Raphaël Kirchner | | 30X |
| Louis Wain | | 20X |
| Caton Woodville | | 20X |
| Harry Payne | | 10X |
| Mucha | | 10X |
| Asti, Ethel Parkinson, Florence Hardy, Ellen Clapsaddle, Arthur Payne | from | 4X |
| Art Gallery Reproductions by Misch & Co., Stengel and Nister | from | 4X |
| Embossed coins, stamps, currency and exchange rates (more for 'gold' coins) | from | 30X |
| Other Embossed cards | from | 8X |
| Crested cards | from | 2X–10X |
| Commemorative cards of disasters and events, value increasing with rarity | | 5X–30X |
| Exhibition cards, according to availability | | 2X–15X |
| Advertisement cards | from | 2X |
| Tinselled cards | from | 2X |
| Appliquéd cards | from | 5X |
| HTL | | 20X |
| Aluminium cards | | 15X |
| Celluloid cards | | 15X |
| Leather cards | | 20X |
| Wood or Peat cards | | 20X |
| Bas-relief | from | 5X |
| Puzzle cards | from | 20X |
| Mechanical cards | from | 20X |
| WWI Silk Embroidered      Sentimental | | 10X |
| Patriotic | | 20X |
| Regimental | | 30X–40X |
| WWI *Daily Mail* Official Pictures | from | 3X |
| Woven Silk card by Stevens | from | 200X |
| Grant | from | 160X |
| Alpha | from | 100X |
| others | from | 30X |
| Tuck's Limited Edition cards | from | 20X |
| Aviation cards | | 10X–50X |
| Autographed cards, depending on fame of signer | from | 8x |
| Prisoner of War cards | from | 25X |
| Boer War cards | from | 25X |
| Before 1900: picture cards posted, or known to have been made before that date | from | 4X |

Before 1900: any special subject cards                          from   10X
1890 Jubilee postal stationery, official cards, unused                 20X
        Posted from Guildhall                                          50X
1891 Royal Naval Exhibition Card showing Eddystone Light-
    house, unused                                                      100X
            used                                                       200X
1st GB Aerial Postcards                                         from   80X
        special violet cards                                    from   200X
Subsequent pre-1918 Aerial cards                                       40X
Postmarks can add from 5 pence to well over £5 to the value of
    your card, depending upon rarity

# 7

# British Exhibitions and other Events Commemorated by Picture Postcards

1901: Glasgow International Exhibition.
1902: Cork International Exhibition, Dublin.
Wolverhampton Exhibition.
1903: Highland and Jacobite Exhibition, Inverness.
Royal Exchange Colonial Exhibition, London.
Bradford Exhibition.
1904: Earls Court Exhibition.
Great Royal Lancs. Agricultural Show.
Pan Celtic Congress, Caernarvon.
1905: Nelson Centennial Exhibition.
1906: I.R. Austrian Exhibition, Earls Court.
Rochdale Jubilee Exhibition.
St John's N.B. International Exhibition.
1907: Miss Cofe's Exhibition, Manchester.
Irish International Exhibition.
Palestine in London Exhibition.
Oxford Pageant.
1908: Franco-British Exhibition, White City.
Bradford Exhibition.
Gloucester Pageant.
Pevensey Pageant.
Scottish National Exhibition, Edinburgh.
Balkan States Exhibition, Earls Court.
1909: Imperial International Exhibition, London.
1910: Japan-British Exhibition, Earls Court.
St John's N.B. Exhibition.
1911: Coronation Exhibition, London.
Festival of Empire, Crystal Palace.
Scottish Exhibition, Glasgow.
1912: Latin-British Exhibition.
1913: Palestine Exhibition, Taunton.
1914: Anglo-American Exhibition, London.
St John's N.B. Exhibition.

# 8

## Some Postcard Dealers and Postal Magazines

DEALERS

Roy Allen, 152 Wheatlands, Heston, Hounslow, Middlesex. Part time, but many classified cards usually available.

H. L. Blechman, HLB Antiques, 940 Christchurch Rd, Boscombe, nr. Bournemouth, Hampshire. Classified postcards.

David Drummond, Pleasures of Past Times, 11 Cecil Crt, Charing Cross Rd, London WC2. Classified postcards.

Mrs Irene H. Farrell, 21 St John's Villas, Friern Barnet Rd, Friern Barnet, London N11 3BA. Postcards of dolls, doll houses and allied subjects.

Ron Griffiths, 47 Long Arrotts, Hemel Hempstead, Hertfordshire. Postcards, greetings and valentines, etc.

John Hall and David MacWilliams, 17 Harrington Rd, London SW7. Classified postcards.

Ingeborg Raymond, The Antique Supermarket, St Christopher's Pl., Barrett St, London W1. Classified postcards.

John Rolph, Coach House Bookstore, Manor House, Pakefield St, Lowestoft, Suffolk. Large stock with over 70 classifications, reasonable prices.

George Wolstenholme, 13 Westroyd Pk, Mirfield, Yorkshire. Postcards, Victorian valentines and animated cards.

POSTAL MAGAZINES

*Birmingham Stamp Auction: Alcester Stamps Ltd*, 23 Mill St, Evesham, Worcestershire. Postal auction; mainly philatelic, but often some interesting deltiological lots.

*Philatelic Literature Auction* (Editor Harry Hayes), 48 Trafalgar St, Batley, Yorkshire. Mainly books, many of interest to deltiologists; also postal history and many postcard lots.

*Northern Postal Auctions* (Editor Lionel Mellors), 116 Victoria Rd, Scarborough, Yorkshire. Postal history, including many officials and picture postcards.

*Rigby Postal History Auction* (Editor B. Rigby-Hall), 31 Richmond Hill, Bournemouth, Hampshire. Many officials and some special picture cards. Expensive as most cards have some philatelic or postmark interest, but a possible outlet for surplus cards of this nature.

*International Postcard Market* (Editor J. H. D. Smith), 96 Idmiston Rd, West
   Norwood, London SE27. Postal auction of classified postcards; also postal
   history section.
*The Magpie's Nest* (Editor Robert G. Woodall), Forest Cottage, Holtwood,
   Wimborne, Dorset. Postal auction of ephemera and postal history, including
   many lots of officials and classified picture postcards.
*Postcard World* (Editor Drene Brennan), 34 Harper House, St James Crescent,
   London SW9. Non-profit making magazine of the Postcard Collectors Club
   of Great Britain. Postcard news, short articles, members wants.

# Bibliography

MAGAZINES

*British Postal Guide Quarterly*, various issues from 1850.
*Collectors' Review*, 1904.
*Girls' Realm*, 1900–1901.
*Picture Postcard Magazine*, July 1900–April 1904.
*Postcard Connoisseur*, March 1904–July 1904.
*Poster and Postcard Collector*, 1903.


BOOKS

R. C. Alcock and F. C. Holland, *British Postmarks. A Short History and Guide*, R. C. Alcock, 1967.
F. Alderson, *The Comic Postcard In English Life*, David & Charles, 1969.
A. J. Butland and E. A. Westwood, *Picture Postcards And All About Them*, The Postcard Collectors' Guide and News.
*A History of Inland Postage Rates Through the Ages*, Post Office Records, HS no. 10, 1968.
R. V. Cannon and F. G. Wallis, *Graphic Reproduction. Copy Preparation And Processes*, Vista Books.
Richard Carline, *Pictures In the Post*, Gordon Fraser, 1959 and 1971.
Rodney Dale, *Louis Wain: The Man Who Drew Cats*, William Kimber, 1970.
Field and Baldwin, *The Coronation Aerial Post 1911*, Frances J. Field, 1934.
Alan Huggins, *British Postal Stationery*, 1970.
Erik Nørgaard, *With Love. The Erotic Postcard*, MacGibbon & Kee, 1969.
Howard Robinson, *Britain's Post Office*, Oxford University Press, 1953.
Walter J. Scott, *All About Postcards*, Leeds, 1903.
Frank Staff, *The Picture Postcard And Its Origins*, Butterworth Press, 1966.
Thieme-Becker, *Kuenstler Lexicon*.
Harry Whetton, ed., *Practical Printing and Binding*, Odhams Press.
John Evelyn Wrench, *Uphill*, Ivor Nicholson & Watson, 1934.

# Index

*Note*: Postcard series titles are given in quotes, Plate numbers and Appendix page numbers in italics.

'A.E.' (artist), 111
'A.L.' (artist), 98
Abeille, Jack, 151
accessories, for post cards, 37, 127, 144–5
'Addled Ads' (Misch & Stock), 96
address side of card, 38, *165*, *170*, *191–4*; trademarks on, *193–4*; Treasury Regulations re, 30, 32; writing on, 32, 38–41, *171*
Adolph, Alfons, 23
advertisement cards, 25–6, 117–28; earliest, 25–6, 34, 117; by Aerial post, 68–69; chocolate, 123–4; competitions, 119–20; exhibitions, 125; fund-raising, 127–8; gift cards, 126–7; hotels, 123; insurance, 120–1; large, 118; local firms, 124–5; novelty, 118; overprinted on series, 119; publishers', 126–7; railway, 121–2; reward, 125–6; shipping lines, 122–3; stage shows, 125; travel, 124; value of, *196*
Aerial Post, first British, 67–9; *142*, *172*, *Plate 4*; value of cards, *197*; Staffs, 75
aeroplanes, early, 74–5, 160, *Plate 30*; Airships, 141; aviators, 75, 108, 138, *196*
airmail, *142*; *see also* Aerial post
Albert, Joseph, *189*
albums, postcard, 15, 51; family, 17, 18, 43; 'historical', 154; purchasing, filled, 44, 45; types of, for storage of cards, 48–49
Alderson, Frederick, *The Comic Postcard . . .*, 86, *174*
Alexandra, Queen, 65, 66–7, 114, 123
Alexandra Palace, p.o.w. cards from, 89, *196*, *Plate 24*
Alfonso, King of Spain, 66, 67, 114
'Alpha' (Stiebel trade name), *183*; silk cards, 136, 137, *183*

'Alphabet Series' (P.P. & P.), 147
Alphalsa Publishing Co., 156–7, *173*
aluminium cards, 135, *196*
Amalgamated Press, *186*
ambulances, 128
Anderson, Martin ('Cynicus'), 97, *175*; *see also* Cynicus
animals, 16, 108–10, *186*; in adverts, 119; fantasy, 157; humanized, 93–4, 109; humorous, 95, 98–9; pets with owners, 103
antique shops, 43, 44
appliqué, 132–3, *191*, *196*
'Aquarette' series (Tuck's), 58
Aristophot Co., *174*
Armstrong, M. H., 102
Army cards, *see* military series *and* regimental cards; Army camps, 83–4; Field Post card, 89; Field Post Offices, 141
art gallery reproductions, 151–3, *196*
'Art & Humour Publishing Co.', 85, *Plate 21*
Art Nouveau, 110, 150, 153
'Art' series (Tuck's), 150, *Plate 22*
artistic cards, 16, 110–11; the first, 37
'Artistique' (Inter-Art Co.), 151, *179*
artists, individual, 47, 149–51; classification of cards by, 149; signatures of on cards, 96; as subjects of cards, 113; *see also individual names*
Arundel, Grace and Sybil, 102
Asti, Angelo, 111, *171*, *184*, *196*
Asti girl, the, 110, 111, *Plate 27*
Atwell, Mabel Lucie, 150
Austen, Alex, 59
Australia: 'Beer and Baccy' card in, 120; formation of Commonwealth of, 70; postage to, *167*, *168*
Austria, issues first post card, 24; Exhibition, *1906*, 73; *see also* Vienna
autochrome system, *190*

autographed cards, 103–4, 142; value of, *196*
Automatic Postcard Machine, 144
automatic vending machines, 37, 145
Aveline, F., 111
Aviation meeting, Blackpool, 75, *Plate 30*
aviators, 75, 108, 138; value of cards, *196*

B. & R. & Co., view cards of, 54, 56
babies, 106, 157
Baird & Sons, Alexander, 73
Bairnsfather, Bruce, 85
Baldwyn, Charles, 150–1
Balkan States Exhibition, 73, *178*
balloon post, 79; cards dropped from balloon, 127
Ballymaclinton, exhibition Irish village, 73, 125, 141
Bamforth & Co., 17, 49, 86, *171*, *174*; history of, 96; humorous cards of, 99; song cards, 155–6; *Titanic*, 158; war cards of, 86–7
Bamforth, James, 86, *174*
Barribal, L., 151, *179*
Bartolozzi, J., 151
Bartholomew & Co., J., 54
bas-relief, *196*
Bateman, Jessie, 102
Beagles & Co., J., 102, 103, *174*
beauties, portraits of, 110–12; artistic, 150, 151; famous, 102–5; 'Hand Coloured', *182*
beauty competitions, 120
Beeching, Messrs, 80
'Beer and Baccy' card, 47, 120, *Plate 4*
Beinne, F. O., 80
Belbin, H. W. G., 143
Belgium, early card from, 34, *170*, *Plate 3*
Bendsdorp, advertisement card, 124
Berkeley, Stanley, 108
Berne, UPU congress in, 27, 170
Bertanza, Cesare, 23
Besnardeau, stationer, 33, 79
bicycling, 106; on water, 143
Billing, M., 153
birds, 109, 150–1; with real feathers, 133, 134; swans, 110
*Birmingham Stamp Auction*, *199*
Birn Bros., 77, 111, 135, *173*, *174*
birthday cards, 33, 77
Blackpool, cards from, 50; Aviation meeting at, 75, *Plate 30*
Blum & Degen, 37, 51, 80, 113, *171*, *174*
Boer War, 37, 47, 79–81, 118, 141, *171*, *184*; end of, 71, 81; value of cards, *196*
Book Post, 118, *171*, *172*, *193*
bookmark cards, 146, *Plate 32*
books, reference, 47–8, *199*, *201*

Bootle, joke card from, 74
Boots (Jesse), (Cash Chemist), 152, *175*; 'Patriotic series', 130; view cards by, 59
Borrow, W. H., 59
Bovril card, 17, 128, *Plate 12*
Boyne, Tom, 59
Bragg, E. A., 158
Bray, Reginald, 'The Autograph King', 142–3
Bréamski, A. de, 59
Brennan, Mrs Drene, 45
Brett's, publishers, 126
bridges, 159–60
Briggate, Leeds, view of, 52
Britain: first postcards in, 24, 25, *Plate 1*; first foreign postcards in, 27, 28, *Plate 1*: and Continental cards, 35; and Ireland, 28; standard of early cards and stamps of, 33; cards of, support of cards of, 60; lack of innovations in, 121; *see also* Post Office
'Britain Prepared!' (film), 86
'British Army' (Tuck's), 80, *Plate 14*
British Museum, 152
'Broderie d'art' (Tuck's), 139
'bromides', 115, *174*
Brooker, W., 51
Browne, Tom ('Tom B.'), 16, 77, 91, 93, 94–5, 98, 123, *172*, *176*
'Bubbles' (Millais), 102, 124
Budapest, Millennium Exhibition, 35, *Plate 3*
buildings, views of, 60; public, cards sold from, 152, *186*
Burns, Robert, centenary of, 57
Burrit, Elihu, 33
'Butterflies on the Wing' (Tuck's), 131
*Bystander*, 85, *Plate 13*

Cadbury's: adverts, 123–4; reward series, 125
calendars, 110
Camburn, Harold H., 74
Campbell & Bright, 33
canal scenes, 159
cancellation of stamps, mechanical, 26–7; *see also* postmarks
*Candid Friend Magazine*, 127
card: coloured, printing on, 51; thin or stout, for Officials, 27, 28, 29, *165*, *166*, *170*; Panel, 160
Carter, Reg, 93, 98
cartoons, 76, 85, 91–100; animal, 95; comic, 91–3; domestic, 98–9; political, 95, 96–7, 98, *186*; regional, 98; sophisticated, 93–6, 97
Cassell's, 126, 152
Cassiers, H., 37, 72

catalogues, postal stationery, 33, 48
catch phrases, 96
cats: photographed, 109; by Louis Wain, 93–4, 109, *Plate 15*
'Caudle, Mr', 98–9
'Celesque' (Photochrom), 58, 59–60, 131, *182*
celluloid, 134–5, *196*
censorship: in wartime, 86, 89, *172*; by Watch committees, 92
Chamberlain, Joseph, 95, 96, 97, 98, 115–116
'Chamberlains at Home', 115–16
charities, fund-raising by, 17, 127–8
Charles I, King, 154
children, on cards, 149–50
Christmas cards, 33, 56, 76–7, *Plate 19*; decorated, 133; embroidered, 139, 140; photographs as, 105
circus cards, 101
'Clan Tartan' (Ja Ja), 53
Clapsaddle, Ellen M., 150, *196*
Clarion Postcards, 154
'classical' series, 153–5
classification of cards, 47, 149; of views, 50
cleaning cards, 48
'Clergymen's cards', 114–15
Clifford, Camille, 104–5, 110, *Plate 26*
Close, Ivy, 120
clubs, collectors', 37, 145; Postcard Collectors', 45
collecting, postcards: accessories for, 37, 127, 144–5; appeal of, 19–20; classification of cards, 47; cleaning and storage of cards, 48–9; completeness of collection, 47–8; craze for, 18, 37, 87, 145; mechanics of, 43–9; obtaining cards, 17–18, 43–6, 144; reasons for, 15; specialization, 47
'Collector's Postcards' (Tuck's), 124
Collectors' Publishing Co., 71, *171*
Collier, R. E., *179*
collotype process, 37, *185*, *188–9*
'Colotype' series, 51–2
colour photography, *190*
colour printing, technique of, *189–90*
coloured card, printing on, 51; coloured picture cards, earliest, 34–5, *189–90*; earliest in Britain, 37, 51; early three-colour, 121; and black and white versions of same card, 102, 103; hand colouring, *190*
comic postcards, 91–3
commemorative cards, 29, 38, 65–78; the first, 34, *170*; aerial post, 67–9; aviation, 75; Boer War, 80–2; current events, 70–2; dating, *191*; disasters,

74–5, 76; exhibitions, 72–4; list of events for, *198*; pageants, 74; Royal occasions, 66–7, 69; seasonal greetings, 76–7; sport, 75; value of, *196*
Commonwealth commemorative card, 70
communication, methods of, 27–8
competitions: beauty, 120; for collecting postcards, 18, 37, 119–20; St Paul's Hospital, 127–8; Tuck's £1000, 37, 119–20, *171*
Conlie, 33
'Connoisseur' (Tuck's), 111, 135
Continental cards, 26, 29, 31–2, 121, 161; accept divided back, 41, *172*, *193*; early Officials, *170*, *Plate 3*; large size, 31, 36; first picture postcards, 32–5; printers used by British, 152–3; tinselling banned, 133
Cook, Thomas, 124, *Plate 18*
Cooper, Gladys, 102–3, 142
Copping, Harold, 153
Corke, C. Essenhigh, 58–9, *183*
Corketts, F. T., 37, *171*
coronation cards: Edward VII, 65, *171*; George V, 67; postmarks, 142
correspondence cards, *see* court cards
costume, 16, 61–2, 105–6
*Country Life*, 41
County series, 57
court cards (correspondence), 24, 31, 36; Official court-sized, 31, *169*, *171*
Crawfords, adverts of, 118, *Plate 28*
crested cards, 53–4; silk, 137; value of, *196*
curiosities, 143–8; *see also* novelties
currency, illustrated, 161
'Current Events', 70, 71, 80, *171*
'Cynicus' (Martin Anderson), 59, 97, 98, *175*, *Plate 25*
Cynicus Publishing Co., 97, 155, *173*, *175*

*Daily Express*, beauty competition, 120
*Daily Mail*: Aeroplane and Water circuits, 75, 142; 'Battle Picture' series, World War I, 41, 87–9, *172*, *Plate 13*; value of, *196*
*Daily Mirror*, beauty competitions, 120
Daniell, Eva, 150
Dare, Phyllis, 102, 103, 104
Dartmoor prison, scenes of, 60, *Plate 6*
dates, important, listed *170–2*
dating cards, 19, 41, 61–4, 105–6, *191–4*; up-dated cards, 147
Davey, George, 96
Davidson Bros., 59, 73, 76, 77, *176*; humorous cards of, 93, 94, 95; star portraits by, 102
Daws, F. T., 108

De la Rue & Co., 24, 26, 29–30, 31, 32, *172*, *190*
dealers in postcards, 45–6; *listed*, *199*
'Defenders of the Empire' (Tuck's), 119
Delittle, Fenwick & Co. (D. F. & Co., Defco), 52, 115, 126, *171*, *176*; 'moonlight' views of, 52, *Plate 6*
Dennis, E. T. W., & Sons, 59, 131, *177*
Dickens cards, 153, 154
Dietrich of Brussels, 72
disasters, 74–5, 76, 143
'divided back' cards, 38–41, *171*, *192–3*; accepted on Continent, 41, *172*, *193*; dates of instructions on, *192–3*
dogs: series, 108–9; adverts, 119; Edward VII's, 114
do-it-yourself portrait cards, 105, 106–7, 144
dolls, 77, 161–2, *199*
Doolin, Bill, 162
Doré, Gustave, 26, *170*, *171*
Downey, W. and D., 66, 67
'Drawing Room Games', 116
Drummond, N., 81
'Ducal' series, 114
Duplex Post Card, 131–2
Dutch pictures, 149–50, 159, *Plate 15*

'E.F.A.' series, 113
E.R.G. & Co., 75
Earls Court, exhibitions at, 73–4, *198*
'Early Days of Sport' (Tuck's), 119
Easter cards, 16, 33, 77, 135
ecclesiastical cards, 17, 114–15
Eddystone lighthouse, 35, *169*, *170*, *197*
Edinburgh, first views of, 36, 37, 51, *171*, *183*
Edward VII, King, 114, *Plate 9*; coronation of, 65, *171*; reign of, 17, 66, 106; funeral of, 66–7, *Plate 11*
Edward, Prince of Wales, 69, 119, 128
Eiffel tower, 18, 34, *170*
embossed cards, 76, *196*; with currency or stamps, 160–1, *196*, *Plate 29*; embossed stamp on private postcards, 26, 29
embroidered cards, silk, of World War I, 137–40, *Plate 23*; greetings, 139; manufacture of, 139–40; patriotic, 137; regimental, 138; sentimental, 138; value of, 44, *196*
'Empire, Defenders of the' (Tuck's), 119, *Plate 14*; 'Links of the' (Wrench), 70, 80, *186*
'Empire series' (Tuck's), 113–14, *184*
Ena, Princess of Battenberg, 114; wedding of, 66
engineering cards, 158–60
Engle, C. J. & Co., 161

engraving process, *187–8*
envelopes: khaki, 81; Mulready, 33, 120; necessary for some cards, 133, 135; pictorial, 33; for silk embroidered cards, 140; silk cards in form of, 138; transparent, 133, *172*
Ettlinger & Co., 77, 93, *177*; midget cards, 146; novelties, 134; stage scenes, 102; still life, 153
Everitt Studios, T. H., 107
Excelsior, 77
exchange clubs, 45, 145
exhibitions, 72–4, 125, *184*; *listed*, *198*; postmarks from, 16, 141; value of cards from, *196*; *see also names of exhibitions*
explorers, 70–1, 108, 128
Eyre & Spottiswoode, 92, 108, 116, 152, *177*

'Fab Patchwork cards', 137, *Plate 31*
Fabian, Maud, 123
facsimiles, 56–9, 136
Faith, Hope and Charity (FHC), 154–5, *Plate 27*
faking, 147; flying machines inserted in view, 75; of moonlight views, 52; superimposition or updating, 147; two prints in reverse, 107, 111, 147; views with towns' names inserted, 147
family albums, 15, 17, 18, 43
family photographs, 17, 105, 106
fantasy compositions, 102, 104, 156–7, *Plate 30*
fashion magazines, 61
Faulkner, C. W. & Co., 51, 67, 81, 87, 128, 153, 154, *171*, *177–8*, *182*; art reproductions, 152; competition cards, 120; crested cards, 53; facsimile views, 59; military heroes, 84, *Plate 12*; painting book, 131; Panel cards, 160; Parkinson series, 149
Field Postcard (Army form), 89
Field Post Offices, 84, 141
Finnemore, J., 74
'Firelight Effects' (Tuck's), 113
first: postcard (world), 24, *170*, *Plate 1*; British postcard, 24, 25, *166*, *170*, *Plate 1*; British Aerial Post, 67–9; British Foreign card, 27, *166*, *170*, *Plate 1*; British view cards, 26, 36, *170*, *171*; coloured cards, 35; British coloured, 37, 51; commemorative, 34, *170*; divided back, 40, *171*; picture postcards, 33–4; reply paid, 29, *167*
first-day used issues, 47, 143
fishing, 112
flaps, 131
Fletcher-Watson, P., 57

*Floral Studies Postcard Painting Book*, 131
'Flower and Beauty Silverette Series' (Tuck's), 102
Flower, Charles E., 48, 57, 125
flowers: appliqué, 132–3; on birthday cards, 77; painting book, 131; pressed, 133; on silk cards, 138
folded cards, 130
forces: abroad, send cards home, 79, 138–139; fund raising for, 17, 83, 128; recruiting, 80–1, 82; *see also* military series
Forces' Post Offices, 139; Field, 84, 141
Foreign Postcard, Official, 29, *167*, *Plate 3*; Britain's first, 27, 28, *166*, *170*, *Plate 1*
'formulas of courtesy', 41–2, *160*
'framed' view cards, 54–5
France: earliest cards from, 33–4; first Official, *170*; commemorative cards in, 71; embroidered cards from, 17, 138, 139–40; accepts divided back, *172*, *193*
Franco–British Exhibition, *1908*, 73, 141, 146
Franco–Prussian war, 33, 79
freaks, 101, 143
French, Sir John, 84–5
Frictograph cards, 129–30
Frith & Co., F., *178*, *193*
Fry's advertisement cards, 119, 123, *Plate 18*
Fulleylove, J., 57, 59
fund raising, 17, 83, 127–8

G. B. & Co., 154, *Plate 27*
Gale & Polden Ltd, 101, *178*; military cards, 73, 75, 81–2
'Gallery Pictures' (Tuck's), 151
Gardening and Forestry Exhibition, 35
Gaston, R., 59
General Union of Posts, convention of, 27; *see also* Universal Postal Union
George V, King: coronation of, 67; accession of, 69
Germany: postcards first suggested in, 24; cards from, 31, 35, 41; embossed, 76; greetings, 76, 77; *Gruss Aus . . .*, 35, 55, *Plate 10*; Officials, *170*, *191*; British cards printed in, 41, 152, 153, *170*; mistranslation on, 147; printing development in, 41, 76, *170*; accepts divided back, *172*, *193*
Giant cards, 146
Gibbons, Stanley, 33, 48
Gibson, Charles Dana, 47, 98, 104, *179*, *Plate 26*
'Gibson Girl', the, 98, 104–5, 110, *Plate 26*

gift cards, 126–7
Gilbert, Allan, 105
girls, sets of, 139; art studies, 150, 151, 152; 'the Gibson', 104–5, *Plate 26*; photographed, 110–12; 'Portrait of a Young -', 152–3
*Girl's Own Paper*, 126
*Girl's Realm*, 20, 53
'Girls we Miss' (Valentine's), 139
Gladstone, William E., 27, 41, 115
Glasgow international exhibition, 72–3
Godden, G. A., *Stevengraphs . . .*, 137
Goethen, E. Van, 152
Goldwyn, J. M., 154
Goss, W. H., *178*
Gossage's adverts, 119
'Grande Bretagne', 28, *167*
Grant & Co.: Doré card, 26, *170*, *171*; silk cards, 136–7
Grapevine cigarettes, 119
*Graphic*, 29
Graphotone Co., 146
Greenaway, Kate, 150
Greenbank, A., *176*
greetings cards, 76–8, *184*, *185*; early German, 35, 55, *Plate 10*; embroidered silk, 139; seasonal, 76–7; town and national, 78
Gretna Green, 147
Gretty, G., 56
Greuze, 'Portrait of a Young Girl', 152–3
gruesome cards, 143
'*Gruss Aus . . .*' cards, 35, 55, *Plate 10*
Guildhall Postal exhibition, *1890*, 29, *168*, *170*

H.M. Stationery Office, 82
H.M.V. trademark, use of, 108
Hadfield Cubley, 57
Haines, Reginald, 84
Hamel, Gustav, 69, 75, 108
Hammond, Noel, 105
hand colouring, *190*
'Hands Across the Sea', 78, 136
Harbour, Jennie, 150
Hardy, Dudley, 93, 95
Hardy, Florence, 149–50, *178*, *196*, *Plate 15*
Hartmann, F., 40–1, 56, 112, 113, 147, *171*, *179*; Frictographs, 130
Hassall, John, 91, 93, 94, *176*
'Hattire' (Valentine's), 132
Haydock Coals, adverts of, 124
Hayes, F. W., 57
'Head Studies', 111, *179*
'heater' cards, 130
Heaton, Henniker, M.P., 30, 39, 121
Heligoland, early card from, 34, *170*

Henderson & Sons, James, 98, 105, 111, *179*, *Plate 26*
'Heraldic Series' (Ja Ja), 53, *Plate 5*
Hermann, Dr Emanuel, 24
heroes, 108, 113, 116, 138; historical, 154; military, 80, 84, 89
Heyermans, John A., 57
Hicks, Seymour, 103, 104, 120
hidden pictures, 130
Hier, Prof. van, 184
'Highland Clan' (Tuck's), 54
Hildesheimer & Co., S., 108, 154, *179*; art reproductions, 152; reward cards, 125; view cards, 59
'Historical' albums, 154
'Historical Series', *181*
Hold-to-the-Light cards, 129, *196*
Holland, cards printed in, 92
hop picking, 112
Horniman's, 129–30
hotel cards, 28, 31, 123
House of Commons, 29, 39
house sales, 15, 17, 45
Huardel & Co., 153
Huggins, Alan, *British Postal Stationery*, *acknowledgements*, 33
Hull trawlers, Russians fire on, 82–3, *171*, *Plate 8*
humorous cards, 16, 17, 91–100; comic, 91–3; political, 95, 96–7, 98; regional, 98; songs, 99; sophisticated, 93–6, 97; value of, *195*; of World War I, 85; *see also* cartoons
hymns, 17, 156

Ibbotson, Ernest, 82
*Idle Moments*, 126
'Illustrated Daily Postcard', 78, *Plate 8*
India: cards from forces in, 79; Prince's ivory cards, 148
information: about postcards, 49, *173*; from postcards, 15, 61, 64; topical, 78, 80
Inland Revenue, Dept. of, embosses stamps, 23, 26, 29
'inserts', 126
insurance cards, 120–1, *186*
intaglio printing process (line drawing), *187–8*
Inter-Art Co., 92, 140, *179*; 'Artistique', 151; 'Comique', 147
international postage, 35, 145; *see also* Universal Postal Union
*International Postcard Market* (*IPM*), 45, 46, 92, 158, 159, *200*
Ireland: the card that upset, 28, *167*, *170*; humorous card from, 124; peat cards from, 135

Irving, Sir Henry, 72, 101, 104, 125
ivory cards, 148

Jackson, Helen, 57
Jackson & Son (Jay Em Jay), 55–6, *179*, *180*
Ja-Ja, *179–80*; 'Heraldic Series', 53, 54
Japan-British Exhibition, *1910*, 73
Japanese: Official Postcard, *Plate 17*; veneered cards, 135; vogue, 82, 83, 107, 110, *Plate 23*; war with Russia, 82–3, *Plate 17*
Japanese series (Tuck's), 135
Jarrold, Antony, 49
Jarrold & Son Ltd, 49, 57, 59, *180*; 'Pageant Series', 74; 'The Great War', 83, *Plate 17*
jewelling, 133, *172*
jigsaw cards, 130, *196*
'John o' Groats Series', 76
Johnson Bros, adverts of, 118
Johnston, W. & A. K. Ltd, 54, 149
Joseph Asher & Co., 92
'Jotter' (W. H. Young), 57–8, *180*, *184*
Jubilee of Penny Postage: card, 29, 35, *168*, *Plate 2*; value of, *197*; postmarks, 142

Karlsruhe, conference at, 24
Kennedy, T., milliners, 119
Khaki card, the, 136
khaki envelopes, 81
King, J. W., 74
'Kings and Queens of England' (Tuck's), 114, *Plate 9*
Kipling, Rudyard, 79–80; 'If', 84
Kirchner Girl, the, 110, *Plate 26*
Kirchner, Nina, 110–11
Kirchner, Raphael, 37, 44, 47, 110–11, *172*, *Plate 26*; value of cards, *196*
Kitchener, Lord, 70, 80; advertising, 118; 'If' card, 84, *Plate 12*
Kiwi Polish Co., 118–19
Knight, Bros, *180*
Knowles, G. Sheridan, 152
Kodak, DIY cards, 105, 107, 144; competition for, 120
Kuroki, Gen., 82, *Plate 17*
Kyd, 154, *185*

L.L. (Lévy?), photos by, 156, *Plate 7*
L.S.D., 109
Ladysmith, relief of, 19, 70, 81, *184*
Landor, W. S., 109; animal studies by, *186*
Landseer, Sir Edwin, 108, 151
Lange, Heinrich, 23
Langhorne sisters, the, 104; *see also* Gibson Girl, the

Langlands of Dumbarton, 54
Langley, Prof. S. P., 160
languages, of vegetables and stamps, 146–7
largest postcard, the world's, 146
Lawrence, Peter, 20
Lawton, J. A., advert of, 118
Laxey, water wheel at, 159, *Plate 11*
leather cards, 135, *196*
letterpress printing, *187, 190*
letter-writing, 27
lifeboats, 112
limited editions, 48, 157–8, *184*; value of, *196*
'Links of the Empire' (Wrench), 70, 80, *186*
lithography, process of, *187, 188–90*; lithographic cards, early, 34
Livermore & Knight, 118
Liverpool, 63; Motor Show, 118; Pageant, 74
*Liverpool Echo*, 31
*Living London*, 126
local events, photos of, 105–7
local firms, adverts of, 124–5
local history, 15
locally produced cards, 76, 80–1
London, Victorian, 63–4; and Aerial post, 68–9; People's Palace, 147; pictures of, 26, 53, 113, 126, 127
'London by Night' (Tuck's), 53
London County Council reward cards, 125–6
London Volunteers, City of, 80–1
Longstaffe, E., 59
Ludovici, Anthony, 74, 93, 95, *176, Plate 20*

MacBrayne, David, 122, *Plate 29*
McCorquodale & Co., 121, 122, *172, 180*
McGill, Donald, 16, 77, 91–3, *179, Plate 25*; career of, 91–3; first cards by, 92, *172*
machines, on cards, 160
Machnow, the giant, 101
MacIntyre, R. F., 57
McKenzie, W., 51
McKinley, President, assassination of, 71
M'Clinton, 73, 125, 141
McNeil, J., 82
magazines, publicizing of, 126–7
magazines: fashion, 61; postal auction, 46, *listed, 199–200*; postcard, 45–6, 145, *listed 201*; *see also names of magazines*
Mailick, 76, 154, *Plate 27*
Mallandain's, 105, 144
map postcards, 54; of war, advert, 118, *Plate 28*
Maria Feodorovna, Dowager Empress, 67

'Mars, message from', 127
Martin, Phil, *179*
materials used for postcards: card, quality of, 27, 28, 29, *165, 166, 170*; Panel, 160; unusual, 134–40, 148
Mathison, W., 57
May, Edna, 102, *Plate 32*
May, Phil, 77, 91, 93, 96, *184, Plate 16*
Mead, Margaret, 20
mechanical cards, 130–1, *191, 196*
Menpes, Mortimer, 149
messages, on cards, 17; on address side, 32, 38–41; convenience of, 27; five-word 'formula of courtesy', 41–2, 131, 160; incur Letter Rate, *193*; looking-glass or tilted, 130; openness of, 23, 25, 41; secret or coded, 19; spread over set of cards, 102; *see also* advertisements
metal cards, 135, *171*
'Meva' (Josephy Salomonson), 115
mezzotint, *187–8*
'Midget postcards', 146, *Plate 32*
military postmarks, 141
military series, 16, 80, 81–2, 128; of Boer War, 79–81; regimental, 80, 81–2, 87, 138, *178*; World War I, battle scenes, 87–9; silk embroidered, 137–8; *see also* forces *and* wars
Millais, Sir John, 125, 152; 'Bubbles', 102, 124
Millar & Lang, 54, *180–1*; 'National Series', 78, 96
Millet, Jean; 'Gleaners', 125; '—'s Masterpieces', 152
mills, 159, 195
'Miniature series' (Hartmann), 56
Minns, F. M., 59
Misch & Co., 16, 77, 96, 135, 150, *181*; art repro., 152–3, *196*
Misch & Stock, 152, *181*
mistakes, 147
'moonlight effects', 52–3, *Plate 6*
'Moonlit Sea' (Tuck's), 53
Morell, Charles, 111
Morris, M., 57
Moss, Henry, 110
motor car: development of the, 62–3; cards, 108; shows, 118; racing, 75, 108; 'round-the-world', 127; substituted on cards for horses, 147
'Motorist's Series', *181*
'Mrs Caudle's Curtain Lectures', 98–9
Mucha, 37, 110, *196*
Muir & Moodie, 161
Muller, A., 108
Mulready envelope, the, 33, 120
*Myra's Journal*, 61

name cards, 135
Napoleon I, 154, 156–7
Nash, A. A., 151, *179*
National Gallery, 152, *191*
National Science Museum, 160
'National Series' (Millar & Lang), 78, 96, 111, 158
'Nelson, Eventful' series, 113
Nestlé's, 128
New Year cards, 139, *182*; the first, 77
news postcard, daily, 78
Newton, G. E., 51, 53, 57
Nicholson & Carter, 147
Nister, Ernest, *181*, *196*
*Northern Postal Auctions, 199*
novel, written on a postcard, 145
novels, titles, cards of, 96
novelties, 129–40; active, 129–32; adverts, 118; something stuck on, 132–4; of unusual materials, 134–40
nudes: artistic, 151, 152; erotic, 99–100
Nuremberg exhibition, *1882*, 23, 34, *170*

obscene cards, 99–100
Official postcards, 24–6, 33, *165*; *serials detailed 166–9, Plate 2*; first British, 24–25, *Plate 1*; address side, *see* address side; card, thin or thick, 27, 28, 29, *165*, *166*, *170*; charge for, 25, 28, 29; collecting, 46, 68; first Commemorative issue, 29; Continental large-size, 32; court size, 31; dating, *191*; Foreign, 27, 28, *Plate 3*; Inland, 23, 24–6, 29; literature on, *acknowledgements and*, 33; 'Pig Control', 42; printers, *see* De la Rue *and*, *172*; Reply paid, 29; stocks of early, 32; value of, 33, *195*
'Oilette' (Tuck's), 50–1, 56, 136, *184*, *Plate 11*; artists for views, 56–8
'Oilette de Luxe', 150
'Oilfacsims', 58
'Old Bill', 85
'Olde Print' (Tuck's), 151
'Opalette series', 108
'Opium Eater', 111
opium dens, 143
Oriental Tea Agency, 117
Orwell, George, 92
Otmar Zieher, 161
'Our Local Express', 97, *Plate 25*
'Our Servants' (Davidsons), 94
Owen, Will, 91, 96
Oxford: college arms of, 54, *180*; 'eights' cards, 75–6; illustrations of, 59; Pageant, *1907*, 74
Oxo, 128, *Plate 28*

P.R.P.C., 54, 59
pageants, 74
painting cards, 131
'Palatine' series, 135
Panel cards, 160
Pankhurst, Emily, 115
'Panoramic Card', 146
'paquebot' marks, 141
Paris: adverts from, 119; erotic cards from, 99–100; Exhibitions, 34, 100; fashions, 61; magazines, 110; siege of, 79, 145; UPU Congress in, *170*
Parisius, Pastor Ludolph, 23
Parkinson, Ethel, 149, *178*, *196*
patchwork cards, 137, *Plate 31*
'Patriotic series' (Boots), 130
patriotism, 17, 37, 79, 137–8
Payne, Arthur C., 56, 59, *196*
Payne, Harry, 59, 69, *196*; career of, 56, 149; military cards by, 37, 80, 119, *184*, *Plate 14*
'Peacock' series, *182*
Pearce, Chas., 123
Pear's soap, 124
peat cards, 135, *196*
'Pelham' series, *175*
Penley, Edwin E., 57
Percival, E. D., 57, 59
personalities, 82; national, 80, 84; stage, 101–5; *see also* portraits
'Phil May Series' (Tuck's), 93, *Plate 16*
*Philatelic Literature Auction, 199*
Philco Publishing Co., 59, 77, 111, *181*; jewelled cards, 133, *172*; star portraits, 102, 103; virtue cards, 155; World War I, 90, *Plate 19*
Phillimore & Co., R. P., 154, *181*; view cards of, 59
Phillips, Godfrey, tobacco company, 126
Phosphor cards, 130
Photochrom Co., 58, 59–60, 84, 85, 86, 108, *181–2*; art repro., 152; largest cards, 146
photographs: amateur, 105, 106–7; family, 17, 105, 106; local, 105–7; by moonlight, 52; portraits, 84–5, 101–4, 105, 107–8, 110, 111–15; reversed, superimposed or tinted, 107, 111, 147; view cards, 59–61
photography, 37–8, 156; printing process of, *188–9*, *190*; in World War I, 83, 87–8
'Photogravure': process of, 84, *187*, *188*; series, 84, 85
photo-lithography, *170*, *189*
phototype process, 35
'Pictorial Comedy' series, 105
Pictorial Postcard Co., 92

'Pictorial' series (Frith's), *193*

Pictorial Stationery Co., 37, 95, 112, *171*, *182*

Picture Postcard Co., 79

*Picture Postcard Magazine*, 41, 45, 80, 92, 114, 120, 121, 144, 146, *178*, *182*; first issue, 37, 64, 99, 145, *171*; on divided back, 40; on erotic cards, 99–100; on faked moonlight views, 52; on Swan fountain pen, 127; on tourists sending cards, 18

picture postcards, earliest, 33–42; attitude to, *c. 1900*, 41; dating, *191*, value of, *196–7*

'Pig Control Postcard', 42, *172*

pigeon post, 145–6

pin-up, creator of the, 110

plastic bags, for postcards, 49

'Political Leaders' (Tuck's), 116

political portraits, 115–16

political satire, 91, 95, 96–7, 98

'Political series' (Tuck's), 113–14

pollution, 97

'Popular series', 76, 133, *Plate 19*

portrait cards, 84, 99, 101–16; animals, 108–10; beauties, 99, 107, 110–12, *Plate 32*; caricatures, 113, *see also* cartoons; do-it-yourself, 105; ecclesiastical, 114–15; family, 105, 106; great men, 113; group, 114; historical, 154; local, 105–7; political, 113–14, 115–16; regional, 112; royal, 65, 113, 114; sports, 108; stage, 99, 101–5; value of, *195–6*; work, 112–13; woven silk, 140; writers and artists, 113

Portugal, royal family of, 114; visits Britain, 66, *Plate 9*

Post Office: deliveries by, speed of, 18, 77; illustrated on cards, 113; monopoly of early cards, 25, 26, 29–30, 35; regulations for post cards, 24, 39–40, 41–2, 119, 142, 160–1, *170*; bans transparent envelopes, 133

*Post Office Circular*, 38–9, 133

*Post Office Guide*, 40, 160

*Post Office Historical Summary 1911*, 39

Post Office Inland Post Warrant, 39

Post Office Postage Rates committee, 31–2; 39–40

postage rate: for aerial post, 68; book post, 118, *171*, *172*, *193*; Inland raised to 1d, 41, 143; overseas, 27, 28, *165*, *167*; Postcard Rate, 24, 25, *191*; regulations qualifying for, 30–1; cards which incurred extra charge, 132, 133, 137, 160, *191*, *193*; 'formula of courtesy' message for ½d, 41–2, 160

postal deliveries, by unusual methods, 75, 79, 145–6

postal auction, 46; magazines *listed*, *199–200*

*Postal Cards and Covers*, 145

postal exchange clubs, 45, 145

Postal Exhibition, Guildhall, 28, 29, *168*, *170*, *Plate 2*

*Postcard* (magazine), 145

Postcard Association, 49

Postcard Collectors' Club of Great Britain, 45

*Postcard Connoisseur*, 60, 97, 126–7, 145, *171–2*

Postcard Publishers' Association, 180, 183

*Postcard World*, 45, 46, *200*

*Poster and Postcard Collector*, 145

posters, 58, 121; on postcards, 106; Tuck's series of, 124

*Postman's Gazette*, 120

postmarks, special, 16, 84, 124, 141–2; aerial, 68; collectors of, 46, 47; in dating cards, *191*; first day issues, 143; value of, *197*

Postmen's Federation, 120

Pressland, A. L., 59

Preston, John, adverts of, 117

printing techniques, 35, *187–90*; for coloured cards, 51; in Germany, 41, 170

prisoner of war cards, 89, *196*, *Plate 24*

Private Postcard (*int. 1894*) with adhesive stamp; allowed, 23, 35, *169*, *170*; conditions for, 30; size of, 30–2, 35–6; first pictures, 35, 36–7

privately printed card (*int. 1872*) stamped by Inland Revenue: allowed, 23; conditions for, 26, *166*; illustrated, 28; stamp embossing on, 26, 29

publishers' adverts, 126–7

publishers, of postcards: Association of; 180, 183; information re, 49, *173–86*; name on cards, location of, *193–4*; records, 36, 49, *173*; registration of, *173*; *see also names of firms*

pullouts, 131

*Punch*, 91, 93, 94, 98; adverts, 69; reproductions of cartoons from, *186*

puzzle cards, 130, *196*

quality of postcards, 37–8, 41

Quatremain, W. W., 59

*Queen, The*, 61

'Queen Series', 123

Quinton, A. R., 57, 58, *183*

railway: cards, 64, 121–2; postmarks, 141

Raphael Tuck & Sons, 41, 73, *184*; campaign for private cards, 32, 36; first cards of, 36–7, *171*
   cards of: advertising, 118, 119, 124; animal, 109; art, 150; reproductions, 151–2; Christmas, 76–7; classics, 153, 154; competition re, 37, 119–20; coronation, 65; dolls, 161–2; Easter, 77; girls, 110, 111; humorous, 93, 98–9; limited editions, 48, 157–8; military, 80–1, 89; 'Notabilities', 84; novelties, 130, 131, 135, 139; Oxford pageant, 74; portraits, 113–14; railway, 122; reward, 125; songs, 155; Star series, 101, 102; views, 50–1, 51–2, 54, 55–8; war, 80–1; work, 113; *Exchange Register*, 145; *see also* Tuck, Sir Adolf
Rapid Photo Printing Co., 73, 102, 103, *182*
'record' breakers, 76
records of card production, 36, 49, *173*
recruiting cards, 80, 82
Reed, E. T., 76
Reflectoscope, 144–5
'Reform' series (Photochrom), *193*
Regal Art Publishing Co. (Rapco), *182*; view cards of, 59
Regent Publishers, 147
regimental cards, 80, 81–2, 87, *178*; silk embroidered, 138, *196*
regional humour, 98, 124
registry of purchases, 158
religious cards, 17; ecclesiastical, 114–15; festivals, 77
reply-paid cards, first, 29, *167*, *170*; double, for advertisers, 117
reproductions, art gallery, 151–3, *186*
reward cards, 125–6
Richard & Mackay, 151
Richardson, Agnes, *179*
Richardson, E. W., 37, *171*
Richardson, F. Esdaile, 57
*Rigby Postal History Auction Catalogue*, 46, *199*
Rigi mtn., cards from, 18–19, 35, *Plate 7*
Roberts, Lord, 80, 84, *Plate 12*
Robey, George, 104, 142
Rosebery, Lord, 98, 113–14, 116
Rotary Photographic Co., 72, 75, 77, 84, 111, 120, 144, 155, *182*, *190*; nudes, 151; portraits, 114–15; reversed and tinted sets, 107; small cards, 146; Star series, 101, 102, 103
rotary presses developed, *170*, *188*, *190*
Rotophot, *183*
'Rough Seas' (Tuck's), 51, *184*
round-the-world trips, 127, 143–4
Rowntrees, adverts, 124

Royal: events, 16, 65–7, *Plate 9*; postmarks for, 142; portraits, 113, 114; in adverts, 119
Royal Naval Exhibition, 35, *169*, *170*; value of cards from, *197*
'Royal Postcard' series (Tuck's), 114
Ruddock & Sons, J. W., *173*, *182*; view cards of, 59
Russo-Japanese war, 82, 118, *171*, *172*, *Plates 8, 28*; Russian navy fires on Hull trawlers, 82–3, *171*, *Plate 8*

St Martins le Grand, P.O., 25
St Paul's Hospital, 127–8
sales: and bazaars, 44; house, 15, 17, 45
Salmon, J., 158, 159, *183*; view cards of, 58–9
Sandoz, A., 61
Saunders, Rev. W. R., card of, 34
Schilling, Geo. M., 143
Schwerdtfeger & Co., F. A. S., 77, 111, *183*
Scopes & Co., 84–5
Scott, Capt., 70–1
Scott, Russell & Co., 53–4
'Scottish Clans' (Tuck's), 54
Scottish exhibition, *180*
Scottish humorous cards, 98
'Scottish Studies', 112
seaside postcards, 91, 92–3
seaside resorts, 16, 56, 131, *Plate 7*
seasons, sets of, 155
'Seldoms, the' (stage act), 151
Senefelder, Alois, 189
sentimental cards, of World War I: Bamforths, 86–7; silk, 138, *196*
sets, 157; limited, 157–8; message spread over, 102
Severn, Walter, 57
sexuality, on cards, 99
Shackleton, Lt. Ernest, 108, 128
Shakespearian cards, 153–4
Shandon steeple, view card of, 51
shape of cards: court, 24, 31, 36, *169*, *171*; oblong, early, 25, 32, *166*; unusual, 146
Sharpe, W. N., 137
*Sheffield Weekly Telegraph*, 120
Shepheard, G. E., 96, *178*
Shepherd, Neame & Co., 117
ships, 136, 158–9; adverts for, 121, 122–3, *Plate 29*; disasters to, 74, 158–9; letter marks from, 141; subscription cards carried by, 70–1; in World War I, 86
shop cards, 127
Shurey's, publishers, 126
silk: embroidered cards, 17, 137–40; value

of, *196*; woven cards, 136–7, 140, *196*,
  *Plate 31*; silks on cards, 132
'Silver' cards, 76
Silver Print style, *176*
'Silverette' series (Tuck's), 135
size: of first British Officials, 25; Official
  serials, *166–9*; of private postcards,
  *1894*, 30, 31, 35; court size, 31; large
  Continental, 31–2, 36; first picture, 35–
  36; minimum raised, *1907*, *172*; extra
  large, 146, *193*; advertising, large, 118;
  miniature, 146; box to check, 145
Smith, John (ed.), 45, 158, 159
Smith, Robert H., 113
Smith, T., 57
*Smith's Weekly*, 127
Sneath, R., of Sheffield, 56
song cards, 86, 99, 155–6; Shakespearian,
  54
South Pole, expeditions to, 70–1, 108, 128
specials, 141–8; autographs, 142; delivery,
  145–6; faking, 147; gadgets, 144–5;
  languages, 146–7; mistakes, 147; postmarks, 141–2; provenance, 144, 145;
  size or shape, 146; stamps, 143; subject
  matter, 143
Spencer, Tom, 89
sports, 16, 75–6, 107–8
Spratt's, 'Portrait Postcards of Champion
  Dogs', 108, 109
Spurgin, Frederick, 85, *179*, *Plate 19*
'Spy' (Sir Leslie Ward), 91, 98
'squeakers', 132, 134
stage: adverts, 125, *Plate 18*; the amateur,
  107; personalities, 16, 99, 101–4, *195*;
  scenes, 101–2, 125
stamp space, *191*
stamps: adhesive, allowed on Officials, *165*,
  *167*; cancellation of, 26–7, *see also* postmarks; collectors of, 16, 44, 46, 143;
  dating cards by, *191–2*; early British, 33;
  embossed illustrations of, 160–1, *Plate
  29*; embossed on privately printed cards,
  26, 29; first day issues, 81; issues *listed*,
  *192*; 'language of', 147; philocartophical clubs, 145
*Standard*, 29
Stannard, Henry, 57
'Star' series, 101–2
stars, stage, portraits of, 101–4; value of, *195*
stationery, 25; pictorial, 33; trade, 25
Stead, Henry, 70, 71, 80, 81, *171*, *186*
Stengel & Co., 47, 153, *181*, *183*, *189*
Stephan, Heinrich von, 24, 27
stereoscopic cards, 144
Stevens, T., silk cards of, 136, 137, *Plate
  31*; value of, *196*
Stewart, George, *183*; Britain's first pic-
ture postcard by, 36, 37, 51, 70, *171*;
  war cards of, 81
Stewart & Woolf, 81, 98, *183*
Stiebel & Son, Alfred, 77, 137, *183*
still life pictures, 153
Stoddart & Co., *180*
storage of cards, 48–9, 50
Studholme, Marie, 103, *Plate 32*
subscription cards, 70–1, *186*
suffragettes, 85, 115
Swan Fountain Pen, 127
swans, 110
Switzerland, 19, 161

'T' stamp, *165*, *172*
*T.A.T. Journal*, 126
tanks, 85–6
*Tatler*, 96
Taylor, A. G., *184*
telephone, the, 18, 27, 28
Tempest, Douglas, 96
Terris, Ellaline, 103
Thackeray, Lance, 96, *172*, *184*, *Plate 16*
Thorneycroft Steam Wagon Co., 118
3-D cards, 132
Tilley, Vesta, 101, 103, 142
*Times, The*, 75, 92, 113, *Plate 30*
tinselling, 133, *172*, *196*
*Titanic*, 158–9
*Tit-Bits*, 126
'Tom B', *see* Browne, Tom
'Tom P', 94
topical cards, 65–7, 69–76, 78; of Boer
  war, 80–2; seasonal, 76–7
topographical cards, *see* view cards
towns: greetings from, 78; photographers
  in, 105; share same view cards, 147;
  scenes, 61; work in, 113
trademarks, publishers', *173–90 passim*;
  position of on cards, *193–4*
transparencies, 129
transport, 16, 62–4; motor buses, 63;
  public, 63–4; railways, 64, 121–2, 141;
  trams, 63–4; *see also* motor car
travel agents, 124
Travelling Post Offices (T.P.O.), 124, 141
Treasury Warrants: *1894*, 30, 39, *191*;
  *1897*, 39, *194*
Trent Bridge Publishing Co., 146
Tuck, Sir Adolph, 29–30, 32, 36, 81, 92,
  113, 119, 120, 121
Tuck & Sons, *see* Raphael Tuck & Sons

United States of America, 33, 110, *172*
Universal Postal Union, 28, 31; accepts
  divided back, 41, *172*, *193*; Convention
  of, 27, *170*
up-dated cards, 147

Upton, Florence K., 77
used and unused cards, 47

Valentine cards, 77, 150, *199*
Valentine & Sons, 41, 158, *184*; cards by: first, 37, *171*; art repro., 152; bridges, 159, 160; greetings, 77; humorous, 98; novelties, 130, 131; Russian war, 82–3; views, 51, 52, 54–5, 56, 59, 73; photographed views, 60, *184*
value of postcards, 16, 33, 44, 46, 47, 48; *guide to, 195–7*
Van Hier, Prof., 57, *184*
*Vanity Fair*, 91, 98
'Varsity Oxford City', *180*
Vaughan, E. H., 57
Velox, 105, 144
vending machines, automatic, 37, 144, 145
Vesuvius, Mt., 35, 124, *Plate 10*
Victoria, Queen, 79, 113, 114; death of, 38, 67, *171*
Vienna, early card suggestions in, 23, 24; *1891* Postal Union Congress in, 141
view cards, 34–5, 50–64, *182, 183*; early Continental, 34; German *Gruss Aus . . .*, 35, 55; first British, 26, 36; classification of, 50; collecting, 48; dating, 61–64; information from, 64; publishers of, 58–9; value of, *195*; types of: beauty spots, 61; buildings, 60; on coloured card, 51; composite, 55–6, *180*; cramped, 51; crested, 53; crowd scenes, 61, *Plate 7*; facsimiles, 56–8; flap, 131; framed, 54–5; Franco–British, 73; 'Giant', 73; hold to light, 129; map, 54; misattributed, 147; 'moonlight', 52–3; photographed, 59–61, *184*; Tuck's series, 51–2; Valentine's, 51, 52, 54–5, 56, 59, 73, 60, *184*
viewing cards, gadgets for, 144–5
Vincent, Kathleen, 107
Virol, 125
virtues, sets of, 154–5, *Plate 27*
Voisey, Charles, stereoscope of, 144

W.H.'s 'Hold-to-Light' cards, 47, *196*
W.R. & S., *185*
Wain, Louis: card by, *Plate 15*; career of, 109; cat cards by, 93–4, 109; value of cards by, *196*; mentioned, 16, 47, *176, 184*
Walker, Harrison & Garthwaites, 119
Walker, John, maps, 54
Walmsley, G. C., 74
Wane & Co., 103
Ward, Herbert, 87
Ward, Sir Leslie ('Spy'), 91, 98
Ward, Marcus, 150
Warrington, Ellen, 57

wars, cards of, 17, 79–90; in adverts, 118; Franco-Prussian, 79; Russo-Jap., 82–3; *see also* Boer War *and* World War I
Water Colour Postcard Co., 59
Waterloo Monument, 147
Watkins & Kracke, 77, *185*
Weary Willie and Tired Tim, 95
'Wedgwood' series, 60, *182*
Welbourne, Ernest, 59
Welch, J., & Sons, 56, 154, *184–5*
'Wellington Series' (Gale & Polden), 81–2, *178*
Welsh cards, 98, 112
Welsh troops, fund raising for, 128
Wennerbery, B., 151
*Westminster Gazette*, 30–1, 71
'When Father says Turn . . .', 96–7, *Plate 21*
'White Label' whisky cards, 118
Whitroy, Henry, 108
Wildt & Kray, 73, 76, 77, 135, 155, *185*; Panel cards, 160
Williams, Warren, 131
'Wiltshire Moonrakers', the, 143
Wimbush, Henry B., 56–7
Windsor Castle, 66; in Aerial Post, 68, 69
Woestyn, H. R., 121, 122
Wolverhampton Art and Industrial Exhibition, *1902*, 73
women: position of, 85, 115
Wood, Lawson, 95, *179*
wooden cards, 135, *196*
Woodville, Richard Caton, 37, 79, 80, 83; value of cards of, *196*
Woolstone Bros, 52, 131, *185*
Woolworths, F. W., 77, 84
work, types of, 112–13
works, mines and factories, 159
World War I, 17, 41, 67, 83–90, *172, Plates 12, 13*; air raids of, 75, 85; postmarks of, 142; silk cards of, 137–40
'World's Galleries' (Misch & Co.), 152–3, *181, 189, Plate 22*
woven silk cards, 136–7, 140, *196, Plate 31*
Wrench, John Evelyn, 41, 59, 65, 67, 70, 71, 98, 109, 130, *171, 172, 188, 191*; art repro., 152; career and Company of, *185–6*; dog series, 108; novel titles series, 96
'Write Away' (Tuck's), 93, 96, 99, 109, *184, Plate 16*

Young, Gwendoline, 58
Young, Walter Hayward, *see* 'Jotter'
Young & Cooper, 112

Zeppelins, 85, *Plates 20, 24*
'Zoo Series', 125–6
Zrenner, Ludwig, 23, 34